21 世纪高等学校专业英语系列规划教材

汽车

专业英语教程

刘 伟 张 良 编著

清华大学出版社

北京交通大学出版社

·北京·

内 容 简 介

本书以中英文对照的方式介绍了当今主流汽车技术及其维护保养知识，其主要内容包括：汽车结构（包括汽车结构简介、发动机、变速器、车桥和车轮、转向系、制动系、悬架系统、空调系统、电气系统和车身结构）、汽车识别（包括车辆类型和车辆识别码）、发动机控制系统（包括发动机控制系统概述、发动机控制系统的组成、传感器和信号、电子燃料喷射系统、电子点火提前系统、怠速控制系统、诊断系统）、汽车维修（包括维护计划、有效的诊断和故障修理、OBD-Ⅱ）。

本书可作为高等院校汽车应用专业的教材，也可作为汽车工程技术人员、汽车维修技师及车主学习汽车专业英语知识的参考书。

图书在版编目（CIP）数据

汽车专业英语教程／刘伟，张良编著. —北京：清华大学出版社；北京交通大学出版社，2008.7（2017.12 重印）

ISBN 978－7－81123－036－9

Ⅰ. 汽…　Ⅱ. ① 刘…　② 张…　Ⅲ. 汽车工程－英语－教材　Ⅳ. H31

中国版本图书馆 CIP 数据核字（2008）第 087560 号

责任编辑：张利军

出版发行：清 华 大 学 出 版 社　邮编：100084　电话：010－62776969　http：//www. tup. com. cn
　　　　　北京交通大学出版社　邮编：100044　电话：010－51686414　http：//press. bjtu. edu. cn
印 刷 者：北京鑫海金澳胶印有限公司
经　　销：全国新华书店
开　　本：185×243　印张：18.75　字数：460 千字
版　　次：2008 年 7 月第 1 版　　2017 年 12 月第 5 次印刷
书　　号：ISBN 978－7－81123－036－9/H・122
印　　数：8 001 ～ 9 000 册　定价：28.00 元

本书如有质量问题，请向北京交通大学出版社质监组反映。对您的意见和批评，我们表示欢迎和感谢。

投诉电话：010－51686043，51686008；传真：010－62225406；E-mail：press@bjtu. edu. cn。

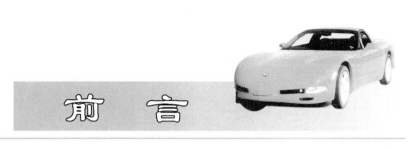

前　言

随着中国国民经济的迅速发展，汽车正在走进千家万户。中国不仅已成为汽车制造大国，而且正在成为汽车出口大国。汽车行业不仅需要大量专业技术人才，更需要大量外向型汽车专业人才。作为汽车行业的从业人员，无论你是汽车设计和制造工程技术人员，还是配件和售后服务人员，不仅要借助英语知识学习更多、更新的汽车专业知识，还要利用英语知识促进中国汽车的出口，到国外去开展汽车销售、技术培训和维修服务。市场竞争日趋激烈，就业形势也日益严峻，要想在竞争中获得优势和发展，汽车专业英语知识将是助你成功的一把钥匙。为此，我们精心编撰了《汽车专业英语教程》一书，旨在帮助读者掌握实用的汽车专业技术英语知识，提高汽车专业英语阅读理解能力。

本书具有以下特点：

1. 内容紧密结合当今最新的汽车技术，读者不仅可以学到最新的汽车技术词汇，同时还可从中学到最新的汽车技术知识；

2. 具有很强的实用性，很多内容来自生产实践，对维修、设计和制造的生产作业具有实际指导作用；

3. 中英文对照，图文并茂，通俗易懂；

4. 后附常用的汽车技术词汇等，学员可以集中查询和记忆；

5. 将随本教材推出相关课件，供教师教学参考。

本书适合作为汽车应用专业的专业英语教材，同时也是汽车维修、设计和制造技术人员学习汽车专业知识和专业英语的一本好书。此外，感兴趣的车主也可从中获得一些车辆的日常养护和正确驾驶知识。

本书主要由刘伟、张良负责编写，白潮、鲁爱萍、张红松、王新宇、鲍晓东、高吕禾等也参与了编写工作。

本书在编写过程中得到了一些汽车制造商、维修站和高等院校的大力支持，并得到了国家劳动部专家委员会汽车维修专业分会各位专家的指点，在此一并表示感谢！

由于编者知识水平所限，书中难免存在不足之处，敬请各位读者批评指正。

编　者

2008 年 7 月于北京

目　录

→ **Part 1　Vehicle Construction 汽车结构**

I

➡ Part 2　Vehicle Identification 汽车识别

➡ Part 3　Engine Control Systems 发动机控制系统

➡ Part 4　Vehicle Maintenance 汽车维修

Part

Vehicle Construction
汽车结构

Unit 1

Introduction to Vehicle Construction 汽车结构简介

Key Terms

vehicle construction	body
chassis	frame

This unit familiarizes you with the "auto part vocabulary" needed to become a successful auto body technician. You will learn to locate and describe the major body panels of an automobile.

本单元将使你熟悉作为成功的汽车车身技术人员所需要的关于汽车部件的词汇表。而且，你将能够定位和描述汽车的主要车身面板。

Knowledge of vehicle construction will help you answer questions such as: What is the name of that part? How are the parts fastened together? What is that part made of? Does the vehicle use a full **perimeter-type frame** or does it have **unibody** construction?

汽车结构知识将帮助你回答这样的问题：那个部件叫什么？部件是如何固定在一起的？那个部件用什么制造？这辆汽车采用周边式车架还是采用承载式车身结构？

1.1 Body and Chassis 车身和底盘

To avoid confusion, the major parts of a vehicle can be **categorized** as part of the **body**, the **chassis**, or the **frame**. You must understand each major division.

为了避免混淆，一辆汽车的主要部件包括车身、底盘、车架。你应该理解每一个主要部件。

The vehicle body provides a protective outer hull（外壳）or "skin" around the outside of an automobile. The body is an attractive, colorful covering over the other parts. Body parts may also contribute to the structural integrity（整体性）（safety and strength）of the vehicle.

汽车车身提供一个保护性的外壳或"皮肤"，包裹在汽车外面。车身是位于其他部件外面的引人注目的彩色覆盖物。车身部件也对汽车结构的整体性（安全性和强度）有益。

The vehicle body can be made from steel, aluminum, fiberglass（玻璃纤维）, plastic, or composite（a combination of materials）. The body is normally painted to give the vehicle its appealing, shiny color and appearance（See Figure 1 – 1）.

汽车车身可以用钢、铝、玻璃纤维、塑料或者复合材料（多种材料的合成物）制造。车身通常会着色，使汽车具有诱人的、闪亮的颜色和外观（见图 1 – 1）。

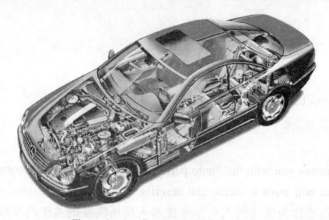

Figure 1 – 1　Construction of a vehicle

The vehicle chassis includes the frame, engine, suspension system, steering system（转向系）, and other mechanical parts with the body removed（See Figure 1 – 2）. The body and chassis are two major categories used to classify the repair areas of a vehicle.

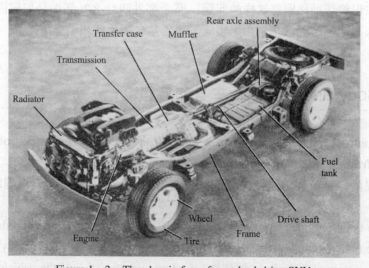

Figure 1 – 2　The chassis for a four-wheel drive SUV

汽车底盘包括车架、发动机、悬架、转向系和去除车身的其他机械部件（见图 1 - 2）。在汽车维修区域的分类中，车身和底盘是两个主要部件。

Description	中文名称	Description	中文名称
radiator	散热器	transmission	变速器
transfer case	分动器	muffler	消声器
rear axle assembly	后轴总成	fuel tank	燃油箱
drive shaft	驱动轴	frame	车架
wheel	车轮	tire	轮胎
engine	发动机		

1.2　Vehicle Frame 车架

The vehicle frame is a high-strength structure used to support all other parts of the vehicle. Besides bolt-on body panels, the frame holds（维持）the engine, transmission, suspension, and other parts in position. Frames are usually made of steel or aluminum and sometimes composite materials. The frame can be separate from the body or integrated into the body shell as in the case of unibody design（Refer to Figure 1 - 3）.

车架是一个高强度结构，用来支撑汽车的其他部件。除了铆接的车身面板，车架使发动机、变速器、悬架和其他部件保持在特定位置。车架通常用钢或铝制成，有时也采用复合材料。车架可以独立于车身，在承载式车身设计中也可以和车身集成在一起（见图 1 - 3）。

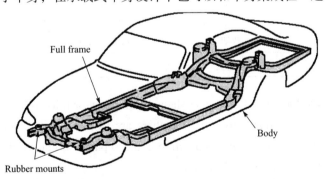

Figure 1 - 3　Frame and body

Description	中文名称	Description	中文名称
rubber mounts	橡胶衬垫	body	车身
full frame	全车架		

Body-over-frame construction has a separate body structure bolted to a thick steel framework. The engine and other major assemblies forming the chassis are mounted on the frame (See Figure 1 – 4). Rubber body mounts fit between the frame and body structure to reduce road noise (unwanted sounds entering the passenger compartment from outside the vehicle).

非承载式车身有单独的车身结构，固定在厚重的车架上。发动机和其他主要部件构成底盘，安装在车架上（见图1 – 4）。为了降低路面噪声（来自车辆外面进入乘员舱的不必要的声音），在车架和车身结构之间安装橡胶车身衬垫。

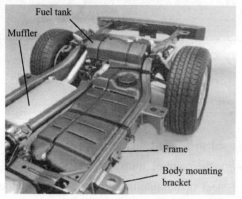
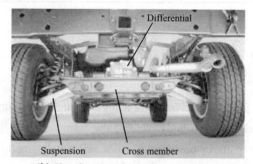

(a) Large brackets on the full frame for the mounted body　　(b) How the suspension mounts to the frame

Figure 1 – 4　Chassis construction

Description	中文名称	Description	中文名称
muffler	消声器	fuel tank	燃油箱
frame	车架	body mounting bracket	车身安装托架
suspension	悬架	cross member	横梁
differential	差速器		

A full frame has a thick metal box or U-shaped stampings or rails welded and/or riveted (用铆钉铆牢的) together. The main structural members are two side rails connected by a series of cross members. For high load-carrying capabilities, the separate frame is made of much heavier gauge (大型量规) steel than the body panels.

全车架是将一个厚重的金属盒或U型冲压件或者横梁焊接或铆接到一起。其主要结构包括连接有多根横梁的两根边梁。为了提高承载能力，车架采用了比车身面板规格高得多的钢材。

The full frame rails extend the entire length of the vehicle. Body-over-frame or full frame construction is commonly used on pickup trucks, sport utility vehicles (SUVs), and most full-size vans.　Some larger luxury cars still use traditional body-over-frame construction.

全车架增大了整车尺寸。非承载式车身或全车架通常用于皮卡、运动型多功能车（SUV）和大部分全尺寸货车。某些大型豪华车仍然使用传统的非承载式车身结构。

A hydro-formed（液压成型的）frame is manufactured by using water under high pressure to force straight box extruded frame rails into the desired shape or contour（轮廓）. A hydro-formed frame is made of a thinner gauge steel than a conventional perimeter frame.　Hydro-formed frames are lighter, almost as strong, and equally as stiff as conventional heavy-gauge steel frames.

液压成型车架是通过高压水迫使车架梁变成设计的形状或轮廓。液压成型车架比传统车架采用更低规格的钢材。与传统的高规格钢车架相比，液压成型车架更轻，强度基本相当，硬度不变。

Unibody construction uses body parts welded or adhesive-bonded（黏合的）together to form an integral（built-in）frame.　The body structure is designed to secure other chassis parts.　No separate heavy-gauge steel frame under the body is needed.

承载式车身将车身部件焊接或黏合到一起，形成一体化结构。车身结构用来确保其他底盘部件的安全，所以不再需要独立的高规格钢制车架。

Today's vehicles are manufactured using both unibody and body-over-frame construction（Refer to Figure 1 –5）.

今天的汽车同时采用承载式车身和非承载式车身结构（见图 1 –5）。

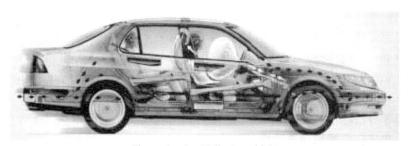

Figure 1 – 5　Unibody vehicle

Unibody construction is a totally different concept in vehicle design that requires more complex assembly techniques, new materials, and a completely different approach to repairs.　In unibody designs, heavy-gauge, cold-rolled（冷轧）steels have been replaced with lighter, thinner, high-strength steel or aluminum alloys（铝合金）. This requires new handling, straightening, and welding techniques.

承载式车身结构是一种完全不同的汽车设计概念，要求更复杂的装配技术、新材料和完全不同的修理方法。在承载式车身设计中，更轻、更薄的高强度钢材或铝合金代替了高规格的冷轧钢。这需要采用新的加工处理方法、强化方法和焊接技术。

Unibody vehicles weld small body panels together to serve as the vehicle frame.　Unibody vehicles are light yet very strong. The front and rear sections are made to crumple（溃缩）while the passenger compartment stays intact（完整无缺的）during a collision.

承载式车身将车身面板焊接到一起充当车架。采用承载式车身的汽车质量轻，强度大。为了在碰撞中乘员舱不变形，在车身前部和后部设计了溃缩区。

1.3　Major Body Sections 车身的主要组成部分

For simplicity and to help communication in auto body repair, a vehicle is commonly divided into three body sections—front, center, and rear. You should understand how these sections are constructed and which parts are included in each.

为了简单及有助于汽车车身维修中的交流，一辆汽车通常被分为三个部分：前部、中部和后部。你应该了解这些部分的结构及所包括的部件。

1. Front Section　前部

The front section, also called the nose section, includes everything between the front bumper and the firewall（车身前围板）. The bumper, grille, frame rails, front suspension parts, and the engine are a few of the items included in the front section of a vehicle.

前部，也被称为鼻梁部，包括前保险杠和车身前围板之间的所有部件。保险杠、冷却格栅、车架梁、前悬和发动机是汽车前部的几个部件。

The nickname "doghouse" is used to refer to the front body section. It is often purchased and cut off from a wreck in one piece from an automotive recycler or salvage yard. The empty engine compartment forms the doghouse.

汽车前部车身俗称"狗窝"。在汽车循环再利用场或废品回购站从汽车残骸上完整地切下汽车前部并出售。空的发动机舱构成"狗窝"。

2. Center Section　中部

The vehicle's center section, or midsection, typically includes the body parts that form the passenger compartment. A few parts in this section include the floor pan（地板）, roof panel, cowl, doors, door pillars, glass, and related parts. The center section is nicknamed the "greenhouse" because it is surrounded by glass.

汽车的核心部分或中部包括构成乘员舱的车身部分。这一部分的几个部件包括地板、顶棚、散热器百叶窗、车门、车门立柱、车窗玻璃和相关部分。中部被昵称为"温室"，因为它被玻璃所环绕。

3. Rear Section　后部

The rear section (the tail section) commonly consists of the rear quarter panels, trunk or rear floor pan, rear frame rails, deck lid (行李箱盖), rear bumper, and related parts. It is often sectioned or cut off of a salvaged vehicle to repair severe rear impact damage.

后部（尾部）通常由后四分之一面板、行李箱或者后部地板底盘、后部车架滑轨、行李箱盖、后保险杠和相关部分组成。为了修理严重的后部碰撞损害，经常需要切割或解体事故汽车的后部。

When discussing collision repair, body shop personnel often refer to these sections of the vehicle. It simplifies communication because everyone knows which parts are included in each section.

在讨论碰撞维修的时候，车身商店经常会提到汽车的这些部分。由于每个人都知道各部分包括哪些部件，这便简化了交流。

4. Vehicle Left and Right Sides　车辆左边和右边

The left and right sides of a vehicle are determined by standing behind the vehicle or sitting in the driver's seat behind the steering wheel. In either position, the vehicle's left side is to your left; the right side is to your right. Panels and parts are often named for the left or right side of the vehicle.

通过站在汽车后部或坐在转向轮后的驾驶员座椅上可确定汽车的左边和右边。在上述位置中的任何一处，汽车的左边就是你的左边，汽车的右边就是你的右边。面板和部件经常根据其在汽车的左边或者右边来命名。

Note that vehicles built for American roads have the steering wheel on the left. Vehicles built for use in other countries may have the steering wheel on the right side of the passenger compartment.

需要注意的是，为行驶于美国而制造的车辆转向轮在左面。为在其他国家使用而制造的车辆转向轮可能位于乘客舱的右面。

5. Drive Line Configuration　驱动线路组成

Drive line configuration refers to how power is transmitted from the engine to the drive wheels. There are six basic drivetrain (动力传动系统) designs: front-wheel drive; rear-wheel drive; rear-engine, rear-wheel drive; mid-engine, rear-wheel drive; four-wheel drive; and all-wheel drive. The vast majority of unibody vehicles on the road today are FWD with the engine in the front. These variations affect vehicle construction and repair methods.

驱动线路组成是指动力如何从发动机传递到驱动轮。共有6种动力传动系统设计：前轮驱动；后轮驱动；后置发动机，后轮驱动；中置发动机，后轮驱动；四轮驱动；全轮驱动。

今天在路上行驶的大量承载式车身的汽车都是前轮驱动，发动机前置。这些变化会影响车辆结构和修理方法。

A transverse（横向的）engine mounts sideways in the engine compartment. Its crankshaft centerline extends toward the right and left of the body. Both front-engine and rear-engine vehicles use this configuration.

横置发动机安装在发动机舱的一侧。它的曲轴中心线通过车身的左面和右面。发动机前置和后置车辆使用这种结构。

A longitudinal（纵向的）engine mounts the crankshaft center-line front to rear when viewed from the top. Front-engine, rear-wheel drive vehicles use this type of engine mounting.

从顶部观察，纵置发动机的曲轴通过在从前到后的中心线。发动机前置，后轮驱动的车辆采用这种发动机安装方式。

A front-engine, front-wheel drive（FWD）vehicle has both the engine and transaxle in the front. Drive axles extend out from the transaxle to power the front drive wheels. This is one of the most common configurations. The heavy drivetrain adds weight to the front drive wheels for good traction on slippery pavement.

发动机前置，前轮驱动（FWD）的车辆，发动机和驱动桥在前面。驱动轴从驱动桥中伸出，驱动前驱动轮。这是最常用的结构之一。为了在光滑的公路上得到良好的牵引性能，重型动力传动系统加大了前驱动轮的负荷。

A front-engine, rear-wheel drive（RWD）vehicle has the engine in the front and the drive axle in the rear. The transmission is usually right behind the engine, and a drive shaft transfers power back to the rear axle.

发动机前置，后轮驱动（RWD）的车辆，发动机在前面，驱动轴在后面。变速器通常在发动机的后面，传动轴传输动力给后轴。

A rear-engine, rear-wheel drive（RRD）vehicle has the engine in the back, and a transaxle transfers power to the rear drive wheels. Traction upon acceleration and cornering is good because more of the weight of the drivetrain is over the rear drive wheels.

发动机后置，后轮驱动（RRD）的车辆，发动机在后面，驱动桥传输动力给后驱动轮。由于动力传动系统的更多重量施加在后驱动轮上，其加速和转弯的牵引性能良好。

A mid-engine, rear-wheel drive（MRD）vehicle has the engine centrally located, right behind the front seat. This helps to place the center of gravity（重心）in the middle so that the front and rear wheels hold the same amount of weight, which improves cornering ability.

中置发动机，后轮驱动（MRD）的车辆，发动机居中安装，在前排座椅的后面。这有助于使重心居中，从而使前轮和后轮承担同样的重量，从而改善过弯性能。

All-wheel drive（AWD）uses two differentials to power all four drive wheels. This is a relatively new design used on several makes of passenger vehicles.

全轮驱动（AWD）使用两个差速器来驱动全部四个驱动轮。这是一种相对较新的设计，只在几种样式的客车上使用。

Four-wheel drive（4WD）systems use a transfer case to send power to two differentials and all wheels. The transfer case can be engaged（啮合的）and disengaged to select two- or four-wheel drive as desired. It is common on off-road vehicles.

四轮驱动（4WD）系统使用分动箱传输动力给两个差速器和所有车轮。通过分动器的啮合或分离来选择两轮驱动或者四轮驱动。它通常用于越野车。

Key Words

perimeter-type frame　周边式车架	body　车身
unibody　承载式车身	chassis　底盘
categorize　分类	frame　车架

Exercises

1. _____ is normally painted to give the vehicle its appealing, shiny color and appearance.

2. The body and chassis are two major categories used to classify _____ of a vehicle.

3. In _____ designs, heavy-gauge, cold-rolled steels have been replaced with lighter, thinner, high-strength steel or aluminum alloys.

4. Four-wheel drive（4WD）systems use a _____ to send power to two differentials and all wheels.

Unit 2
Engine 发动机

Key Terms

air duct	oil pump
throttle	cooling system
manifold	thermostat
volume	radiator
exhaust system	engine block
integrated catalytic converter	oil sump
exhaust flap	crankcase
cylinder head	crankshaft
camshaft	connecting rod
gasket	piston
Valvetronic	flywheel
drag lever	lubrication system
worm gear	oil filter
chain drive	oil cooler
camshaft	

Internal combustion engines（内燃机）convert potential chemical energy（化学能）into mechanical energy（机械能）. Engine components commonly include the air ducts（进气道）, exhaust system（排放系统）, cylinder head（气缸盖）, cooling system（冷却系统）, engine block（气缸体）and lubrication system（润滑系统）. The following literature on components is about an engine. It is available in two engine capacity（发动机排量，有时称为"engine size"）versions, B36 = 3.6 L and B44 = 4.4 L.

内燃机将化学能转化为机械能。它由进气道、排放系统、气缸盖、冷却系统、气缸体和润滑系统组成。下文描述了一台发动机各部件的情况。该发动机有两种排量：B36 = 3.6 升和 B44 = 4. 4 升。

2.1　Air Ducts 进气道

2. 1. 1　Fresh Air System　新鲜空气系统

As shown in Figure 2 – 1, the intake passes through the **air intake ducts** from the air cleaner（空气滤清器，有时称为"air filter"）to the **throttle** section in the variable intake manifold（可变进气歧管），and on to the two cylinder head intake ducts.

如图 2 – 1 所示，吸入的空气通过进气道接头从空气滤清器到节气门部件，再进入可变进气歧管，最后到达两个气缸盖的进气道。

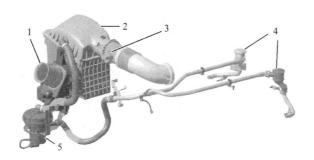

Figure 2 – 1　Air routing

Index	Description	中文名称
1	Air intake duct	进气道
2	Air cleaner housing with intake air silencer	带消音器的空气滤清器
3	Intake pipe with HFM (hot-film air-mass flow sensor)	带 HFM（热膜式空气质量流量传感器）的进气管
4	Secondary air valves	二次空气阀
5	Secondary air pump	二次空气泵

2. 1. 2　Throttle Valve　节气门

The throttle valve（节气门阀）is not necessary for engine load control（发动机负荷控制）. This is carried out by the intake valves' variable lift（进气门可变升程）adjustment. The tasks of the throttle valve are：

— To provide support for and optimal（最佳的）engine start；

— To ensure a constant 50 mbar vacuum（真空）in the **intake pipe** in all load ranges.

发动机负荷控制不需要节气门阀，发动机负荷控制是通过进气门的可变升程变化来实现的。节气门完成下列任务：

——为得到最佳发动机起动性能提供支持；

——确保在所有负荷范围内进气管中真空度恒定为 50 mbar。

The intake manifold is located in the V of the engine, and is mounted on the cylinder head intake ducts. The variable intake manifold housing is made from a **magnesium alloy**（See Figure 2-2）.

进气系统位于发动机的 V 形区域并被安装在气缸盖的进气道上。可调式进气系统的壳体由镁合金制成（见图 2-2）。

Figure 2-2　Interior view of the variable intake manifold

Index	Description	中文名称
1	Intake port	进气口
2	Funnel	漏斗
3	Rotor	转子
4	Shaft	轴
5	Spur gears	直齿圆柱齿轮
6	Manifold volume	集气箱腔体

Each cylinder has its own intake pipe（1）which is connected to the manifold volume（6）via a rotor（3）. The rotors are supported by one shaft（4）per cylinder bank（每列气缸）. The shaft for the cylinder bank 1-4 rotors is adjusted by a drive unit, an electric motor with speed-transforming transmission, depending on the engine speed. The second shaft, from which the rotor for the opposite cylinder bank is adjusted, is turned by the driven shaft active through spur gears（5）in the opposite direction. The intake air flows via the manifold volume through the funnel（2）and on to the cylinders. The intake path length is set as the rotor turns.

　　每一个气缸都有一个自己独用的进气道（1），进气道通过一个转子（3）与集气箱腔体（6）连在一起。每一个气缸列都有一个轴（4），所有转子固定在轴上。一个驱动单元（一个带变速装置的电动马达）根据转速调节气缸列 1～4 的转子轴。调节对置气缸列转子的第二根轴通过正齿轮（5）由被调节的轴逆向转动。经集气箱腔体的进气通过漏斗（2）流向各气缸。进气行程的长度通过转子的旋转调节。

The drive motor is controlled by the DME（digital engine-management system）and is intended for providing feedback about the funnel position via a potentiometer（电位计）.

　　驱动马达由 DME（数字式发动机管理系统）控制。为了反馈漏斗位置，驱动马达带有一个电位计。

The intake path length can be adjusted according to the engine speed（See Figure 2-3 and Figure 2-4）. Adjustment from long to short intake path begins at 3,500 rpm. As the engine speed increases, the intake path length is reduced linearly, up to 6,200 rpm.

　　进气行程长度根据发动机转速调节（见图 2-3 和图 2-4）。从长进气行程到短进气行程的调节在转速为 3 500 rpm 时开始，随着发动机转速的上升，在转速达到 6 200 rpm 之前进气行程线性缩短。

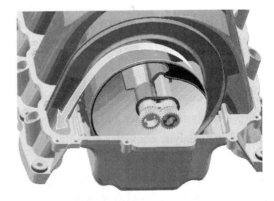

Figure 2-3　Intake manifold set to short intake path　　Figure 2-4　Intake manifold set to longer intake path

2.2　Exhaust System 排气系统

Figure 2-5 shows the exhaust system.

图 2-5 所示为排气系统的构成。

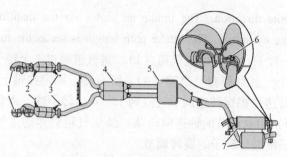

Figure 2 – 5　Exhaust system

Index	Description	中文名称
1	Manifolds with integrated catalytic converter	内置催化转换器的排气歧管
2	Broadband oxygen sensor	宽带氧传感器
3	Secondary oxygen sensor（steep characteristic curve）	辅助氧传感器（跳跃式特性线）
4	Exhaust pipe with front silencer	排气管，带消音器
5	Centre silencer	中央消音器
6	Exhaust flap	排气风门
7	Rear silencer	后消音器

2. 2. 1　Exhaust Manifold with Catalytic Converter
带废气触媒转换器的排气歧管

A four-into-two-into-one manifold has been fitted on each cylinder bank. The manifold and the catalytic converter housing are integrated into a single component. A ceramic-bed（陶瓷载体）pre-catalytic converter and a ceramic-bed main catalytic converter are arranged one behind the other in the catalytic converter housing.

每一个气缸列侧都安装了一个四变二变一结构的弯管排气歧管。它与废气触媒转换器的壳体组成一个部件。在废气触媒转换器壳体中依次安装有一个陶瓷载体前部废气触媒转换器和一个陶瓷载体主废气触媒转换器。

The supports for the broadband oxygen sensors and the secondary oxygen sensors are located upstream and **downstream** of the catalytic converter in the head pipe（前置管）or catalytic converter outlet funnel（漏斗形出口）.

宽带氧传感器和监控用传感器安装在废气触媒转换器的前面和后面，位于前置管及废气触媒转换器的漏斗形出口中。

2. 2. 2　Silencer　消音器

An absorption-type, 1. 8L capacity front silencer has been fitted for each cylinder bank. An absorption-type, 5. 8L centre silencer is fitted downstream of the two front silencers. The rear silencers are of the resonator type（谐振型）, and have capacities of 12. 6 and 16. 6 liters.

每一个气缸列侧都安装了一个吸收型容积为 1. 8 升的前消音器。在两个前消音器后连接了一个吸收型容积为 5. 8 升的中间消音器。后消音器为谐振型，容积有 12. 6 升和 16. 6 升两种。

2. 2. 3   Exhaust Flap   排气风门

The rear silencer is fitted with an exhaust flap to keep noise to a minimum. The exhaust gas flap is opened when a gear is **engaged** and the engine speed is above 1, 500 rpm. This activates an additional rear silencer capacity of 14 liters.

为了把噪音降到最小，后消音器装备了一个排气风门。在车辆挂入挡位且发动机转速超过 1 500 rpm 时排气风门打开，这样就给后消音器增加了 14 升的容量。

2.3   Cylinder Heads 气缸盖

2. 3. 1   Description   概述

The two **cylinder heads** are fitted with the variable **valve timing system**（Refer to Figure 2 - 6）. The cylinder heads are cooled according to the cross-flow（横流）principle. The **camshaft** and the eccentric shaft（偏心轴）are jointly guided by means of a bridge support. The cylinder heads are made from aluminum（铝）.

为进行气门控制，气缸盖装备有可变气门正时系统（见图 2 - 6）。气缸盖按横流原理进行冷却。凸轮轴和偏心轴借助于一个轴承支座一起控制。气缸盖由铝合金制成。

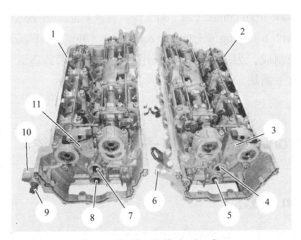

Figure 2 - 6   Cylinder heads

Index	Description	中文名称
1	Cylinder head for cylinder bank 1 – 4	1～4 缸侧气缸盖
2	Cylinder head for cylinder bank 5 – 8	5～8 缸侧气缸盖
3	Upper timing chain guide with oil jet	带机油嘴的上正时链导向件
4	Hole for variable camshaft adjustment intake solenoid valve	进气电磁阀安装孔
5	Hole for variable camshaft adjustment outlet solenoid valve	排气电磁阀安装孔
6	Chain tensioner mount	链条张紧器托架
7	Hole for variable camshaft adjustment intake solenoid valve	进气电磁阀安装孔
8	Hole for variable camshaft adjustment outlet solenoid valve	排气电磁阀安装孔
9	Oil pressure switch	机油压力开关
10	Chain tensioner mount	链条张紧器托架
11	Upper timing chain guide with oil jet	带机油嘴的上正时链导向件

2. 3. 2　Cylinder Head Gaskets　气缸盖密封件

The cylinder head gasket（密封件）is a multi-layer steel gasket with a rubber coating.
气缸盖密封件是一个带橡胶层的多层钢质密封件。

2. 3. 3　Cylinder Head Bolts　气缸盖螺栓

The cylinder head **bolts** for the engine are M10 × 160 necked-down bolts（应力螺栓）. These bolts should always be replaced when repairs are carried out. The lower part of the timing chain housing is bolted to the cylinder head using two M8 × 45 bolts.

气缸盖螺栓都是 M10 × 160 的应力螺栓。这些螺栓在维修时每次必须更换。正时齿轮箱下部部件用两个 M8 × 45 螺栓固定在气缸盖上。

2. 3. 4　Camshafts　凸轮轴

The camshafts are made from chilled cast iron（淬火铸铁）and are hollow to reduce their weight. The camshafts are fitted with balancing weights for equalizing（补偿）imbalances in the valve gear.

凸轮轴由淬火铸铁制成，为了减轻重量采用空心铸造技术铸造。为补偿气门机构中的不平衡，在凸轮轴上装有平衡块。

2. 4　Valvetronic 无级可变电子气门控制系统

2. 4. 1　Description　概述

The Valvetronic system is a combination of variable camshaft adjustment（可调式凸轮轴调

节机构）and valve lift adjustment. This combination of abilities allows it to control when the intake valves are opened and closed, and also the opening lift（开启升程）. The intake air flow is set by adjusting the valve lift while the throttle valve is opened. This enables optimum cylinder filling, and reduces fuel consumption. Each cylinder head in the engine has a Valvetronic unit (See Figure 2 – 7). This Valvetronic unit consists of a bridge support with eccentric shaft, the intermediate levers（中间杠杆）with retaining springs（固定弹簧）, the **drag lever** and the inlet camshaft（凸轮轴）. In addition, the following components belong to the Valvetronic system：

— A Valvetronic motor for each cylinder head;

— A Valvetronic control unit;

— An eccentric shaft sensor for each cylinder head.

无级可变电子气门控制系统是可调式凸轮轴调节机构和一个气门升程调节系统的总称。它以这种组合方式控制进气门的开启时刻和关闭时刻及开启升程。在节气门打开情况下进气量通过调节气门升程设定。这样就能确定出最佳的气缸进气量并降低耗油量。发动机上每一个气缸盖有一个电子气门控制单元（见图 2 – 7）。电子气门控制单元由带偏心轴的轴承支座、带止动弹簧的中间杠杆、摇臂和进气凸轮轴组成。另外，还有下列部件属于电子气门控制系统：

——每个气缸盖有一个电子气门控制马达；

——一个电子气门控制的控制单元；

——每个气缸盖有一个偏心轴传感器。

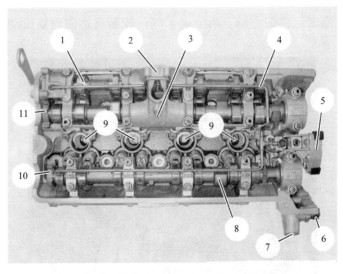

Figure 2 – 7　Cylinder head for cylinder bank 1 – 4

Index	Description	中文名称
1	Eccentric shaft	偏心轴
2	Valvetronic motor mount	电子气门控制马达托架
3	Bridge support	轴承支座
4	Valve gear oil supply	气门机构供油
5	Upper timing chain guide	上正时链导向件
6	Oil pressure switch	油压开关
7	Chain tensioner mount	链条张紧器托架
8	Exhaust camshaft	排气凸轮轴
9	**Spark plug** threads	火花塞螺纹
10 + 11	Camshaft sensor wheels	凸轮轴传感器的传感器轮

2.4.2 Valve Lift Adjustment Components　气门升程调节组件

1. Electric Motor for Eccentric Shaft Adjustment　用于偏心轴调节的电动马达

Valve lift adjustment is driven by two electric motors controlled by a separate control unit（控制单元）which receives its commands from the DME. The eccentric shafts are rotated by a worm gear（蜗杆）which is guided by a bridge support（cam carrier 凸轮轴支座）for each cylinder head. The two Valvetronic motors are located towards the inside of the engine's V（发动机的 V 型区域）（See Figure 2 – 8）.

气门升程的调节通过两个电动马达实现。一个独立的控制单元从 DME 接收控制命令并对这两个电动马达进行控制。偏心轴由一个蜗杆传动装置带动旋转。每个气缸盖都借助一个轴承支座凸轮轴支座来定位偏心轴。两个电子气门控制马达向内朝发动机 V 型区域安装（见图 2 – 8）。

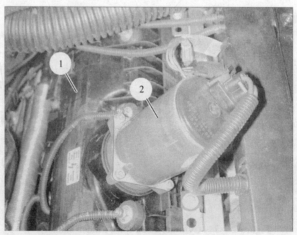

Figure 2 – 8　Valvetronic motor

Index	Description	中文名称
1	Cylinder head cover for cylinder bank 1 – 4	1～4缸侧的气缸盖罩
2	Valvetronic motor for eccentric shaft adjustment	用于偏心轴调节的电子气门控制马达

2. Eccentric Shaft Sensor　偏心轴传感器

The eccentric shaft sensors are mounted in each of the two cylinder heads above the eccentric shaft rotors. They use a data telegram（信号）to convey（传输）the precise position of the eccentric shafts on the Valvetronic control unit.

偏心轴传感器在两个气缸盖中都是安装在偏心轴的磁轮上方。它们借助一个数据电码向电子气门控制系统的控制单元传输偏心轴的准确位置数据。

The eccentric shaft（1）rotors（2）contain strong magnets（磁铁）（See Figure 2 – 9）. These allow the eccentric shaft sensors to determine the precise position of the eccentric shafts （1）. The rotors are secured to the eccentric shafts using non-magnetic stainless steel bolts（不锈钢螺栓）. On no account（绝不）must magnetic bolts be used, since this could cause the eccentric shaft sensors to produce inaccurate results.

偏心轴（1）上的磁轮（2）有很强的磁性（见图2 – 9）。在它们的帮助下通过偏心轴传感器能确定出偏心轴（1）的精确位置。这些磁轮用无磁性的不锈钢螺栓固定到偏心轴上。在任何情况下都不允许使用磁性螺栓，否则的话，偏心轴传感器会传递出有错误的数值。

On the engine, the roller-type fingers（滚子式摇臂）are made from sheet metal（金属板材）. The intake valve lift can be adjusted to anywhere between 0. 3 mm and 9. 85 mm（See Figure 2 – 10）.

在发动机上滚子式摇臂由板材制成。进气门的气门升程可以在0. 3 mm～9. 85 mm之间进行调节（见图2 – 10）。

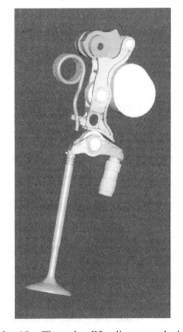

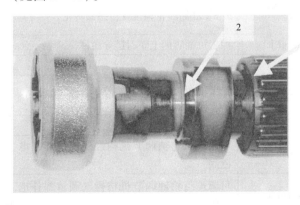

Figure 2 – 9　Rotor on eccentric shaft

Figure 2 – 10　The valve lift adjustment device

2.5 Chain Drive 链条传动

Figure 2 – 11 shows the chain drive.

链条传动的结构如图 2 – 11 所示。

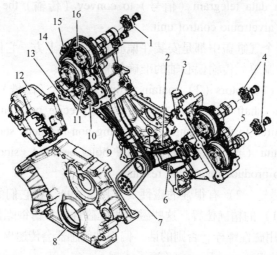

Figure 2 – 11　Chain drive

Index	Description	中文名称
1	Sensor wheels for the camshaft position sensor, cylinder bank 1–4	1~4 缸侧凸轮轴位置传感器转轮
2	Tensioning rail, cylinder bank 5–8	张紧导轨，5~8 缸侧
3	Chain tensioner, cylinder bank 5–8	链条张紧器，5~8 缸侧
4	Sensor wheels for the camshaft position sensor, cylinder bank 5–8	5~8 缸侧凸轮轴位置传感器转轮
5	Upper timing chain guide with integrated oil jet	内置机油嘴的上正时链导向件
6	Guide rail	滑轨
7	Sprocket for oil pump drive	机油泵驱动链轮
8	Lower timing chain cover	下正时链盖
9	Tensioning rail, cylinder bank 1–4	1~4 缸侧张紧导轨
10	Solenoid valve, variable camshaft adjustment intake	可调式凸轮轴调节机构进气调节部件电磁阀
11	Solenoid valve, variable camshaft adjustment outlet	可调式凸轮轴调节机构排气调节部件电磁阀

continued

Index	Description	中文名称
12	Upper timing chain cover	上正时链盖
13	Chain tensioner, cylinder bank 1–4	1～4缸侧链条张紧器
14	variable camshaft adjustment outlet	可调式凸轮轴调节机构排气调节部件
15	Upper timing chain guide with integrated oil jet	内置机油嘴的上正时链导向件
16	variable camshaft adjustment intake	可调式凸轮轴调节机构进气调节部件

The camshafts are driven by a **toothed chain**, one for each cylinder bank. The oil pump is driven by a separate roller chain（滚子链）.

每个气缸列的凸轮轴都由一个齿形带驱动。机油泵由一个单独的滚子链驱动。

2.6   Cooling System 冷却系统

Coolant flow has been optimized. The engine is warmed up as quickly as possible after a cold start, and sufficient engine cooling while the engine is running is also ensured（保证）(See Figure 2 – 12). The cylinder heads are supplied with coolant in a cross-flow pattern (previously longitudinal). This ensures more even temperature distribution to all cylinders.

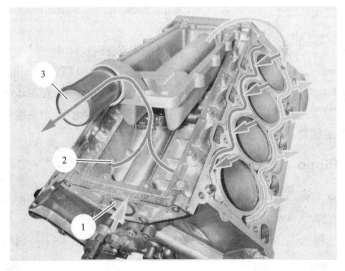

Figure 2 – 12   Coolant flow in the engine block

Index	Description	中文名称
1	Coolant from the coolant pump through the feed pipe to the rear face of the engine	冷却液从冷却液泵经过进流管路流向发动机后端
2	Coolant from the cylinder walls to the thermostat	冷却液从气缸壁流向节温器
3	Connection to water pump/thermostat	至水泵/节温器的接口

冷却液导流系统已进行优化。这样在冷机起动后就能尽快使发动机暖机，并在运行过程中保证均匀且充分地使发动机冷却（见图 2 – 12）。冷却液横向流过气缸盖（迄今为止其他发动机都是纵向流过），这样所有气缸的温度都是均匀分布的。

The coolant flows from the water pump through the feed pipe (1) in the engine's V, and to the rear side of the **engine block**. This area has a cast aluminum cover.

水泵输送的冷却液经过发动机 V 型区域中的进流管路（1）流向发动机，缸体后端这个区域装有一个铸铝盖。

From here, the coolant flows to the external（外面的）**cylinder walls**, and from there into the cylinder heads.

冷却液从这里流向气缸外壁，并从那里流进气缸盖。

The coolant then flows from the cylinder heads in the engine block V and through the connection (3) to the **thermostat**.

冷却液从气缸盖中流入发动机缸体的 V 型区域并经接口（3）流向节温器。

The still cold coolant flows from the thermostat back to the engine block via the water pump (short circuit).

较冷的冷却液从节温器流出后直接由水泵送回到发动机缸体中（小循环回路）。

When the engine reaches operating temperature（85℃ – 110℃）, the thermostat closes the small coolant circuit and opens the large coolant circuit, including the **radiator**.

在发动机工作温度达到 85℃～110℃时，节温器关闭这个小冷却系统管路，并打开包括散热器的大冷却系统回路。

2.6.1 Water Pump 水泵

The water pump（See Figure 2 – 13）is combined with the thermostat housing and is screwed（用螺丝拧紧的）to the lower timing chain case cover.

水泵（见图 2 – 13）与节温器壳组合在一起，并用螺栓固定在下正时链箱盖上。

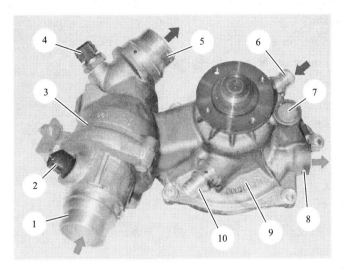

Figure 2 – 13　Water pump

Index	Description	中文名称
1	Map-controlled thermostat（radiator return flow）	电子节温器（水箱出水管）
2	Electrical connection for map-controlled thermostat heating element	电子节温器加热元件电气接头
3	Thermostat mixing chamber（in water pump）	节温器混合室（在水泵中）
4	Temperature sensor（engine outlet temperature）	温度传感器（发动机出水口温度）
5	Radiator in-flow	水箱进水管
6	Heat exchanger transmission oil return flow	变速箱油热交换器回流管路
7	Leakage chamber（evaporation space）	泄漏室（气化室）
8	Alternator in-flow	发电机进流管路
9	Water pump	水泵
10	Expansion tank connection	接口热膨胀平衡罐

2. 6. 2　Map-controlled Thermostat　电子节温器

The map-controlled thermostat allows the engine to be cooled in accordance with（与……一致）the relevant operating conditions. This reduces fuel consumption by around 1% – 2%.

通过电子节温器发动机冷却系统能精确地与发动机当前工作状态进行适配，这样耗油量能降低大约 1% ~ 2%。

The cooling module（See Figure 2 – 14）contains the following main **cooling system** components：

— Cooling radiator；

— Air conditioning condenser（冷凝器）；

— Transmission oil-water heat exchanger with control unit；

— Hydraulic fluid radiator；

— Engine oil radiator；

— Main electric fan；

— Fan shroud for viscous coupling fan（硅油离合器风扇）.

冷却模块（见图2-14）包括冷却系统的下列主要组件：

——冷却液散热器；

——空调冷凝器；

——带调节单元的变速箱油-水热交换器；

——液压油冷却器；

——发动机机油冷却器；

——嵌入式电动风扇；

——硅油离合器风扇的集风罩。

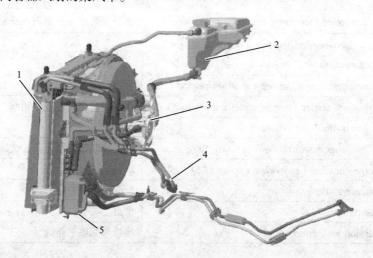

Figure 2-14　Cooling module

Index	Description	中文名称
1	Cooling radiator	冷却液散热器
2	Expansion tank	热膨胀平衡罐
3	Water pump	水泵
4	Engine oil-air heat exchanger connection	发动机机油-空气热交换器接口
5	Transmission oil-water heat exchanger（ÖWT）	变速箱油-水热交换器

2. 6. 3 Cooling Radiator 冷却液散热器

The radiator is made from aluminum and is divided into a high-temperature part and a low-temperature part by a partition wall (隔板), both are connected in series.

该散热器由铝制成，并由一个隔板分隔成高温部分和低温部分，这两个部分串接在一起。

The coolant first flows into the high-temperature section, and then back to the engine, cooled.

冷却液首先流入高温部分并在那里冷却后流回到发动机内。

Some of the coolant flows through an opening in the radiator partition wall to the high-temperature section, then on to the low-temperature part where it is cooled further.

冷却液流入高温部分后，一部分冷却液通过冷却器隔板上的孔到达低温部分，并在那里继续冷却。

The coolant then flows from the low-temperature part (when the thermostat is open) into the oil-water heat exchanger.

从低温部分出来的冷却液（当节温器已打开时）到达油 – 水热交换器内。

2. 6. 4 Coolant Expansion Tank 热膨胀平衡罐

The coolant expansion tank has been removed from the cooling module and installed in the engine compartment on the right hand of the wheel-housing (轮罩).

热膨胀平衡罐已从冷却模块中移出，安装在发动机室中轮罩右边。

2. 6. 5 Transmission Oil-water Heat Exchanger 变速箱油 – 水热交换器

The transmission oil-water heat exchanger ensures that the transmission oil is heated up quickly and also that it is safely and appropriately cooled.

变速箱油水 – 热交换器首先快速提升变速箱油的温度，随后确保变速箱油充分冷却。

When the engine is cold, the thermostat switches the transmission oil water heat exchanger to the engine's shorter circuit. This allows the transmission oil to heat up as quickly as possible.

当发动机冷机启动时节温器把变速箱油 – 水热交换器切换到发动机的小循环回路，这样可以尽快使变速箱油升温。

From an thermostat return flow water temperature of 82℃, the thermostat switches the transmission oil-water heat exchanger to the low-temperature coolant radiator circuit. This cools the transmission oil.

节温器回流管路的水温在 82℃ 以上时，节温器把变速箱油 – 水热交换器切换到冷却液水箱的低温回路，这样变速箱油将冷却下来。

2.6.6 Electrically Operated Fan 电动风扇

The electric fan is integrated in the cooling module and is fitted flush（齐平的）against the radiator. The speed is regulated（控制）by the DME.

电动风扇集成在冷却模块内，并嵌入到散热器上，其转速由 DME 进行无级调节。

2.6.7 Viscous Coupling Fan 硅油离合器风扇

The viscous coupling fan is driven by the water pump.

这个硅油离合器风扇通过水泵驱动。

The viscous coupling fan is the last cooling level and switches on at an air temperature of 92℃.

在空气温度达到 92℃ 以上时，这个硅油离合器风扇作为最后一级冷却而启动。

2.7 Engine Block 发动机缸体

2.7.1 Oil Sump 油底壳

Figure 2 – 15 shows the oil sump.

油底壳如图 2 – 15 所示。

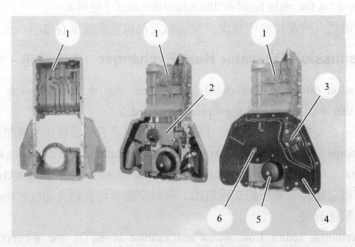

Figure 2 – 15　Oil sump

Index	Description	中文名称
1	Upper section of the oil sump	油底壳上部分

continued

Index	Description	中文名称
2	Oil pump	机油泵
3	Oil condition sensor	机油状态传感器
4	Lower section of the oil sump	油底壳下部分
5	Oil filter element	机油滤清器元件
6	Oil drain plug	放油螺塞

The **oil sump** consists of two parts. The upper section of the oil sump is made from cast aluminum and is sealed（密封）to the **crankcase** with a rubber-coated（涂橡胶层的）sheet steel gasket. The double-skinned lower section of the oil sump is flanged to（用螺栓连接）the upper section of the oil sump.

油底壳由两部分组成。油底壳上部分由压铸铝合金制成，与曲轴箱之间用涂橡胶层的钢板密封件进行密封。由双层板材制成的油底壳下部用螺栓固定在油底壳上部。

2.7.2   Crankcase   曲轴箱

The crankcase（See Figure 2 – 16）has a one-piece "open deck" design and is made entirely from Alusil（铝硅合金）.

曲轴箱（见图 2 - 16）是以开盖结构方式制造的单个部件，全部由铝硅合金制成。

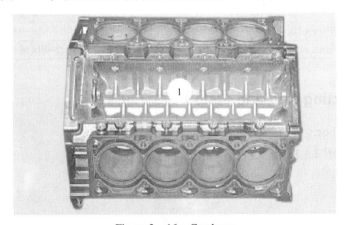

Figure 2 – 16   Crankcase

Index	Description	中文名称
1	V（coolant collection area）	V 形区域（冷却液聚集区域）

2.7.3　Crankshaft　曲轴

The **crankshaft**（See Figure 2–17）is made from grey cast iron and is inductively hardened. To save weight, the crankshaft has been hollowed around bearings（2）,（3）, and（4）. It has five bearings. The fifth bearing is also the thrust bearing（轴向止推轴承）.

曲轴（见图 2–17）由灰口铸铁制造并进行了高频感应淬火。为减轻重量,曲轴在轴承（2）、（3）、（4）的区域内采用了空心铸造。它有 5 个轴承,第 5 个轴承同时是轴向止推轴承。

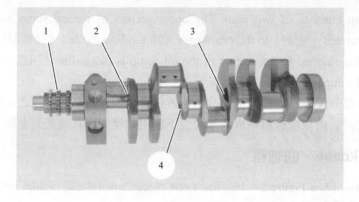

Figure 2–17　Crankshaft

Index	Description	中文名称
1	Crankshaft sprocket	曲轴链轮
2–4	Hollowed area of the crankshaft	曲轴的空心浇铸区域

2.7.4　Connecting Rod and Piston　连杆和活塞

Figure 2–18 shows the piston and connecting rod.

连杆和活塞如图 2–18 所示。

Figure 2–18　Piston and connecting rod

The cast piston is a weight-optimized box piston with integrated valve pockets（避阀坑）in the piston crown（活塞顶）.

以铸造方式制造的活塞是一个做过重量优化的箱形活塞，在活塞顶中带有避阀坑。

The pistons are made of high-temperature aluminum alloy and fitted with three **piston rings**：

— 1st piston ring groove（活塞环槽）＝square ring；

— 2nd piston ring groove＝taperface ring（锥面环）；

— 3rd piston ring groove＝three-part oil control ring.

这种活塞用一种耐高温的铝合金制造并带有 3 个活塞环：

——第一道活塞环槽＝矩形环第一道气环；

——第二道活塞环槽＝锥面环第二道气环；

——第三道活塞环槽＝三件式挡油环。

The steel forged **connecting rod** is split. As the connecting rod end is split at 30°, it is possible to carry out the cranking in a very compact space. The **pistons** are cooled by oil jets（喷油嘴）on the exhaust side of the piston crown.

锻钢连杆的斜切口采用裂开工艺制造。因为连杆大头有一个 30°斜切口，所以可以设计一个特别紧凑的曲轴箱。活塞的冷却通过曲轴箱内的喷油嘴在活塞顶排气侧喷油实现。

2.7.5　Flywheel　飞轮

The **flywheel** is made from laminated plate. The starter rim（启动齿圈）and increment wheel（for recording the engine speed and crankshaft positioning detection）are riveted（铆接的）directly on the drive disc while warm. The flywheel diameter is 320 mm.

飞轮为复合板材结构。起动马达齿圈和信号齿轮（用于测得发动机转速和识别曲轴位置）直接热铆接到从动盘上。飞轮的直径是 320 毫米。

2.7.6　Vibration Damper　扭振减震器

The vibration damper is a torsional vibration absorber（扭转减震器）in an axial（轴向的）non-interacting design.

扭转减震器是一种轴向去耦合结构的扭转减震器。

2.7.7　Engine Suspension　发动机支座

The engine suspension（发动机支座）is provided by means of two hydraulic damping engine mounts. The engine mounts are located on the front axle carrier.

发动机支座由两个液压减震的发动机支座构成。这两个发动机支座安装在前桥架梁上。

2.8 Lubrication System 润滑系统

2.8.1 Oil Circuit 机油回路

The engine oil is filtered（过滤）by the oil pump to the lubrication and cooling points in the engine block and pumped in the cylinder head. The following components are supplied with engine oil in the crankcase and cylinder head.

Crankcase（See Figure 2 – 19）：

— Crankshaft bearing；

— Oil jets for cooling the piston crowns；

— Oil jets for the chain drive on cylinder bank 5 – 8；

— Tensioning rail（张紧导轨）for chain drive on cylinder bank 1 – 4.

Cylinder head：

— Chain tensioner（链条张紧器）；

— Guide rail on cylinder head；

— Hydraulic tappet（液压推杆）（hydraulic valve adjustment elements）；

— VANOS；

— Camshaft bearing；

— Oil jet strips（喷油轨）for the valve gear.

发动机机油经过滤后由油泵泵至发动机缸体和气缸盖的润滑和冷却点。在曲轴箱和气缸盖中下列部件会由发动机机油供应。

曲轴箱（见图 2 – 19）：

——曲轴轴承；

——活塞顶冷却用喷油嘴；

——气缸列 5 – 8 链条传动的喷油嘴；

——气缸列 1 – 4 链条传动的张紧导轨。

气缸盖：

——链条张紧器；

——气缸盖上的滑轨；

——液压推杆（液压阀调节元件）；

——可调式凸轮轴控制系统；

——凸轮轴轴承；

——气门机构的喷油轨。

Figure 2 – 19   Crankcase with oil jets

Index	Description	中文名称
1	Oil jets for chain drive cylinder bank 5 – 8	喷油嘴用于气缸 5 ~ 8 的链条传动
2	Oil jets for cooling the piston crown	喷油嘴用于冷却活塞顶

2. 8. 2 Oil Check Valve 机油单向阀

Three oil check valves are inserted into each cylinder head from the outside（See Figure 2 – 20）. This prevents the engine oil from flowing back out of the cylinder head and the VANOS units.

在每个气缸盖中都从外部安装了三个机油单向阀（见图 2 – 20），用于阻止发动机机油从气缸盖和可调式凸轮轴控制系统单元中回流。

Figure 2 – 20   Oil check valves in the cylinder head

Index	Description	中文名称
1	Oil check valve for VANOS intake	VANOS 的进气机油单向阀
2	Oil check valve for VANOS exhaust	VANOS 的排气机油单向阀
3	Oil check valve for cylinder head oil supply	气缸盖供油的机油单向阀

2.8.3　Oil Pump　机油泵

The oil pump（See Figure 2-21）is secured onto the crankshaft bearing cap（轴承盖）by threaded connections inserted at an angle and is driven by the crankshaft using a roller chain.

油泵（见图 2-21）通过斜置螺栓连接固定在曲轴轴承盖上并由曲轴通过管筒型链驱动。

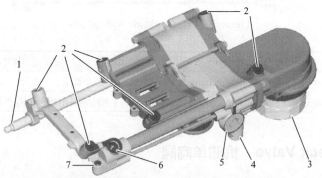

Figure 2-21　Oil pump

Index	Description	中文名称
1	Drive shaft	驱动轴
2	Threaded connection	螺栓连接
3	Oil filter	机油滤清器
4	Pressure relief valve	过压阀
5	Control valve	调节阀
6	Oil pressure from the oil pump to the engine	从油泵到发动机的压力油
7	Oil pressure control cable from the engine to the control valve	从发动机到调节阀的油压控制管

The oil pump is a two level gear oil pump with two parallel switched gear clusters.

油泵是一个两级齿轮油泵，有两个并列连接的齿轮组。

2.8.4   Oil Filter   机油滤清器

The **oil filter** is located beneath the engine by the oil sump. The support for the oil filter element is integrated in the rear oil pump cover.

机油滤清器安装在发动机下面油底壳区域内。机油滤清器滤芯的托架集成在油泵后盖板上。

The oil filter cover is screwed to the rear oil pump cover through an opening in the oil sump. An oil drain plug is integrated in the oil filter cover for emptying the filter element before the cover is unscrewed.

机油滤清器盖穿过油底壳中的一个开口用螺栓固定在油泵后盖板上。在机油滤清器盖中集成了一个放油螺塞，以便在松开并拆下盖板前排空滤清器元件。

The filter element support dome contains a bursting pressure valve（旁通阀）. If the filter element is blocked, this valve guides the unfiltered engine oil around the filter element to the engine's lubrication points.

在滤清器元件的定位罩中有一个旁通阀。当滤清器元件堵塞时，这个阀门控制发动机机油不经滤清器元件过滤而直接到达发动机的润滑点。

2.8.5   Oil Cooling   机油冷却装置

An **oil cooler** is built into vehicles in hot countries. The oil cooler is located in front of the engine coolant heat exchanger above the **condenser** in the cooling module.

在热带国家使用的车辆中安装了一个机油冷却器。这个机油冷却器安装在发动机冷却液热交换器前冷凝器上面的冷却模块内。

The engine oil flows from the oil pump through a channel in the crankcase to a connection on the generator support. The generator support has an oil thermostat. A wax element（蜡制元件）in the oil thermostat continuously opens the inflow to the oil cooler when the oil temperature is between 100℃ to 130℃.

发动机机油从机油泵出来经曲轴箱中的一个通道流向在发电机支座上的一个接口。在发电机支座上安装有一个机油节温器。在机油温度从 100℃～130℃时，机油节温器内的一个蜡制元件持续打开流经机油冷却器的支路。

Some of the engine oil always flows past the oil thermostat and through the engine without being cooled, even when the oil thermostat is fully open.

即使机油节温器完全打开，也有一部分发动机机油不经机油节温器不断流动，不经冷却而从发动机内流过。

This ensures that oil is supplied even if the oil cooler is faulty（损坏的）.

通过这一措施保证在机油冷却器损坏时也能保证供油。

Key Words

air intake duct	进气道	cylinder wall	气缸壁
throttle	节气门	thermostat	节温器
intake pipe	进气管	radiator	散热器
magnesium alloy	镁合金	cooling system	冷却系统
downstream	下游的，后面的	oil sump	油底壳
engage	（齿轮）啮合	crankcase	曲轴箱
cylinder head	气缸盖	crankshaft	曲轴
valve timing system	气门正时系统	piston ring	活塞环
camshaft	凸轮轴	connecting rod	连杆
bolt	螺栓	piston	活塞
drag lever	摇臂	flywheel	飞轮
spark plug	火花塞	oil filter	机油滤清器
toothed chain	齿形带	oil cooler	机油冷却器
engine block	机体	condenser	冷凝器

Exercises

1. The intake passes through the air intake ducts from the air cleaner to _____ in the variable intake manifold, and on to the two cylinder head intake ducts.

2. The second shaft, from which the rotor for the opposite cylinder bank is adjusted, is turned by the driven shaft active through _____ in the opposite direction.

3. Adjustment from long to short intake path begins at _____ .

4. _____ and the catalytic converter housing are integrated into a single component.

5. The rear silencers are of _____ , and have capacities of 12. 6 and 16. 6 liters.

6. The rear silencer is fitted with _____ to keep noise to a minimum.

7. _____ and the eccentric shaft are jointly guided by means of a bridge support.

8. These bolts should always be replaced when _____ are carried out.

9. The camshafts are fitted with _____ for equalizing imbalances in the valve gear.

10. This Valvetronic unit consists of a bridge support with eccentric shaft, the intermediate levers with retaining springs, _____ and the inlet camshaft.

11. The eccentric shafts are rotated by _____ which is guided by a bridge support (cam

carrier) for each cylinder head.

12. ＿＿＿＿＿＿＿＿＿＿ must magnetic bolts be used, since this could cause the eccentric shaft sensors to produce inaccurate results.

13. The camshafts are driven by ＿＿＿＿＿＿＿＿＿＿, one for each cylinder bank.

14. The coolant flows from ＿＿＿＿＿＿＿＿＿＿ through the feed pipe in the engine's V, and to the rear side of the engine block.

15. ＿＿＿＿＿＿＿＿＿＿ allows the engine to be cooled in accordance with the relevant operating conditions.

16. From an thermostat return flow water temperature of 82℃, the thermostat switches the transmission oil-water heat exchanger to ＿＿＿＿＿＿＿＿＿＿ .

17. The viscous coupling fan is ＿＿＿＿＿＿＿＿＿＿ and switches on at an air temperature of 92℃.

18. The crankcase has a one-piece ＿＿＿＿＿＿＿＿＿＿ design and is made entirely from Alusil.

19. To save weight, the crankshaft has been ＿＿＿＿＿＿＿＿＿＿ around bearings (2), (3), and (4).

20. The pistons are made of high-temperature aluminum alloy and fitted with ＿＿＿＿＿＿＿＿＿＿ piston rings.

21. The pistons are cooled by ＿＿＿＿＿＿＿＿＿＿ on the exhaust side of the piston crown.

22. The engine oil is filtered by ＿＿＿＿＿＿＿＿＿＿ to the lubrication and cooling points in the engine block and pumped in the cylinder head.

23. ＿＿＿＿＿＿＿＿＿＿ prevents the engine oil from flowing back out of the cylinder head and the VANOS units.

24. An oil drain plug is integrated in the oil filter cover for emptying the filter element before the cover is ＿＿＿＿＿＿＿＿＿＿ .

25. Some of the engine oil always flows past the oil thermostat and through the engine without being cooled, even when ＿＿＿＿＿＿＿＿＿＿ is fully open.

Unit 3
Transmission 变速器

Key Terms

automatic gearbox	planetary gear train
transmission	CAN bus
clutch	shifting gear
gearshift	Hall sensor
overrunning clutch	neutral position
turbine	electronic-hydraulic control
stator	solenoid valve
impeller	electronic pressure control valve

3.1   Introduction 简介

3.1.1 Mechanical Design of the Gearbox   变速箱的机械结构

The mechanical power **transmission** of the gearbox has been optimized with regard to **gearshift** comfort, fuel consumption reduction and product quality.

变速箱机械传动装置在换挡便捷性、降低油耗和产品质量方面进行了优化。

Figure 3 – 1 shows the mechanical design of the gearbox.

变速箱的机械结构如图 3 – 1 所示。

The torque developed by the engine is transferred to the gearbox via a torque converter with a controlled converter lockup **clutch**. The gears are shifted by means of multi-disc（多片式）clutches. The six forward gears, used in automatic gearboxes, and the reverse gear are produced by a planetary gear train（行星齿轮组）.

发动机输出的扭矩通过带自调节变矩器离合器的变矩器传递到变速器。换挡通过多片式离合器实现。自动变速箱中使用的 6 个前进挡和倒车挡由行星齿轮组产生。

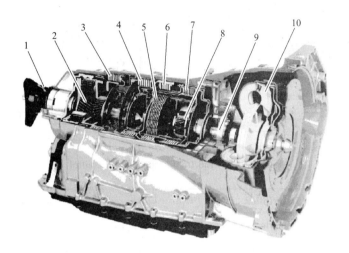

Figure 3 – 1　Mechanical design of the gearbox

Index	Description	中文名称	Index	Description	中文名称
1	Output shaft	输出轴	6	Clutch B	离合器 B
2	Double gear train	双排齿轮组	7	Clutch A	离合器 A
3	Clutch D	离合器 D	8	Single gear train	单排齿轮组
4	Clutch C	离合器 C	9	Oil pump	机油泵
5	Clutch E	离合器 E	10	Torque converter with converter lockup clutch	带变矩器离合器的变矩器

3.1.2　Transmission Control　变速箱控制系统

The gearbox is controlled by a so-called mechatronics module that is made up of a combination of hydraulic gearshift unit and electronic control unit. The following system overview (See Figure 3 – 2) shows the main components of the electronic control system.

变速箱由一个所谓的机械电子装置模块控制，该模块由液压换挡机构和电子控制单元组合而成。以下的系统一览图（见图 3 - 2）列出了电子控制系统的基本组件。

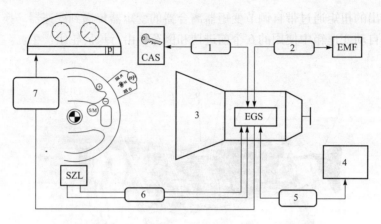

Figure 3 – 2　Electronic transmission control

Index	Description	中文名称
1	Key signal, starter interlock	钥匙信号，起动锁止
2	Redundancy（parking lock）	备用信号（驻车锁止器）
3	Automatic gearbox	自动变速箱
4	Controls in vehicle interior（for emergency release）	车内操纵机构（用于紧急解锁装置）
5	Mechanical emergency release for parking lock	驻车锁止器的手动紧急解锁装置
6	Driver's choice P, R, N, D, S, M, +, –	驾驶员希望值 P、R、N、D、S、M、+、–
7	Shift pattern（shift gate） Position indicator P, R, N, D, S, M1 ... M6 Shift lock indicator Error messages	换挡示意图 位置显示 P、R、N、D、S、M1……M6 换挡自锁功能提示 故障信息
CAS	Car access system	便捷进入系统
EMF	Electromechanical parking brake	电动机械式驻车制动器
EGS	Electronic transmission control（in mechatronics module）	电子变速箱控制系统（在机械电子装置模块内）
SZL	Steering column switch centre	转向柱开关中心

　　The driver's choice is transmitted in the form of an electrical signal from a **selector lever** on the steering column or from several control buttons in the multifunction steering wheel（多功能方向盘）and transferred via a CAN bus to the transmission control. In the gearbox, the commands are implemented（执行）while evaluating various ambient conditions. The relevant positions are indicated in the instrument cluster.

驾驶员希望值由转向柱上的选挡杆或多功能方向盘上的多个操作按钮生成，并作为电信号通过一条 CAN 总线继续传输到变速箱控制系统。在变速箱内，分析各种外界条件后再执行这些命令。变速箱挡位在组合仪表中显示。

Pure electronic transmission control（shift by wire）realized in this way renders（放弃）the conventional gearshift lever in the **center console** and the associated components unnecessary.

在以此方式实现的变速箱纯电子控制系统（"导线换挡"）中可不再使用传统的中央控制台换挡杆及其附属的组件。

The automatic parking lock which is active, for instance, when the ignition key is removed, represents a further important increase in comfort and convenience.

例如，当点火钥匙拨出后，自动驻车锁就被激活，从而进一步提高了舒适性。

3.2   Components and Functional Description 部件及功能描述

The components and functional description follow the power transmission progression（顺序）in the gearbox, i. e.（也就是）from the torque converter with converter lockup clutch up to the output shaft. The component arrangements are shown in the illustration（示意图）below（See Figure 3 – 3）.

部件及功能描述按变速箱内的动力传递顺序进行，即从带变矩器离合器的变矩器直至输出轴。部件的结构布置可见下面的示意图（见图 3 – 3）。

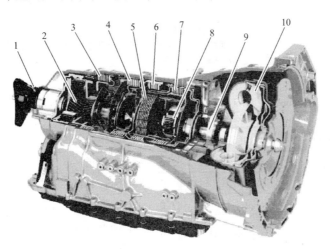

Figure 3 – 3   Components of the gearbox

Index	Description	中文名称	Index	Description	中文名称
1	Output shaft	输出轴	6	Clutch B	离合器 B
2	Double gear train	双排齿轮组	7	Clutch A	离合器 A
3	Clutch D	离合器 D	8	Single gear train	单排齿轮组
4	Clutch C	离合器 C	9	Oil pump	机油泵
5	Clutch E	离合器 E	10	Torque converter with converter lockup clutch	带变矩离合器的变矩器

3.2.1 Torque Converter and Converter Lockup Clutch
变矩器和变矩器离合器

Figure 3 – 4 shows the torque converter and converter lockup clutch.

变矩器和变矩器离合器如图 3 – 4 所示。

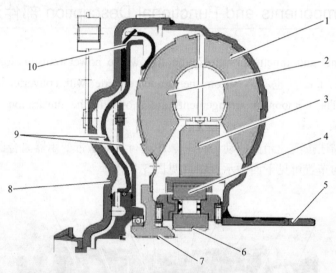

Figure 3 – 4　Torque converter and converter lockup clutch

Index	Description	中文名称	Index	Description	中文名称
1	Pump	泵	6	Stator shaft	导轮轴
2	Turbine	涡轮	7	Turbine shaft	涡轮轴
3	Stator	导轮	8	Torque converter casing	变矩器壳
4	Overrunning clutch	单向离合器	9	Piston for converter lockup clutch	变矩器离合器活塞
5	Torque converter hub	变矩器轮毂	10	Lined plate	从动盘片

The torque converter acts as the linking element for power transmission between the engine and gearbox. As is the case with other automatic gearboxes （自动变速器）, it has the task of converting high speed/low torque into low speed/high torque. The converter lockup clutch is used for the purpose of eliminating slip （速度差） during rotary speed transmission.

变矩器是发动机与变速箱之间动力传输的连接部分。像其他自动变速箱一样，它的任务也是将高转速/低扭矩转换为低转速/高扭矩。变矩器离合器用于消除传输过程中的转速差。

The converter lockup clutch is designed as a two-friction surface （双摩擦面） clutch. It is slip-controlled in the gears 1 to 6. Consequently, the operating points with the converter lockup clutch disengaged （分离） are reduced thus also reducing fuel consumption.

变矩器离合器也设计为双摩擦面离合器。在1～6挡时控制该离合器的转速差。这样就减少了变矩器离合器"分离"的工况，因此也降低了燃油消耗。

The converter lockup clutch is not closed or engaged up to a gear oil temperature of 35℃.

变速箱油温在35℃以下时不控制变矩器离合器的转速差，该离合器也不被接合。

At other operating points, the control of the converter lockup clutch depends on various factors such as load requirement signal, engine load status, vehicle speed, gearbox oil temperature, selected gearshift program.

在其他工况下，变矩器离合器的转速差控制取决于各种因素：负荷希望值信号、发动机负荷状态、车速、变速箱油温、所选换挡模式。

For this reason, it is not possible to provide a general statement as to when control of the converter lockup clutch begins or when it engages.

因此，无法简单地描述变矩器离合器何时开始执行转速差控制及接合。

3.2.2   Oil Pump   机油泵

The oil pump （See Figure 3 – 5） supplies the required oil pressure and lubricating oil for the automatic gearbox. As on other gearboxes, it is designed as a crescent-type pump （内啮合齿轮泵） and has a delivery capacity of approx. 16 cm^3 per revolution. A delivery control valve is not fitted. The converter in the pump is mounted in a needle bearing （滚针轴承）.

机油泵（见图3 – 5）为自动变速箱提供所需要的油压和润滑油。像其他变速箱一样，该油泵也设计为内啮合齿轮泵，其输送能力为每转约16立方厘米，但是未安装流量调节阀。油泵内变矩器的轴承座带有一个滚针轴承。

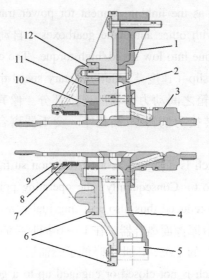

Figure 3 – 5　Oil pump

Index	Description	中文名称	Index	Description	中文名称
1	Intermediate plate	夹板	7	Bearing	轴承
2	Centring plate	定心板	8	Snap ring	卡环
3	Stator shaft	导轮轴	9	Rotary shaft seal	轴密封环
4	Intake	进油道	10	Impeller	泵轮
5	To oil strainer (intake pipe)	至机油滤网（进油管）	11	Internal gear	齿圈
6	O-ring	圆形密封环	12	Pump housing	泵壳

3.2.3　Multi-disc Clutches　多片式离合器

Figure 3 – 6 shows the multi-disc clutches.

多片式离合器如图 3 – 6 所示。

The gearbox requires only 5 clutches to shift 6 gears. The clutches are divided into drive clutches and brake clutches. Clutches A, B and E are drive clutches while clutches C and D are brake clutches. The drive clutches A, B and E are balanced with respect to（关于）the dynamic pressure.

变速箱只需要 5 个离合器用于 6 个挡位的换挡。这些离合器分为传动离合器和制动离合器。离合器 A、B 和 E 是传动离合器，离合器 C 和 D 是制动离合器。传动离合器 A、B 和 E 的平衡状态与动态压力有关。

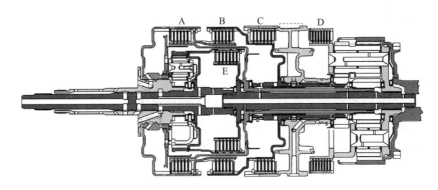

Figure 3 – 6   Multi-disc clutches

Index	Description	中文名称	Index	Description	中文名称
A	Drive clutch	传动离合器	D	Brake clutch	制动离合器
B	Drive clutch	传动离合器	E	Drive clutch	传动离合器
C	Brake clutch	制动离合器			

In the gearbox, all gearshifts from 1st to 6th gear and from 6th to 1st gear are executed as overlap shifts（重叠换挡）. Free-wheel gearshifts are no longer required as on a gearbox where the shift from 1st to 2nd and 2nd to 3rd took place via overrunning clutches. The overlap gearshift system saves weight and space.

在变速箱中所有从 1 挡至 6 挡及从 6 挡至 1 挡的换挡都设计为重叠换挡，因此可不再像从 1 挡到 2 挡再从 2 挡到 3 挡通过超越离合器实现换挡的变速箱那样，而是取消了自由轮换挡装置。通过重叠换挡，减轻了重量并节省了空间。

The electrohydraulic gearshift is executed by valves in the hydraulic shift unit that are controlled by pressure regulators（压力调节器）.

电子液压换挡是由液压换挡机构内的液压阀及压力调节器的控制执行的。

3.2.4 Planetary Gear Train   行星齿轮组

The planetary gear train（行星齿轮组）is used in the gearbox. Six forward gears and one reverse gear are possible with this planetary gear train.

在变速箱中使用了行星齿轮组，通过这个齿轮组实现了 6 个前进挡和 1 个倒车挡。

The planetary gear train consists of a single carrier（单排星架）planetary gear train and a downstream double planetary gear train.

这个齿轮组由一个单排单行星架行星齿轮组和一个附加连接的双排行星齿轮组组成。

The single carrier planetary gear train（See Figure 3 – 7）is made up of：

— 1 sun gear;

— 3 planet gears;

— 1 planet carrier;

— 1 internal gear.

单排单行星架行星齿轮组（见图 3 - 7）由以下部件组成：

——1 个太阳轮；

——3 个行星轮；

——1 个行星架；

——1 个齿圈。

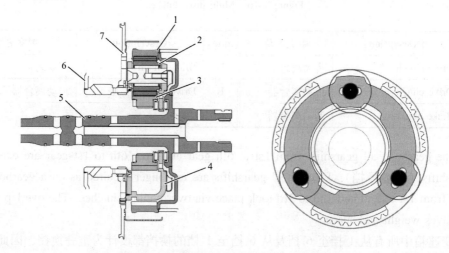

Figure 3 - 7　Single carrier planetary gear train

Index	Description	中文名称	Index	Description	中文名称
1	Internal gear 1	齿圈 1	5	Turbine shaft	涡轮轴
2	Planet gear	行星轮	6	Cylinder A	油缸 A
3	Sun gear 1	中心轮 1	7	Pressure plate A	挡板 A
4	Planet carrier	行星架			

The subsequently（附加）connected double planetary gear train（See Figure 3 - 8）is made up of:

— 2 differently sized sun gears;

— 3 short planet gears;

— 3 long planet gears;

— 1 planet carrier;

— 1 internal gear.

附加连接的双排行星齿轮组（见图 3 - 8）由以下部件组成：

——2 个大小不同的太阳轮；

——3 个短行星轮；

——3 个长行星轮；

——1 个行星架；

——1 个齿圈。

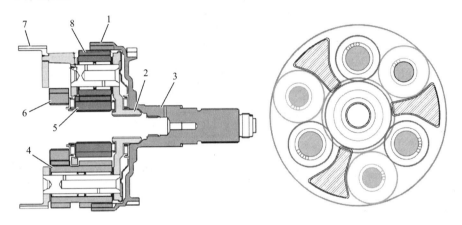

Figure 3 - 8   Double planetary gear train

Index	Description	中文名称	Index	Description	中文名称
1	Internal gear 2	齿圈 2	5	Sun gear 3, clutch E	中心轮 3，离合器 E
2	Planet carrier, clutch E	离合器 E 的行星架	6	Sun gear 2, clutch A	中心轮 2，离合器 A
3	Output	输出轴	7	Planet carrier 1	行星架 1
4	Double planet gear (long)	双排行星轮（长）	8	Planet gear (short)	行星轮（短）

3.2.5 Parking Lock   驻车锁止器

As shown in Figure 3 - 9, the **parking lock** is a facility that secures the vehicle to prevent it rolling away. When the vehicle is stationary it is applied via the selector lever, depending on the version, by purely mechanical means or, as is the case in this new gearbox, electrically via an actuating magnet（执行电磁铁）.

如图 3 - 9 所示，驻车锁止器是防止车辆自行移动的装置。该锁止器在车辆停车时的锁止取决于规格。在其他规格中通过选挡杆纯机械锁止，在安装了这种新型变速箱时则通过选挡杆以电动方式由一个执行电磁铁锁止。

The parking lock blocks the output shaft of the gearbox by means of a pawl（棘爪）(4) that engages in the gearing of the parking lock gearwheel (1).

驻车锁止器通过啮合在驻车锁止棘轮（1）内的棘爪（4）来锁死变速箱的输出轴。

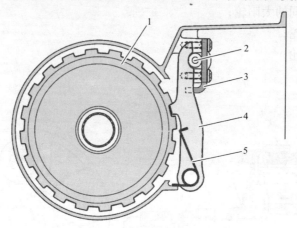

Figure 3 – 9　Parking lock

Index	Description	中文名称	Index	Description	中文名称
1	Parking lock gearwheel	驻车锁止棘轮	4	Parking lock pawl	驻车锁止棘爪
2	Linking rod	连接杆	5	Leg spring	蝶形弹簧
3	Guide plate	导板			

The parking lock is designed such that the vehicle is always reliably held on uphill or downhill gradients of up to 32% and at a speed below 2 km/h. The parking lock must not engage at driving speeds above 5 km/h.

驻车锁止器的设计目标是上坡或下坡坡度小于32%且车速低于2公里/小时时完全保证车辆安全地停住。如果车速超过5公里/小时，则不允许驻车锁止器锁止。

In the electrical version of the parking lock, a differentiation（区别）must be made between mechanical engagement of the lock and corresponding electrical activation.

对电动规格的驻车锁止器必须区分锁止器的机械锁止部分和所属的电动控制部分。

The parking lock is engaged in the gearbox by means of a mechanical spring system, see graphic above（Figure 3 – 9）.

驻车锁止器通过变速箱内的机械弹簧系统锁止，参见上面的示意图（图3 – 9）。

The notched disc（卡盘）in the gearbox is replaced by a parking disc, a parking lock cylinder, a solenoid valve and an electric magnet.

取消变速箱内的卡盘，采用一个驻车棘轮、一个驻车锁止缸、一个电磁阀和一个电磁铁。

Electrical activation of the parking lock is triggered（引发）by a pushbutton on the selector lever or by the radio remote control key transmitter. Activation by the solenoid valve and electric magnet is controlled by the electronic transmission control unit.

锁止器的电动操纵通过选挡杆上的按钮或无线电遥控钥匙实现。电磁阀和电磁铁的控制通过电子变速箱控制单元实现。

The solenoid valve is located in the hydraulic shift unit and the electric magnet on the cylinder for the parking lock.

电磁阀位于液压换挡机构内，电磁铁安装在驻车锁止器缸上。

The electric magnet for the parking lock cylinder is switched off when the parking lock is engaged. Consequently, the mechanical lock is cancelled and the piston released. The solenoid valve in the shift unit is also switched off. The valve assumes（回到）its rest position and the cylinder chamber of the parking lock cylinder is vented（通气）. The piston is pulled in the direction of the parking lock by a preloaded（预张紧的）leg spring on the parking disc and engaged by the linking rod secured to the parking disc.

锁止驻车锁止器时，用于驻车锁止缸的电磁铁被关闭。这样就取消了机械锁止，并释放了活塞，同时换挡机构内的电磁阀也被关闭。这个阀返回关闭位，驻车锁止缸通气。通过驻车棘轮上预张紧的蝶形弹簧，活塞被拉向驻车锁止器，并经过固定在驻车棘轮上的连接杆锁止。

On leaving the parked position, the solenoid valve in the shift unit is switched on and the main pressure is applied in the cylinder chamber of the parking lock cylinder thus pushing back the piston to release the parking lock.

在退出驻车位置时，换挡机构内的电磁阀被接通，主油路压力油进入驻车锁止缸内，并将活塞推回，驻车锁止器解锁。

The electric magnet on the parking lock cylinder is also switched. Consequently, the piston is additionally locked by the locking balls, i. e. held only in position N when the engine is stationary.

驻车锁止缸上的电磁铁也被接通。这样活塞通过锁止钢球被附加锁止或在发动机停机状态下挂入 N 挡时保持不动。

In certain situations, e. g.（举例来说）in the event of power failure in the emergency program, the parking lock can be released manually by means of an additional bowden cable（附加拉线）on the parking disc.

在特殊情况下，例如在电路故障紧急模式下，通过驻车棘轮上的一个附加拉线可以将驻车锁止器手动解锁。

3.3　Electronic Transmission Control Unit 电子变速箱控制单元

The electronic transmission control unit is an integral part（组件）of the mechatronics module that is installed in the oil pan of the gearbox. The electronic inputs are evaluated（分析）

in the control unit and electronic actuating variables are output. The control unit is integrated in the electrical system via a CAN bus（CAN 总线）connection and a separate data link.

电子变速箱控制单元是机械电子装置模块的组件，安装在变速箱油底壳内。在这个控制单元内，分析电子输入信号并输出电子调节参数。该控制单元通过一个 CAN 总线口和一条独立的数据导线集成在车辆电子系统内。

3.3.1　CAN Bus and Serial Line　CAN 总线和串行导线

The signal transfer between the individual components takes place via the CAN bus（See Figure 3 – 10）.

各组件之间的信号传输原则上通过 CAN 总线实现（见图 3 – 10）。

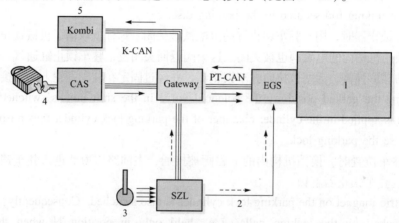

Figure 3 – 10　CAN bus and serial line

Index	Description	中文名称	Index	Description	中文名称
1	Automatic gearbox	自动变速箱	Gateway	Central gateway module	中央网关模块
2	Serial, unidirectional line	串行单向导线	EGS	Electronic transmission control	电子变速箱控制系统
3	Selector lever	选挡杆	SZL	Steering column switch centre	转向柱开关中心
4	Key	钥匙	PT-CAN	Power train CAN	动力传动系 CAN
5	Display	显示	K-CAN	Body CAN	车身 CAN
CAS	Car access system	便捷进入及起动系统	SI-Bus	Safety and information bus	安全信息总线

For safety reasons, in addition to the bus line, the signal transfer between the steering column switch centre and the electronic transmission control system additionally takes place via a unidirectional serial line（单向的串行导线）from the steering column switch centre to the electronic transmission control system. The serial line must exhibit（表现出）comparable reliability as the CAN connection.

出于安全性考虑，除总线导线外，转向柱开关中心与电子变速箱控制系统之间还有一根从转向柱开关中心至电子变速箱控制系统的单向串行导线供信号传输使用。这根串行导线必须同 CAN 一样安全。

The CAN bus features mechanisms（check sums, etc.）that ensure data transmission with a high degree of reliability. The central gateway module is a link in the data transfer chain for data transfer from one bus to another, e. g. from body CAN to power train CAN.

CAN 总线带有保证数据高度安全传输的机构（校核数据等）。在从一个总线向其他总线进行数据传输时，例如从车身 CAN 向动力传动系 CAN 传输时，中央网关模块是数据传输链中的一个环节。

The data that the transmission control unit requires for shifting gears, such as injection timing, engine speed, throttle valve angle（节气门角度）, engine temperature and engine intervention（发动机干预）, are transmitted from the central gateway module via the power train CAN bus to the transmission control unit. The solenoid valves and the pressure actuator（压力调节器）are activated directly by the mechatronics module.

变速箱控制单元所需的用于换挡的数据，例如喷射正时、发动机转速、节气门角度、发动机温度和发动机干预，由中央网关模块通过动力传动系 CAN 总线传输到变速箱控制单元内。电磁阀和压力调节器的控制直接由机械电子装置模块完成。

Signals that are sent via the power train CAN bus to the electronic transmission control unit and from the electronic transmission control unit to the other control units are：

Signal	Transmitter	Receiver
Selector switch	SZL	EGS
Terminal status	CAS	EGS
Central locking system（中控锁）	CAS	EGS
Transmission data	EGS	CAS
Engine data	DME/DDE	EGS
Wheel speeds	DSC	EGS
Deceleration request（减速要求）	EMF	EGS
Display, transmission data	EGS	Instrument cluster（组合仪表）
Check control message	EGS	Instrument cluster
Torque requirement	EGS	DME
Battery voltage（蓄电池电压）	Power module	EGS
Electric loads	EGS	Power module

通过动力传动系 CAN 总线发送至电子变速箱控制单元及从电子变速箱控制单元发送至其他控制单元的信号是:

信号	发射器	接收器
变速箱选挡开关	SZL	EGS
总线端状态	CAS	EGS
中控锁	CAS	EGS
变速箱数据	EGS	CAS
发动机数据	DME/DDE	EGS
车轮转速	DSC	EGS
减速要求	EMF	EGS
变速箱数据显示	EGS	Instrument cluster
检查控制信息	EGS	Instrument cluster
扭矩要求	EGS	DME
蓄电池电压	Power module	EGS
停车时用电器	EGS	Power module

The turbine and output speeds of the gearbox are determined with Hall sensors（霍尔传感器）that transfer their values directly to the mechatronics module. The position switch also transfers directly to the mechatronics module.

通过霍尔传感器测定变速箱涡轮转速和输出转速后，测量值将直接传输到机械电子装置模块内。同样，挡位开关信号也直接传输到机械电子装置模块内。

The processor of the transmission control unit features a 440 KB internal flash memory（内置式可擦写存储器）. Approx. 370 KB of this are taken up by the basic transmission program. The remaining approx. 70 KB contain the vehicle-specific（车辆专用的）application data.

变速箱控制单元的处理器有一个 440 KB 的内置式可擦写存储器。其中约 370 KB 由变速箱基本程序占用，剩余约 70 KB 的内容为车辆专用的应用数据。

3.3.2 **Warm-up Program** 暖车程序

The warm-up program（暖车程序）is selected after every engine start at an engine temperature below approx. 60℃. The gears are held longer, i. e. extended further, during the warm-up program. In this way, the engine and catalytic converter reach their operating temperature faster.

如果发动机温度低于约 60 ℃，则每次启动发动机后都调用这个暖车程序。在执行暖车程序时，保持在各挡位的时间较长。也就是说，在较高转速下才换到某一挡位，这样发动机和废气触媒转换器将很快达到工作温度。

The warm-up program is exited on exceeding（超过）an engine temperature of approx. 60℃ or after approx. 120 seconds.

发动机温度超过约 60 ℃ 时或发动机起动约 120 秒钟后将退出这个暖车程序。

3.3.3 Downshift Inhibitor 换低挡锁止机构

This function prevents a downshift when this would mean that the maximum engine speed would be exceeded. It therefore avoids damage being incurred（招致）to the engine and gearbox.

如果换低挡时转速会超过发动机最高转速，则该锁止机构将阻止换低挡，借此避免损坏发动机和变速箱。

3.3.4 Reverse Interlock 倒车挡锁止机构

This function prevents shifting into reverse gear at a driving speed above 5 km/h. If the driver selects reverse gear at a speed above 5 km/h, the gearbox will assume the **neutral position** and N is indicated accordingly in the instrument cluster.

在行驶速度高于 5 km/h 时，该锁止机构禁止换到倒车挡。如果车速高于 5km/h 时驾驶员选择倒车挡，那么变速箱将挂入空挡位置且在组合仪表内相应显示 N。

Only when the vehicle has reached a speed of less than 5 km/h is it possible to select reverse gear by operating the selector lever once again.

直到车辆速度低于 5 km/h，才能再次按压选挡杆挂入倒车挡。

3.4 Electronic-hydraulic Control 电子液压控制（系统）

The **electronic-hydraulic** transmission control installed in connection with the gearbox features 3 solenoid valves and 6 electronic pressure control valves. The gearshifts in the gearbox are controlled with the aid of the valves.

安装在变速箱中的电子液压变速箱控制系统拥有 3 个电磁阀和 6 个电子压力控制阀。借助这些阀可控制变速箱的换挡。

3.4.1 Solenoid Valves 电磁阀

3 solenoid valves are fitted on the hydraulic gearshift unit. They are designed as **3/2-way valves**, i. e. valves with 3 connections and 2 switch positions.

在液压换挡机构上安装了 3 个电磁阀。它们是 3/2 换向阀，即阀门带有 3 个接头和 2

个开关位置。

The solenoid valves are driven by the electronic transmission control and have the settings "open" or "closed" therefore making it possible to switch over the hydraulic valves.

电磁阀由电子变速箱控制系统控制，有"开启"和"封闭"两个位置，这样就可以转换液压阀的工作状态。

3.4.2 Electronic Pressure Control Valves 电子压力控制阀

The electronic pressure control valves convert electrical current into a proportional hydraulic pressure. They are driven by the electronics module and activate the hydraulic valves belonging to the gearshift elements.

电子压力控制阀将电流成正比地转换为液压压力。这些阀由电子装置模块控制，并操纵属于换挡元件的液压阀。

Two types of electronic pressure control valves are fitted.

目前使用的电子压力控制阀有两种类型。

1. Electronic Pressure Control Valves with Rising Characteristic Curve
特性线上升的电子压力控制阀

There are three electronic pressure control valves with rising characteristic curve (see Figure 3–11).

共有三个特征线上升的电子压力控制阀（见图 3–11）。

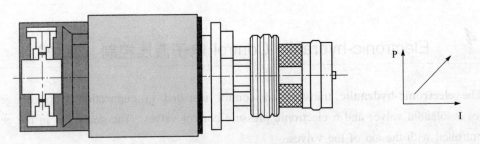

Figure 3–11　Electronic pressure control valves with rising characteristic curve
(0 mA = 0 bar/700 mA = 4.6 bar)

2. Electronic Pressure Control Valves with Falling Characteristic Curve
特性线下降的电子压力控制阀

There are three electronic pressure control valves with falling characteristic curve (See Figure 3–12).

共有三个特征线下降的电子压力控制阀（见图 3 – 12）。

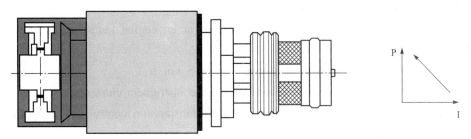

Figure 3 – 12　Electronic pressure control valves with falling characteristic curve

(700 mA = 0 bar/0 mA = 4. 6 bar)

K ey Words

transmission　变速器	parking lock　驻车锁止器
gearshift　换挡杆	neutral position　空挡
clutch　离合器	electronic-hydraulic　电子液压的
selector lever　选挡杆	3 /2-way valve　3 /2 换向阀
center console　中央控制台	

Exercises

1. The torque developed by the engine is transferred to the gearbox via _____ with a controlled converter lockup clutch.

2. The gearbox is controlled by _____ that is made up of a combination of hydraulic gearshift unit and electronic control unit.

3. In the gearbox, _____ are implemented while evaluating various ambient conditions.

4. As is the case with automatic gearboxes, _____ has the task of converting high speed/low torque into low speed/high torque.

5. The electrohydraulic gearshift is executed by valves in _____ that are controlled by pressure regulators.

6. The planetary gear train consists of _____ and a downstream double planetary gear train.

7. _____ is designed such that the vehicle is always reliably held on uphill or downhill gradients of up to 32% and at a speed below 2 km/h.

8. _____ (ZGM) is a link in the data transfer chain for data transfer from one bus to another, e. g. from K-CAN to PT-CAN.

9. _____ is selected after every engine start at an engine temperature below approx. 60℃.

10. If the driver selects reverse gear at a speed above 5 km/h, _____ will assume the neutral position and N is indicated accordingly in the instrument cluster.

11. The solenoid valves are driven by the electronic transmission control and have the settings "open" or "closed" therefore making it possible to switch over _____ .

12. _____ are driven by the electronics module and activate the hydraulic valves belonging to the gearshift elements.

Unit 4

Transaxle & Wheel
车桥和车轮

front axle	swinging arm
carrier	stabilizer bar
arm	rim
stabilizer bar	forged wheel
rear axle	cast aluminum

4.1 Front Axle 前桥

As shown in Figure 4 – 1, the tried and tested double joint spring strut axle（双横臂减振支柱前桥）with tension struts（拉杆）is used.

如图 4 – 1 所示，验证合格的带拉杆的双横臂减振支柱前桥投入使用。

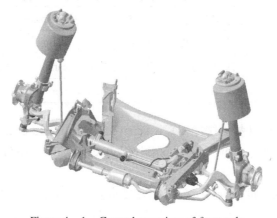

Figure 4 – 1   General overview of front axle

The unsprung mass is reduced which is of particular importance in vehicle construction. Nearly all the axle components are made of aluminum. This results in weight reduction of the chassis（底盘）by about 30% compared to an axle made of steel components.

对车辆结构有特殊意义的是非簧载质量降至最低。几乎所有车桥零件都是铝合金制造的。与钢制部件的车桥相比，底盘的重量减少了约 30%。

4.1.1 Front Axle Carrier 前桥架梁

The **front axle** carrier（架梁）（See Figure 4 – 2）is now also manufactured using light alloy. It consists of cast alloy preformed sections which are welded（焊接）into the extruded sections.

现在前桥架梁（见图 4 – 2）也由轻合金制成。它由铸铝成型件构成，这些铸铝成型件是由条形铝材焊在一起的。

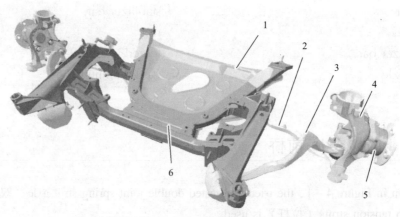

Figure 4 – 2 Front axle carrier with wheel suspension

Index	Description	中文名称	Index	Description	中文名称
1	Reinforcement plate	推力缓冲板	4	Swivel bearing	摆动轴承
2	Control arm	横向摆臂	5	Wheel bearing	车轮轴承
3	Tension strut	拉杆	6	Axle carrier	车桥架梁

A reinforcement plate（推力缓冲板）is screwed on to increase the transversal rigidity（横向刚度）of the front car. This has a positive effect on the handling, acoustics and crash performance.

为提高车头的横向刚度而安装了一个推力缓冲板，它可改善行驶性能，减低噪音并改善防撞性能。

4. 1. 2   **Arms**   转向控制臂

The arms are located with a wishbone and a tension strut containing a hydro（液压轴承）mount at the front. The layout of the arms, combined with the **track rods** fitted in front of the wheel centre, guarantees balanced steering when cornering.

转向控制臂带一个横向摆臂和一个内有液压轴承的拉杆。转向控制臂与安装在车轮中线前面的转向横拉杆一起保证了转向时转向力均衡分布。

The hydro mount in the tension strut（See Figure 4 – 3）damps wheel vibrations through its fluid filling. Vibrations which are felt on the steering wheel are thus avoided.

拉杆内的液压轴承（见图 4 – 3）通过内部的液体减缓车轮的振动，这样就避免了在方向盘上感觉到有振动。

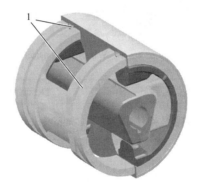

Figure 4 – 3   Hydro mount in the tension strut

Index	Description	中文名称
1	Fluid duct	油道

4. 1. 3   **Stabilizer Bar**   稳定杆

As shown in Figure 4 – 4 and Figure 4 – 5, the **stabilizer bar** is designed as a tubular stabilizer bar, which minimizes the body tilt inclination（侧倾）. It is directly connected to the spring strut by means of stabilizer links to achieve the best performance level.

如图 4 – 4 和图 4 – 5 所示，稳定杆被设计为可以将车身侧倾降至最小的管状稳定杆。为保证性能最佳，将该稳定杆通过稳定杆的支撑杆直接与减震支柱相连。

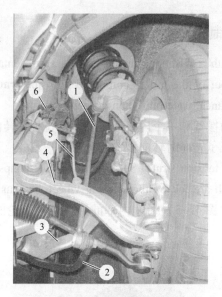

Figure 4 – 4　Wheel suspension

Index	Description	中文名称	Index	Description	中文名称
1	Pendulum support on stabilizer bar	稳定杆的支撑杆	4	Control arm	横向摆臂
2	Stabilizer bar	稳定杆	5	Coupling rod for ride level sensor	高度传感器的连接杆
3	Tension strut	拉杆	6	Ride level sensor	高度传感器

Figure 4 – 5　General overview of front axle from below

Index	Description	中文名称
1	Stabilizer bar	稳定杆

The high connection on the spring strut is selected so that when you are driving straight ahead and when driving over a bump（碰撞）on one side, nothing can cause the spring strut to turn （扭转）. This would make driving straight ahead bumpy（颠簸）.

因此，选择减震支柱上的连接位置时要尽可能高，以便直线行驶时及在单侧不平路面上驶过时不会有作用力使减震支柱发生扭转。这会造成直线行驶时不平稳。

4.2　Rear Axle 后桥

4.2.1　Introduction　引言

A particular focal point（非常重要的问题）of running gear development is weight reduction for the purpose of achieving optimum comfort and safety properties.

为保证最佳的舒适性和安全性，在进行底盘开发设计时减轻重量特别重要。

4.2.2　Rear Axle Carrier　后桥架梁

Figure 4 – 6 is a general view of rear axle.

图 4 – 6 为后桥的概览图。

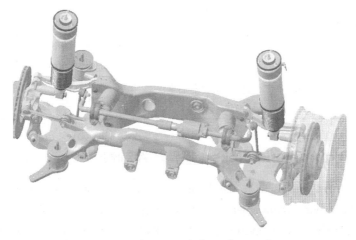

Figure 4 – 6　General view of rear axle

The rear axle carrier（See Figure 4 – 7）is a welded structure made of hydraulically formed （液压成型）aluminum sections and cast aluminum joints or nodes.

后桥架梁的结构（见图 4 – 7）为液压成型的铝型材与铸铝接头焊接而成。

The rear axle **differential**（final drive）is mounted flexibly in the rear axle carrier, now with two mount points at the front and only one at the rear. This modification offers advantages with regard to the acoustics and vibration characteristics. The rear rubber mount features kidney-shaped recesses（肾形）to allow for varying vibrations in horizontal or vertical direction.

后桥差速器以弹性方式悬挂连接在后桥架梁上，现在前面有两个支撑点，后面只有一个。这一更改的优点是降低了噪音和振动。为了让后部橡胶支座能在水平方向和垂直方向承受不同振动，该支座冲压成肾形。

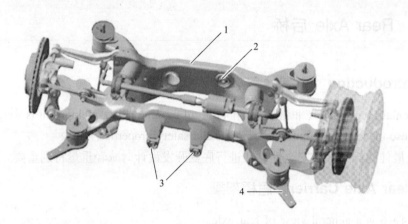

Figure 4 – 7　View of rear axle carrier

Index	Description	中文名称	Index	Description	中文名称
1	Rear cross member	后部横梁	3	Rear axle differential bearing bush, front	后桥主减速器前部轴套
2	Rear axle differential bearing bush, rear	后桥主减速器后部轴套	4	Thrust rod	推杆

4. 2. 3　Swinging Arm and Links　摆臂和控制臂

The **swinging arm** and links（See Figure 4 – 8）are made of aluminum and adapted geometrically to the driving requirements. When observed on the lifting hoist（升降台）, the swinging arm has a very twisted appearance（较大扭转）. Compressed in the normal position, it is parallel to（平行于）the road and creates an air guidance effect for favorable（有利的）aerodynamic flow of the air to the rear area of the vehicle.

摆臂和控制臂（见图4 – 8）由铝合金制成，在几何上适合驾驶要求。车辆在升降台上时可看到摆臂有较大扭转。处于标准位置时摆臂与路面平行，因此非常有利于空气流向车尾。

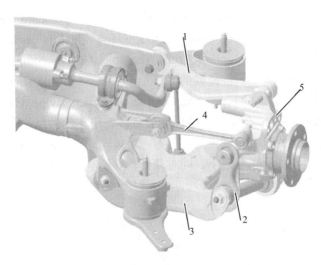

Figure 4 – 8   Wheel suspension rear axle

Index	Description	中文名称	Index	Description	中文名称
1	Control arm	横向摆臂	4	Upper traction strut	上部导向臂
2	Integral link	连接导杆	5	Wheel carrier	轮架
3	Swinging arm	摆臂			

4.2.4　Stabilizer Bar　稳定杆

A stabilizer bar is always fitted on the rear axle. The stabilizer bar is connected by means of stabilizer links（稳定杆支撑杆）between the rear axle carrier and swinging arms. The connection at the swinging arm is now designed as an axial ball joint（轴向球头铰接）. It is secured by means of a taper seat（锥形座）with nut（螺母）and Torx socket head screw（螺杆）.

在后桥上一直使用稳定杆。稳定杆铰接通过后桥架梁与摆臂之间的稳定杆支撑杆实现。与摆臂的连接现在设计为轴向球头铰接形式。固定件是一个用螺母和带有内星形头部的螺杆固定的锥形座。

4.3　Wheels/Tires 车轮/轮胎

4.3.1　Introduction　引言

The chassis is fitted as standard with light-alloy（轻合金）wheels（See Figure 4 – 9）. The

spare wheel is designed in the same way as the road wheels. The standard **rim** of the chassis is a weight-optimized （重量优化的） forged wheel （锻造车轮） which is partly covered by a glass-fibre-reinforced （玻璃纤维加强的） plastic trim. The object of this composite design （复合结构） is to minimize the unsprung （非簧载的）, rotating masses while simultaneously achieving good aerodynamic （空气动力学的） properties and an attractive, stylish visual appearance.

轻合金车轮 （见图4-9） 在底盘上是标准装备。备用车轮的结构与标准车轮相同。标准轮辋是已进行重量优化的锻造轮辋，局部盖有一个玻璃纤维塑料装饰罩。采用这种复合结构的目的是将非簧载旋转质量降至最小，同时获得较好的空气动力学性能及漂亮的外观。

Figure 4 - 9　Lightweight forged wheel with trim

Index	Description	中文名称	Index	Description	中文名称
1	Lightweight forged wheel	轻合金结构锻造车轮	2	Trim	装饰罩

Adhesive （粘结的） weights are used on the chassis for balancing purposes. These weights are cut to length in series assembly as seamless weights as needed and stuck to the inside of the rim on the designated （预留的） precision-cut areas （精车面） for dynamic balancing.

在底盘上利用粘接式平衡重块使车轮平衡。在流水线上装配时根据需要把整条平衡重块切短，并粘接在轮辋内侧预留的精车面上，以便起到动态平衡作用。

4.3.2　Styling Overview for Wheels　车轮式样一览

Styling	No.	零件名称	Description
90	8J×17 Forged wheel with trim	8J×17 带装饰罩的轻合金结构锻造车轮	
91	8J×18 Cast aluminum	8J×18 铸铝	
92	9J×19（Front） 10J×19（Rear） Forged wheel	9J×19（前） 10J×19（后） 锻造车轮	
93	8J×18 Cast aluminium	8J×18 铸铝	
94	8J×18 Cast aluminium	8J×18 铸铝	
95	9J×19（Front） 10J×19（Rear） Cast aluminium	9J×19（前） 10J×19（后） 铸铝	

Key Words

front axle	前桥	swinging arm	摆臂
track rod	转向横拉杆	spare wheel	备用车轮
stabilizer bar	稳定杆	rim	轮辋
differential	差速器		

Exercises

1. _____ results in weight reduction of the chassis by about 30% compared to an axle made of steel components.

2. _____ is screwed on to increase the transversal rigidity of the front car.

3. The hydro mount in _____ damps wheel vibrations through its fluid filling.

4. _____ is directly connected to the spring strut by means of stabilizer links to achieve the best performance level.

5. _____ offers advantages with regard to the acoustics and vibration characteristics.

6. Compressed in the normal position, _____ is parallel to the road and creates an air guidance effect for favourable aerodynamic flow of the air to the rear area of the vehicle.

7. The stabilizer bar is connected by means of _____ between the rear axle carrier and swinging arms.

8. The standard rim of the chassis is a weight-optimized _____ which is partly covered by a glass-fibre-reinforced plastic trim.

9. Adhesive weights are used on the chassis for _____ purposes.

Unit 5
Steering System 转向系

Key Terms

| steering gear | power steering pump |
| track rod | steering column |

Steering components include the **steering gear**, track rod （转向横拉杆）, power steering pump （转向助力泵）, and **steering column**.

转向系的部件包括转向器、横拉杆、转向助力泵和转向柱。

5.1 Steering Gear 转向器

Figure 5 – 1 shows the steering gear.

转向器如图 5 – 1 所示。

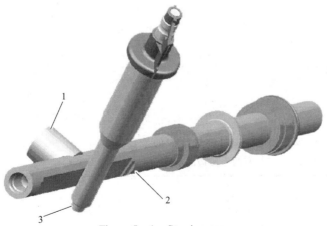

Figure 5 – 1　Steering gear

Index	Description	中文名称	Index	Description	中文名称
1	Thrust piece	压块	3	Steering shaft	转向轴
2	Variable gear tooth pitch	可变齿距的齿条			

The steering gear is rigidly bolted at 4 points to the axle carrier. The gear ratio of the steering gear is variable from 47.0 to 59.0 mm rack movement per steering wheel revolution. The gear ratio is variable in order to keep the number of total steering wheel revolutions when turning to full lock as low as possible. The greater the steering wheel lock the more direct the gear ratio.

转向器有 4 处与车桥架梁刚性拧在一起。转向器的传动比是可变的，方向盘每转一圈，齿条就会移动 47.0 ~ 59.0 mm。为保证方向盘转到极限位置时总圈数较少，传动比被设计为可变传动比。方向盘转角越大，传动比就越小。

5.2　Track Rod 转向横拉杆

Figure 5 – 2 shows the track rod.

转向横拉杆如图 5 – 2 所示。

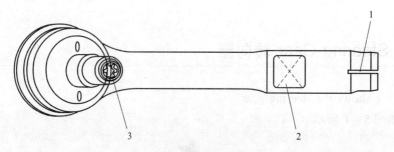

Figure 5 – 2　Track rod

Index	Description	中文名称	Index	Description	中文名称
1	Thread clamp	螺纹锁紧槽	3	Torx for bracing when loosening nut	用于松开螺母的星形着力槽
2	2-edge area for bracing when releasing clamp	用于打开锁紧件的带有两个棱边的着力面			

5.3   Power Steering Pump 转向助力泵

Different power steering pumps are used depending on the vehicle equipment. Vehicles without dynamic drive are equipped with only one vane pump（叶片泵）. The oil reservoir（液压油箱）is a standard reservoir. A tandem（一前一后）pump is fitted if the vehicle is equipped with dynamic drive. This pump consists of a radial piston pump with a maximum output of 180 bar and a vane pump section with a maximum output of 135 bar. These vehicles are also equipped with large oil reservoirs with oil level monitoring.

车辆装备不同，使用的转向助力泵也不同。不带动态驾驶装置的车辆只装备了一个叶片泵。液压油箱是一个标准液压油箱。如果车辆装备了动态驾驶装置，那么会安装一个串联泵。它由一个最大压力 180 bar 的径向活塞泵和一个最大压力 135 bar 的叶片泵组成。同样，这些车辆也装备了带油位监控装置的大液压油箱。

5.4   Steering Column 转向柱

When the steering column is subject to driver load in the event of a crash, the upper steering shaft can be compressed telescopically by 70 mm（See Figure 5－3）. This telescopic action is controlled by a characteristic-controlled crash element made of glass fiber reinforced plastic.

当发生正面碰撞，驾驶员在转向柱上施加了载荷时，上部的转向轴将像望远镜一样自行缩回 70 mm（见图 5－3）。由玻璃纤维增强塑料制成的碰撞元件根据特性线控制缩回过程。

This makes it possible for two metal sleeves to slide together when the glass fiber reinforced plastic element surrounding the metal sleeves is broken over a defined length（See Figure 5－4）. This occurs at force application of 3 to 7 kN.

如果套在两个金属套管外的玻璃纤维增强塑料元件按规定长度裂开，那么这两个金属套管就会缩到一起（见图 5－4）。作用力为 3 至 7 kN 时就会产生这样的结果。

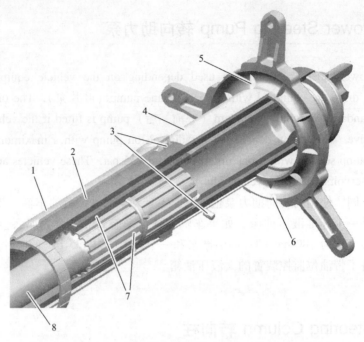

Figure 5 – 3   Sectional view of upper steering column

Index	Description	中文名称	Index	Description	中文名称
1	Steering column tube	转向柱套管	5	Webs	接合边
2	Slide tube	位移管	6	SLZ carrier	SLZ 架梁
3	Shear pin	剪力销	7	Forward/backward adjustment	纵向调节
4	Crash element	碰撞元件	8	Steering column	转向柱

Figure 5 – 4   Crash element (before and after crash situation)

Index	Description	中文名称
1	Crash element	碰撞元件

Key Words

| steering 转向系 | steering gear 转向器 | steering column 转向柱 |

Exercises

1. The gear ratio is variable in order to keep the number of _____ when turning to full lock as low as possible.
2. A tandem pump is fitted if the vehicle is equipped with _____ .
3. The upper steering shaft can be _____ telescopically by 70 mm.

Unit 6
Brake System 制动系

Key Terms

service brake	parking brake
brake disc	electromechanical actuating unit
brake guard	emergency release
brake caliper	indicator lamp

6.1 Service Brake 行车制动器

The chassis features a hydraulic（液压的）dual-circuit brake system with "black/white" distribution. One brake circuit for the front axle and one brake circuit for the rear axle.

底盘上安装了一个以黑白色分类的双回路液压制动系统。一个制动回路用于前桥，另一个制动回路用于后桥。

6.1.1 Brake Control 制动器操纵

The brake system is controlled in the conventional manner with a vacuum（真空的）booster（助力器）and tandem master brake cylinder. The design is based on an 8″/9″ aluminum brake booster with tandem master brake cylinder and brake fluid reservoir（制动液平衡罐）.

常规情况下制动器操纵通过真空助力器和串联式制动主缸执行。按规格分为带串联式制动主缸和带制动液平衡罐的铝制 8 英寸/9 英寸制动助力器。

6.1.2 Brake Discs 制动盘

Vehicles will be equipped on the front and rear axle with inner-vented **brake discs** made of high carbon（碳）cast iron.

车辆的前桥和后桥都使用内通风式高碳灰口铸铁制动盘。

6.1.3   Brake Guard   制动器防护板

As shown in Figure 6 – 1, the ventilation-optimized brake guards（针对通风优化的制动器防护板）on the front axle and rear axle are made of aluminum. They are shaped such that water can drain off（排水）most effectively.

如图 6 – 1 所示，前桥和后桥上针对通风进行优化的制动器防护板由铝合金制成。它们的形状可以保证排水最佳。

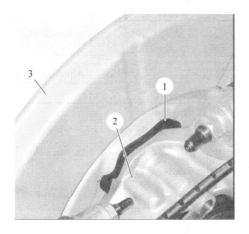

Figure 6 – 1   Brake guard on wheel carrier

Index	Description	中文名称	Index	Description	中文名称
1	Rubber element between wheel carrier and guard plate	轮架与防护板之间的橡胶件	3	Brake guard of rear axle	后桥制动器防护板
2	Wheel carrier	轮架			

6.1.4   Brake Calipers   制动钳

1. Front Brake Calipers   前桥制动钳

The housing of the front axle **brake calipers**（See Figure 6 – 2）is made of aluminum. The frame surrounding the brake caliper prevents V-shaped spread of the brake caliper as the result of contact pressure on the brake disc. The brake caliper holder is made of zinc-nickel coated spheroidal cast iron.

前桥制动钳（见图 6 – 2）的壳体由铝合金制成。在压紧力作用在制动盘上时，围绕着制动钳的框架可防止制动钳开成 V 形。制动钳支架由涂有锌镍涂层的球墨铸铁制成。

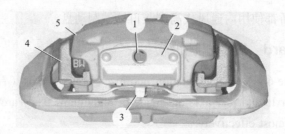

Figure 6 – 2　Front axle brake caliper

Index	Description	中文名称	Index	Description	中文名称
1	Opening for measuring brake pad thickness	用于测量制动摩擦片厚度的开口	4	Spherical cast iron mounting bracket	球墨铸铁支架
2	Cover	饰板	5	Aluminum housing	铝合金壳体
3	Retaining spring	饰板固定弹簧			

2. Rear Brake Calipers　后桥制动钳

The brake calipers on the rear axle are made of zinc-nickel（锌镍合金）coated spheroidal cast iron（球墨铸铁）based on the known version.

后桥制动钳由涂有锌镍涂层的球墨铸铁按我们熟知的结构制成。

3. Stage Brake Pad Wear Sensors　两级制动摩擦片磨损传感器

The 2-stage brake pad wear sensors（两级制动摩擦片磨损传感器）at the front left and rear right relay their voltage signals to the dynamic stability control unit where they are used for continuous calculation of the brake pad wear in the dynamic stability control unit.

左前和右后的按两级设计的制动摩擦片磨损传感器将其电压信号传输给动态稳定控制单元，并以此为动态稳定控制单元内持续计算制动摩擦片磨损量提供支持。

In the first stage, the brake pad wear indicator operates in the same way as on previous models. A resistor（电阻）has now been additionally integrated in the second stage. The control unit is informed of the current wear status based on the changed voltage measurement.

制动摩擦片磨损指示灯同现有类型一样，磨损到第一级即开始工作。在第二级中附加集成了一个电阻。通过电压测量值的变化将当前磨损状态传输给控制单元。

The first stage of the wear indicator is activated at 6 mm remaining brake pad, the second stage at 4 mm remaining brake pad.

在摩擦片剩余厚度为 6 mm 时开始执行第一级磨损显示，4 mm 时执行第二级磨损显示。

4. Wheel Speed Sensors　车轮转速传感器

A new wheel speed sensor that operates in accordance with the Hall principle is used. A special feature of this sensor is that it detects forward and reverse movement.

车辆使用了一个按霍尔原理工作的新型车轮转速传感器。其特点是可以识别向前行驶和倒车行驶。

The sensor contains three Hall-effect elements accommodated next to each other in **housing**. The signals of the first and of the third Hall element form a differential signal for determining the signal frequency and the air gap（clearance）to the sensor wheel.

在传感器内有三个并排安装在一个壳体内的霍尔元件。第一个和第三个霍尔元件的信号形成一个信号差，用于确定信号频率和脉冲信号齿的空气间隙。

Clockwise or anticlockwise rotation is detected by means of the temporal（时间的）offset of the signal from the middle element with respect to the differential signal.

通过中间元件信号与该信号差在时间上的错位即可识别顺时针运行或逆时针运行。

6.2　Parking Brake 驻车制动器

The **parking brake**, also termed as the electromechanical parking brake（EMF）, will be used for the first time in series production in the chassis.

驻车制动器亦称电子机械式驻车制动器（EMF），将首次在底盘中批量使用。

In principle, the parking brake is used to secure the stationary vehicle to prevent it rolling away（移动）. It firmly brakes（locks）the vehicle when parked.

驻车制动器主要用于防止停着的车辆自行移动。它可以使静止状态的车辆以制动方式驻车。

The push-button of parking brake in the instrument panel is shown in Figure 6 – 3.

仪表板上的驻车制动器按钮如图 6 – 3 所示。

Figure 6 – 3　Parking brake push-button in the instrument panel

The task of the system is to lock the vehicle mechanically when parked and, in addition to (另外) the service brake, to provide a further independent brake system as required by law. Added to this, the parking brake offers additional comfort and safety functions.

该系统的任务是车辆静止时以机械方式驻车，并按法规要求为行车制动器提供另一个独立的备用制动系统。此外，该驻车制动器还具有便捷功能和安全功能。

Figure 6 – 4 shows the components of parking brake.

驻车制动器的构成如图 6 – 4 所示。

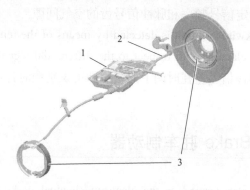

Figure 6 – 4　The components of parking brake

Index	Description	中文名称	Index	Description	中文名称
1	EMF actuator	EMF 伺服单元	3	Drum brake	鼓式制动器
2	Bowden cable	拉线			

6.2.1　Functional Description　功能描述

There are two different types of parking brake functions depending on the operating status of the vehicle.

根据车辆的运行状态，驻车制动器有两种不同的功能。

1. Locking（Brake Applied）　驻车

（1）With the engine running or the vehicle rolling, with the aid of the dynamic stability control, the parking brake acts on the disc brakes of the front axle and rear axle.

发动机运转时或车辆移动时，驻车制动器通过动态稳定控制系统作用在前桥和后桥的盘式制动器上。

（2）When the engine is not running and the vehicle is stationary（静止的）, with the aid of the electromechanical actuator in connection with bowden cables（拉线）, the parking brake acts on the duoservo drum brake（双自增力鼓式制动器）of the rear axle. The actuator is located in the **luggage compartment** floor between the spare wheel recess and stiffener wall of the rear bench seat. The parking brake is always applied as defined in the control unit when the actuator is activated.

发动机关闭且车辆静止时，驻车制动器通过电动机械伺服单元操纵拉线作用在后桥双自增力鼓式制动器上。伺服单元位于备胎凹坑与后排座椅隔板之间的行李箱底板内。如果伺服单元工作，就会执行控制单元内规定的驻车制动。

2. Dynamic Braking   *动态制动*

Defined braking（deceleration）takes place via the dynamic stability control system if the parking brake push-button is pressed while driving. The braking procedure is monitored by the ABS control function and takes place for as long as the push-button is pressed.

如果行驶期间按下驻车制动按钮，则会通过动态稳定控制系统执行规定的制动。该制动由 ABS 调节功能监控，在按住按钮期间会进行制动。

6.2.2 System Structure   系统的结构

Figure 6 – 5 shows the bus network.

图 6 – 5 展示了汽车控制网络。

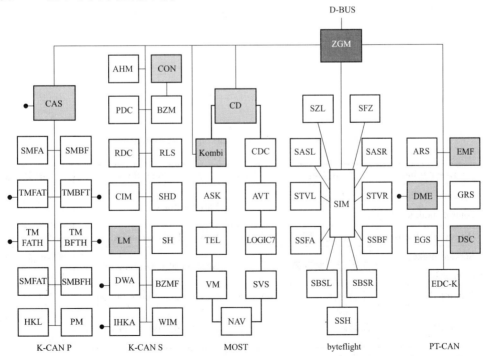

Figure 6 – 5   Bus structure

1. The Parking Brake in the Bus Network   汽车网络中的驻车制动

Figure 6 – 6 is a overview of parking brake system.

汽车网络中驻车制动系统的概览如图 6 – 6 所示。

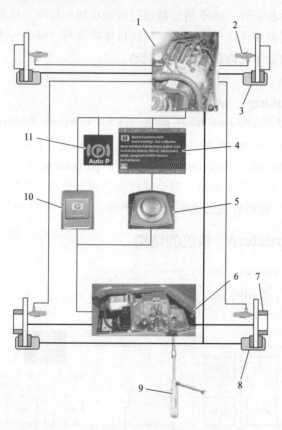

Figure 6 – 6   Overview of parking brake system

Index	Description	中文名称	Index	Description	中文名称
1	dynamic stability control module	动态稳定控制系统模块	7	Parking brake	驻车制动器
2	Wheel speed sensor	车轮转速传感器	8	Service brake, rear axle	后桥行车制动器
3	Service brake, front axle	前桥行车制动器	9	Mechanical emergency release	手动紧急解锁装置
4	Control Display	控制显示	10	Parking brake push-button	驻车制动按钮
5	Controller	控制器	11	Display in instrument cluster	组合仪表中的显示
6	Actuating unit	伺服单元			

2．Components　*部件*

1）End Stop　挡块

The end stop serves as the zero stop for standardizing the actuating position（this component raised is the set position for installing the brake bowden cable assemblies）. The balance arm（平衡杆）rests against the end stop the first time the brake is released after "ignition on". The control unit detects the zero stop（zero stop = released position）by way of the increase in current（电流）.

挡块用于将标准操纵位置限制在零位置（抬起这个部件即可得到制动拉线的安装位置）。"点火开关打开"后第一次松开制动器时，平衡杆靠在挡块上。随着电流的升高，控制单元识别到这个零位置（零位置＝已松开的位置）。

2）Electromechanical Actuating Unit　电动机械式伺服单元

The motor of the actuating unit turns the spindle（丝杆）via the gear mechanism. Driven by the spindle, the balance arm moves for the purpose of right-left compensation of the cable assemblies. With the aid of connecting levers, it pulls the cable pulleys corresponding to the direction of rotation of the spindle. The cable assemblies attached to the cable pulleys apply or release the duo-servo drum brake. The brake is released by means of return springs（复位弹簧）fitted in the duo-servo drum brake.

伺服单元的马达通过变速装置转动丝杆。用于拉线左右平衡的平衡杆因丝杆被驱动而发生移动。这个平衡杆会根据丝杆的旋转方向通过连接杠杆拉动拉线盘。挂在拉线盘上的拉线拉紧双自增力鼓式制动器或将其松开。松开制动器是由双自增力鼓式制动器内的复位弹簧完成的。

The electromechanical actuating unit is shown in Figure 6 – 7.

电动机械式伺服单元如图 6 – 7 所示。

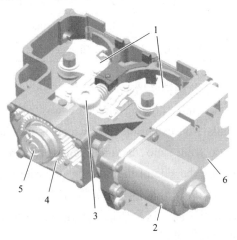

Figure 6 – 7　Electromechanical actuating unit

Index	Description	中文名称	Index	Description	中文名称
1	Cable pulleys	拉线盘	4	Gear mechanism	变速装置
2	Actuator	伺服马达	5	Spindle	丝杆
3	Balance arm	平衡杆	6	Add-on control unit	附加控制单元

3) Gear Mechanism with Wrap Spring   带缠绕式弹簧的变速装置

This is designed as a three-stage step-down gear mechanism consisting of **worm**, **spur gear** and spindle (See Figure 6 – 8). As the gearwheels of the gear mechanism are made of plastic, the entire parking brake holding force is supported by the wrap spring in the housing cover of the spindle.

这是一个由蜗杆、圆柱齿轮和丝杆组成的三级减速器（见图6 – 8）。因为变速装置的齿轮由塑料制成，所以全部的驻车制动力都由丝杆壳体盖内的缠绕式弹簧承受。

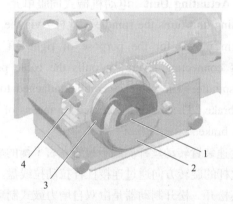

Figure 6 – 8   Gear mechanism and wrap spring (cover half)

Index	Description	中文名称	Index	Description	中文名称
1	Spindle	丝杆	3	Wrap spring	缠绕式弹簧
2	Wrap spring cover	缠绕式弹簧盖罩	4	Emergency release drive	紧急解锁驱动装置

4) Emergency Release   紧急解锁装置

It is possible to release the entire holding effect by way of direct intervention in the gear mechanism. To release the brake, an extension rod, which is provided separately in the vehicle tool kit, is inserted through a guide into the **emergency release** gear wheel. The insertion direction is defined by a guide on the side of the housing opposite the gear mechanism.

直接操纵驻车制动器的传动装置可将整个驻车制动器松开。紧急解锁时可通过一个导向管将一个加长杆推入紧急解锁齿轮内，这个加长杆单独放在随车工具箱内。插入方向由位于变速装置对面壳体侧的辅助导向件决定。

5) Control Unit   控制单元

The add-on（附加的）parking brake control unit integrated in the actuating unit is linked to the dynamic stability control unit and the vehicle periphery（外围设备）（instrument cluster, digital motor electronics, transmission）via CAN. The ECD（electronic controlled deceleration, 电子减速控制系统）interface is used in the dynamic stability control unit for the purpose of hydraulic break activation. When the parking brake push-button is pressed with the engine running, a fixed brake pressure is requested which is then built up by the hydraulic unit of the dynamic stability control system and transferred to the parking brakes.

集成在伺服单元内的驻车制动器附加控制单元通过 CAN 与动态稳定控制单元和车辆外围设备（组合仪表、数字式发动机电子伺控系统、变速箱的控制单元）连接。动态稳定控制单元内的 ECD（电子减速控制系统）接口用于液压制动控制。发动机运转时按压驻车制动按钮即可要求建立固定的制动压力，此压力由动态稳定控制系统液压组件建立，并被传送到驻车制动器。

6.2.3   Indicator Lamps   指示灯

The driver is constantly informed of the parking brake system status and of the system availability. This is achieved by means of an indicator lamp in the instrument cluster（See Figure 6 – 9）and, in the case of a fault, by means of an additional action prompt in the control display. The parking brake control unit is linked with the instrument cluster and the control display via the CAN. The lamp bulb is checked as part of the pre-drive check when the ignition is switched on.

驾驶员可随时获得有关驻车制动系统状态和系统可用性的信息。为此，组合仪表内的一个指示灯（见图 6 – 9）会提醒驾驶员，出现故障时还会在控制显示屏内显示处理提示。驻车制动器控制单元通过 CAN 与组合仪表和控制显示屏连接。打开点火开关时通过驾驶前检查功能检查灯泡的功能。

Parking brake indicator lamp ——

Figure 6 – 9   Display in the instrument cluster

In the basic function, application of the parking brake is indicated by a red LED in the brake symbol and by the letter P on the inside. The letters "PARK" are illuminated in the indicator lamp for as long as the parking brake is applied. The P symbol signals that the requested status "released" or "applied" has been reached. If the parking brake is operated while driving (dynamic braking), an acoustic warning signal is additionally activated (multiple gong).

驻车制动器按基本功能接合时，将通过带制动符号且其内部带字母 P 的红灯显示出来。持续操作时指示灯内的字符"PARK"亮起。P 符号表示已达到所要求的已松开或已接合状态。如果行驶期间操纵了驻车制动器（动态制动），还会发出一个声音报警信号（多频蜂鸣声）。

K ey Words

brake disc　制动盘	luggage compartment　行李箱
brake caliper　制动钳	worm　蜗杆
housing　外壳，壳体	spur gear　圆柱齿轮
parking brake　驻车制动器	emergency release　紧急解锁装置

Exercises

1. The chassis features a _____ brake system with "black/white" distribution.

2. All vehicles will be equipped on the front and rear axle with _____ brake discs made of high carbon cast iron.

3. The frame surrounding _____ prevents V-shaped spread of the brake caliper as the result of contact pressure on the brake disc.

4. In principle, the parking brake is used to secure the stationary vehicle to prevent it _____ .

5. There are two different types of parking brake functions depending on the operating status of the vehicle.
   (1) _____ .
   (2) _____ .

6. Driven by the spindle, _____ moves for the purpose of right-left compensation of the cable assemblies.

7. It is possible to release the entire holding effect by way of _____ in the gear mechanism.

8. The add-on parking brake control unit integrated in the actuating unit is linked to _____ and the vehicle periphery via CAN.

Unit 7
Suspension System
悬架系统

7.1　Suspension 悬架

Key Terms

suspension   shock absorber
damping

The chassis features a conventional helical （螺旋状的） or coil （盘绕的、卷的） compression spring as standard on the front and rear axle. It has a linear characteristic. Both at the front as well as at the rear axle, the springs are combined with the **shock absorbers** to form the spring strut （［悬架］滑柱）（McPherson strut，麦弗逊式滑柱）. The optional pneumatic spring （空气弹簧） on the rear axle serves the purpose of adjusting the level at high payloads （高负荷）. It has the advantage of maintaining a constant level of the vehicle irrespective （不考虑） of the load status （载荷状况）. As a result, the full spring compression and deflection travel （偏转运动） range is made available. A pneumatic spring is not fitted on the front axle as the load differences are not so great at this point.

系列化底盘的前桥和后桥上安装了常规螺旋压簧。该类型弹簧的特性线是线性的。在前桥及后桥上都采用弹簧与减震器一起组装成弹簧滑柱（麦弗逊式滑柱）。后桥上选装的空气弹簧用于高负荷时进行高度补偿。它的优点是不论负荷多大都能保证车辆高度恒定，所以在车轮整个上下移动行程中也可以保证这一要求。因为在前桥上负荷变化不太大，所以不必安装空气弹簧。

7.2 Damping 减振

The chassis is equipped with two-tube gas pressurized shock absorbers as standard. The chassis features aluminum McPherson struts at the front and rear. A locking device/positioning aid is used on the front axle. The clamping area （紧固区域） of the spring struts is shot-peened （喷丸处理） to increase the strength. In view of the improved response characteristics and in order to avoid cavitation （气蚀）, the low pressure dampers are filled with nitrogen at a pressure of 5 bar.

系列化的底盘上安装了双筒减振器。前部和后部使用了铝合金麦弗逊式烛式独立悬架。减震支柱的紧固区域进行了喷丸处理，提高了强度。低压减振器充有 5 bar 压力的氮气，它的响应特性较好且可避免气蚀。

Key Words

shock absorber　减振器

Exercises

1. Both at the front as well as at the rear axle, the springs are combined with _____ to form the spring strut （McPherson struts）.

2. In view of the improved response characteristics and in order to avoid cavitation, the _____ are filled with nitrogen at a pressure of 5 bar.

Unit 8

Air Conditioning System
空调系统

Key Terms

refrigerant	evaporator
refrigerant oil	reservoir
compressor	restrictor
condenser	

8.1　Introduction 简介

8.1.1　Basics of Air Conditioning Technology　空调技术基础知识

1．Physical Principles　物理法则

The four familiar states of water apply to air conditioning refrigerants as well：

(1) Gaseous（not visible）；

(2) Vapour（蒸汽）；

(3) Liquid；

(4) Solid.

水的4个常见状态同样适用于空调制冷剂：

(1) 气态（看不见）；

(2) 蒸汽；

(3) 液体；

(4) 固态。

When water is heated in a vessel（容器）（heat absorption），water vapour can be seen to rise. If the vapour is further heated through heat absorption，the visible vapour turns into invisible gas. The process is reversible. If heat is extracted（释放）from gaseous water, it changes first to vapour, then to water and finally to ice.

当水在容器中加热时（吸收热量），可以看到水蒸气不断升起。如果将水蒸气进一步加热，看得见的水蒸气就会变为看不见的气体。此过程是可逆的。如果将热量从气态水中排出，它将变为水蒸气，然后变为水，最后变为冰。

2. Pressure and Boiling Point　压力和沸点

The boiling point given in tables for a liquid is always referenced to an atmospheric pressure（大气压力）of 1 bar. Changing the pressure on a liquid also alters its boiling point. Water, for instance, is known to boil at lower temperatures at lower pressures.

一般在表格中给出的沸点都指 1 个大气压（1 巴）下的沸点。改变作用在液体上的压力也将改变其沸点。例如，水的沸点随着压力的降低而降低。

The vapour pressure curves for water and refrigerant R134a show for example that, at constant pressure, reducing the temperature changes vapour to liquid（in condenser 冷凝器）or that, for instance, reducing pressure causes the refrigerant to change from liquid to vapour state（in **evaporator**）.

以水和制冷剂 R134a 为例，蒸汽压力曲线显示：当压力一定时，降低温度将使蒸汽变为液体（在冷凝器）；降低压力将使液体变为气体（在蒸发器）。

3. How Air Conditioning Works　空调是怎样工作的

The temperature in the **passenger compartment** depends on the amount of heat radiated（辐射）through the windows and conducted（传导）by the metal parts of the body. In hot weather it is possible to achieve a more comfortable temperature for the passengers by pumping off（泵出）some of the heat.

乘客舱内的温度取决于通过车窗辐射的热量和通过车身金属件传导的热量。天热时，通过将热量泵出乘客舱，就可能获得更舒适的温度。

As heat spreads into cooler areas, the passenger compartment is fitted with a unit for generating low temperatures in which refrigerant is constantly evaporated. The heat required for this is extracted from the air flowing through the evaporator.

因为热量只能向温度较低的区域扩散，因此乘客舱内要安装一个装置，使制冷剂不断地蒸发，才能产生低温。空气流经蒸发器时，热量将从空气中吸收出来。

After absorbing heat, the refrigerant is pumped off through the **compressor**. The work of compression increases the heat content（热容量）and temperature of the refrigerant. Its temperature is now substantially（充分地）higher than that of the surrounding air.

制冷剂在吸收热量后，由压缩机泵出。压缩机的作用是增加制冷剂的热容量，使制冷的温度远高于外界环境温度。

The hot refrigerant flows with its heat content to the condenser, where the refrigerant dissipates (散发) its heat to the surrounding air via the condenser due to the temperature gradient (温差) between the refrigerant and the surrounding air.

高温制冷剂带着其热量流到冷凝器，因为制冷剂与外界大气之间存在温差，制冷剂在通过冷凝器时会将热量散发到大气中。

The refrigerant thus acts as a heat transfer medium. As it is to be re-used, the refrigerant is returned to the evaporator.

这样，制冷剂就充当了传递热量的媒介。因为要重复使用，制冷剂将返回蒸发器。

For this reason all air conditioning systems are based on the refrigerant circulation principle. There are however differences in the composition (组成) of the units.

因此，所有空调系统都建立在制冷剂的循环原理基础上，但具体结构却不尽相同。

8.1.2   Refrigerant R134a   制冷剂 R134a

Use is made in vehicle air conditioning systems of the evaporation and condensation (冷凝) process, employing a substance with a low boiling point (沸点) referred to as the refrigerant (制冷剂). The refrigerant used is tetrafluoroethane R134a, which boils at $-26.5\,°C$ at a vapour pressure of 1 bar. The physical data of refrigerant R134a is shown in Table 8-1.

用于汽车空调系统蒸发和冷凝过程的物质具有较低的沸点，称为制冷剂。目前所用的制冷剂为诺氟烷，在 1 bar 蒸汽压力下，其沸点为 $-26.5\,°C$。制冷剂 R134a 的物理数据如表 8-1 所示。

Table 8-1   Physical data of refrigerant R134a

Chemical formula	化学分子式	**CH2F-CF3 or CF3-CH2F**
Chemical designation	化学名称	Tetrafluoroethane
Boiling point at 1 bar	1 巴下的沸点	$-26.5\,°C$
Solidification point	凝固点	$-101.6\,°C$
Critical temperature	临界温度	$100.6\,°C$
Critical pressure	临界压力	40.56 bar (absolute)

1. Critical Point   临界点

The critical point (临界点) (critical temperature and critical pressure) is that above which there is no longer a boundary between liquid and gas. A substance above its critical point is always in the gaseous state. At temperatures below the critical point, all types of refrigerant in pressure vessels exhibit both a liquid and a gaseous phase; i.e. there is a layer of gas above the liquid. As long as both gas and liquid are present（存在）in the vessel, the pressure depends on the ambient（环境）temperature.

临界点（临界温度和临界压力）是指：超过这个点液体和气体就不再有边界。物质超过其临界点时通常为气态。压力容器中的各种制冷剂，在低于临界温度时都表现为液体和气体两种状态，也就是说，在液体上面有一层气体。只要容器中气体和液体都存在，其压力就取决于外界温度。

2. Trade Names and Designations 商品名称

The refrigerant R134a is currently available under the following trade names：

- H-FKW 134a
- SUVA 134a
- KLEA 134a

制冷剂 R134a 目前有以下几种商品名称：

- H-FKW 134a
- SUVA 134a
- KLEA 134a

Of the wide range of refrigerants available, this is the only one which may be used for vehicles. The names Frigen（氟利根）and Freon（氟利昂）are trade names. They also apply to refrigerants which are not to be used in vehicles.

在很多制冷剂当中，它是唯一一种用于车辆的。氟利根和氟利昂是商品名称，它们也用于那些非汽车用途的制冷剂。

8.1.3 Refrigerant Oil 冷冻机油

Refrigerant oil（冷冻机油）mixes with the refrigerant（about 20% – 40%, depending on compressor type and amount of refrigerant）and circulates（循环）constantly in the system, lubricating the moving parts.

冷冻机油与制冷剂混合（大约20%～40%，与压缩机的类型和制冷剂的量有关），在空调系统中不断地循环，润滑运动的零部件。

Special synthetic（合成）refrigerant oils, e. g. polyalkylene glycol（PAG）oil, are used in conjunction with R134a air conditioning systems. This is necessary as mineral oil, for example, does not mix with R134a. In addition, the materials of the R134a air conditioning system could be corroded（腐蚀）as the mixture flows through the refrigerant circuit under pressure at high temperatures or the lubricating film（润滑油膜）in the compressor breaks down. The use of non-approved oils can lead to the failure of the air conditioning system; exclusive use is therefore to be made of authorized（认可的）oils.

R134a 空调系统使用专用的合成冷冻机油，如聚链烷甘醇（PAG）机油。这点很重要，因为矿物油（举例而言）一方面不能与 R134a 混合，另外，这种混合物在高温高压下流经制冷管路时，还可能会腐蚀 R134a 空调系统的材料，或者会破坏压缩机的润滑膜。使用非认可的机油会导致空调系统故障，因此只能使用经认可的冷冻机油。

8.1.4   Comfort   舒适性

A basic requirement for concentrated and safe driving is a feeling of comfort in the passenger compartment. Especially when it is hot and humid（潮湿）, comfort can only be attained through the use of air conditioning. Comfort can of course also be enhanced（增加）by opening windows/**sun roof** or increasing the air output. Such a course of action is however associated with certain drawbacks（负面影响）for the occupants of the vehicle, e. g. : more noise, exhaust fumes and unfiltered pollen（unpleasant for allergy sufferers ［花粉过敏者］）.

集中精力和安全驾驶的一个基本要求是乘员舱要有舒适的感觉，尤其是在天气比较热和潮湿的情况下。此时，只能通过使用空调才能获得舒适的感觉。当然，通过开窗/天窗或增加空气流动也可以增加舒适感，但这些措施都会给车内的乘客带来一些负面的影响，如噪声更大、废气和未过滤的花粉（对于花粉过敏者不利）。

Climate control together with a good heating and ventilation（通风）system concept can create a sense of well being and comfort by regulating temperature, humidity（湿度）and air circulation in the passenger compartment to suit ambient conditions, both when the vehicle is stationary and moving.

无论车辆是静止的还是在行驶过程中，气候控制与良好的加热和通风系统一起，通过调节乘客舱中的温度、湿度和空气循环以适应车外的气候状况，可以创造出很好的舒适感。

8.2   Components of Refrigerant Circuit 冷却管路的组成

8.2.1   Distribution of Refrigerant Circuit Components
冷却管路部件的分布

On the high-pressure side, there are the condenser, the **reservoir** and, as a division between the high-and low-pressure fluid sides, the restrictor（限流器）or the expansion valve（膨胀阀）.

冷凝器、储液器位于高压段，限流器或膨胀阀是高压段和低压段液体的分界点。

High pressure develops because the **restrictor** or the expansion valve creates a narrow point and the refrigerant builds up, leading to increased pressure and temperature.

由于限流器或膨胀阀形成了一个小孔，制冷剂产生了阻塞，压力和温度上升。

Overpressure develops when there is too much refrigerant, the condenser is dirty, the radiator fan is defective（有缺陷的）, the system is plugged or moisture（湿气）is present in the refrigerant circuit（icing［结冰］on the restrictor）.

当制冷剂过多、冷凝器不洁、散热器风扇有缺陷、系统阻塞或冷却管路中存在湿气（限流器结冰）时，就会产生过压。

On the low pressure side, there are the evaporator, the evaporator temperature sensor and, as a division between the high-and low-pressure gas sides, the compressor.

蒸发器、蒸发器温度传感器位于低压段，压缩器是高压段和低压段气体的分界点。

A drop in system pressure can be caused by loss of refrigerant, restrictor or expansion valve（no narrow point）, a defective compressor or an iced-over evaporator.

制冷剂的损耗、限流器或膨胀阀（无小孔）、压缩器故障或蒸发器结冰都会造成系统压力的下降。

8.2.2 Compressor 压缩机

The compressor（See Figure 8－1）is driven via a ribbed belt by the vehicle's engine.

汽车发动机（见图8－1）通过皮带驱动压缩机。

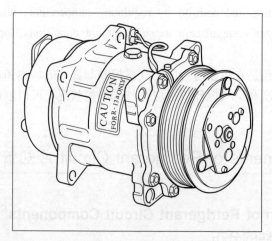

Figure 8－1 Compressor

Compressor with magnetic coupling：

An electromagnetic coupling attached to the compressor completes the power transfer between belt pulley（皮带轮）and compressor crankshaft when the air conditioning is switched on.

带有磁耦合机构的压缩机：

当空调开启时，连接在压缩机上的电磁耦合器将动能从皮带轮传递给压缩机曲轴。

Compressor without magnetic coupling：

An overload safety attached to the belt pulley of the compressor releases if the compressor turns with difficulty, protecting the belt drive from overload.

没有磁耦合机构的压缩机：

如果压缩机转动困难，压缩机皮带轮上的过载安全装置启动，防止皮带驱动装置过载。

The compressor draws refrigerant gas from the evaporator, compresses it and pushes it on to the condenser.

压缩机抽取蒸发器中的制冷剂气体，压缩它，再把它送入冷凝器。

8.2.3   Condenser   冷凝器

The condenser (See Figure 8 – 2) transfers heat from the compressed refrigerant gas to the surrounding air. When this happens, the refrigerant gas condenses to liquid.

冷凝器（见图 8 - 2）把压缩过的制冷剂气体中的热量排入环境空气中，同时制冷剂气体冷凝成液体。

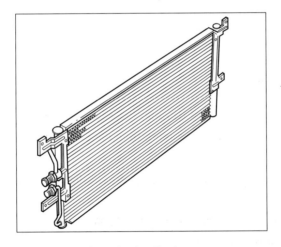

Figure 8 – 2   Condenser

8.2.4   Evaporator   蒸发器

The liquid refrigerant evaporates in the tubes of the evaporator (See Figure 8 – 3). The required heat is extracted from the air flowing past the evaporator ribs （肋片）. The air cools off. The refrigerant evaporates and, together with the absorbed heat, is drawn away by the compressor.

液态制冷剂在蒸发器（见图 8 - 3）的管子中蒸发。所需热量从流经蒸发器肋片的空气中吸取。空气被冷却。制冷剂蒸发，并在压缩机的作用下带着吸收的热量流出。

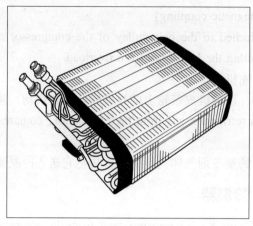

Figure 8 – 3   Evaporator

A restrictor or an expansion valve allows a defined quantity（定量的）of refrigerant to flow to the evaporator. The flow is regulated in systems with expansion valves so that only gaseous refrigerant exits the evaporator.

限流器或膨胀阀使一定数量的冷却剂流向蒸发器。膨胀阀控制系统中冷却剂的流动，因此只有气态冷却剂离开蒸发器。

8.2.5   Reservoir   储液器

To ensure that the compressor draws in only gaseous refrigerant, the reservoir（See Figure 8 – 4）traps the mixture of vapor and gas coming from the evaporator. The vapor becomes gaseous refrigerant.

为保证压缩机只抽取气态制冷剂，储液器捕集蒸汽和来自蒸发器的气体的混合物。蒸汽变为气态制冷剂。

Refrigerant oil flowing in the circuit does not remain（呆在）in the reservoir, as an oil extraction hole has been provided.

由于有机油排出孔，管路中的冷冻机油不会呆在储液器中。

Any moisture which has entered the refrigerant circuit during assembly will be trapped（收集）by a filter（dryer, 干燥剂）in the reservoir.

在装配过程中进入冷却管路的潮气由储液器中的过滤器（干燥剂）收集。

Gaseous refrigerant with oil is drawn in by the compressor.

带有机油的气态制冷剂在压缩机的作用下流入储液器。

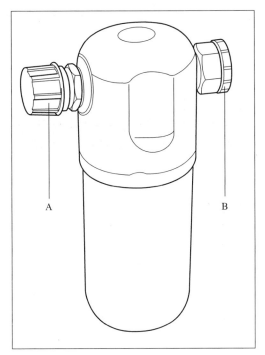

Remove sealing plugs A and B only immediately before installation.

Figure 8 – 4   Reservoir

8. 2. 6   Restrictor   限流器

The restrictor (See Figure 8 – 5) creates a narrow point. This narrow point restricts the flow, separating the refrigerant circuit into high-pressure and low-pressure sides. Upstream (上游) of the restrictor, the refrigerant is warm due to the high pressure. Downstream (下游) of the restrictor, the refrigerant is cold due to the low pressure. Upstream of the narrow point is a strainer (过滤器) to catch dirt and downstream of the narrow point is a strainer to atomize the refrigerant before it enters the evaporator.

限流器（见图 8 – 5）形成了一个小孔。这个小孔起限流的作用，它把制冷管路分成高压段和低压段。在限流器的上游，由于压力高，制冷剂是热的。在限流器的下游，由于压力低，制冷剂是冷的。小孔上游的过滤器捕集杂质，小孔下游的过滤器在制冷剂进入蒸发器之前使它变成雾状。

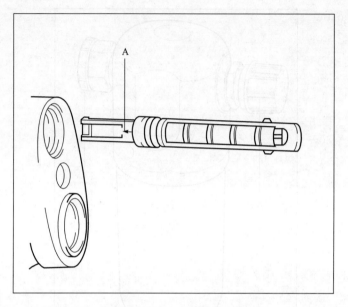

Arrow A on restrictor faces evaporator.

Figure 8 – 5   Restrictor

K ey Words

evaporator　蒸发器	sun roof　天窗
passenger compartment　乘员舱	reservoir　储液器
compressor　压缩器	restrictor　限流器

Exercises

1. Water, for instance, is known to boil at _____ temperatures at lower pressures.

2. Use is made in vehicle air conditioning systems of the evaporation and condensation process, employing a substance with a low boiling point referred to as the _____.

3. The use of non-approved refrigerant oils can lead to the _____ of the air conditioning system; exclusive use is therefore to be made of authorized oils.

4. _____ together with a good heating and ventilation system concept can create a sense of well being and comfort.

5. All air conditioning systems are based on _____ principle.

6. _____ is a division between the high- and low-pressure fluid sides.

7. If the compressor turns with difficulty, _____ protects the belt drive from overload.

8. The flow is regulated in systems with _____ so that only gaseous refrigerant exits the evaporator.

9. Any moisture which has entered the refrigerant circuit during assembly will be trapped by a filter (dryer) in the _____ .

10. Upstream of _____ is a strainer to catch dirt and downstream of _____ is a strainer to atomize the refrigerant before it enters the evaporator.

Unit 9
Electrical System 电气系统

Key Terms

exterior lighting	central-locking functions
headlight	power windows
clearance light	closing and opening of windows
number-plate lamp	emergency close
fog lamp	child lock
interior lighting	seat heating
ambient lighting	backrest
instrument lighting	exterior rearview mirrors
anti-theft alarm system	mirror adjustment
installed position	mirror heating
components of the anti-theft alarm	windscreen
system	functional description
functional description	tailgate lift
central locking	park distance control (PDC)
central-locking master	PDC acoustic warning

9.1   Exterior Lighting 外部照明

9.1.1   Introduction 引言

The vehicle's **exterior lighting** is controlled by the light module. This makes a significant contribution to roadworthiness（车辆性能）and safety. The load currents are switched by means of semiconductor components, thus resulting in high service-life reliability. There is also the option of self-diagnosis.

车辆的外部照明由灯光模块控制。这对交通安全性非常有益。负载电流通过半导体元件开关，因此寿命可靠性高，同样也使自诊断成为可能。

9.1.2　Functional Description　功能描述

The light module（LM）comprises the electronics for controlling and monitoring the complete exterior vehicle lighting. The following tasks are part of the LM's scope of functions:

（1）Control and monitoring exterior vehicle **headlights** and lamps including flashing and hazard-warning function;

（2）Function of dimmer for instrument and locator lighting（terminal 58 g，总线端 Kl.58 g）and function and locator lighting for hazard warning button（报警按钮）;

（3）Evaluation of messages from rain/driving-light sensor（晴雨/行车灯传感器）for effecting automatic driving-light control;

（4）Communication with a trailer（挂车）module（if fitted）;

（5）Management of diagnostics and monitoring functionality;

（6）CAN communication;

（7）Limp-home functions.

灯光模块由控制和监控整个外部车辆照明的电子元件组成。以下工作是灯光模块的一部分功能：

（1）控制和监控位于外部的车辆大灯和具有转向信号功能和闪烁报警功能的车灯；

（2）用于组合仪表照明和查寻照明的亮度调节器功能总线端 Kl.58 g 及用于闪烁报警按钮的功能照明和查寻照明；

（3）分析晴雨/行车灯传感器信息，用于实现行车灯自动控制；

（4）与挂车模块通信（如安装）；

（5）管理诊断功能和监控功能；

（6）CAN 通信；

（7）紧急运行功能。

9.1.3　Lamp Monitoring　车灯监控

1. Power Limitation　功率限制

In order to increase their service life, the vehicle lamps are activated under dimmed（暗淡的）conditions once the system voltage rises above a coded value.

一旦车辆电源系统电压大于设定值，在昏暗条件下车灯就会点亮，以便提高车灯的使用寿命。

2. Cold Monitoring　冷态监控

Cold monitoring is initiated through a brief activation of the lamp drivers（车灯驱动装置）. The ON period is so short that bulbs（灯泡）do not light up on account of their thermal inertia（热滞后性）. LED and xenon（氙）lights are not cold-monitored. LEDs respond so fast that any brief lighting up would be visible；on principle，xenon lights must not be pulsed.

短暂接通车灯驱动装置即可触发冷态监控。这个接通时间很短，以保证白炽灯泡因自身的热滞后性而不亮起。系统不对 LED 指示灯和氙气灯照明进行冷态监控。LED 指示灯响应非常快，只要接通就会短暂亮起一下；受工作原理限制，氙气灯照明不允许以脉冲方式加载。

3. Hot Monitoring　热态监控

Hot monitoring involves checking the nominal current of an activated lamp via the status output of the lamp drivers which indicates among others if there is an overload or open circuit.

热态监控是指通过车灯驱动装置的状态输出端检查一个已接通灯泡的额定电流，该输出端还显示是否有过载或导线断路的情况。

9.1.4　Light Functions　灯光功能

1. Parking Light　停车灯

From terminal 30 and with the light switch in the parking-light or low-beam setting（近光灯底座）, the parking-light function is activated with **clearance lights**, front and rear side-marker lamps（侧面示廓灯）, rear lamps and number-plate lamps（牌照灯）. The function can likewise（同样地）be activated by automatic driving-light control.

从总线端 Kl. 30 接通位置起且灯开关在停车灯或近光灯位置上，则停车灯功能与示宽灯，前部和后部侧示廓灯，尾灯和牌照灯一起打开。该功能也可以通过行车灯自动控制启用。

2. Low Beam　近光灯

The low-beam headlights are activated when：

— at terminal 15 the light switch is in the low-beam setting；

— darkness has been signaled by the rain sensor in the automatic driving-light control function；

— low beam is requested via the CAN by an anti-theft Alarm system（防盗报警系统）alarm；

— the hardware limp-home mode is active.

在下列情况下近光灯接通：

——在总线端 Kl. 15 接通时且灯开关在近光灯位置上；

——在行车灯自动控制功能下由晴雨传感器发出了昏暗信号；

——防盗报警系统通过 CAN 请求近光灯接通；

——硬件紧急运行模式处于工作状态。

3．High Beam　远光灯

The high-beam headlights are activated when：

— from terminal R the turn-signal/dipping switch（转向开关/近光灯开关）is in the headlight-flasher setting；

— at terminal 15 and with the light switch in the low-beam setting, the turn-signal/dipping switch is in the high-beam setting；

— high beam is requested via the CAN by an anti-theft alarm system alarm.

在下列情况下远光灯接通：

— 从总线端 Kl. R 接通位置起且转向开关/近光灯开关在远光灯瞬时功能位置上；

— 在总线端 Kl. 15 接通时且灯开关在近光灯位置上，转向开关/近光灯开关在远光灯位置上；

— 防盗报警系统通过 CAN 请求远光灯接通。

4．Turn-signal Indication and Hazard-warning Flashing　转向显示和闪烁报警

From terminal R ON and with the turn-signal/dipping switch in the flashing left/right position, the turn-signal lamps on the corresponding side are switched on and off with a pulse rate of 640 ms and a **duty factor** of 50：50.

从总线端 Kl. R 接通位置起且转向开关/近光灯开关在左/右转向信号灯位置上时，相应一侧的转向信号灯以 640 毫秒的脉冲重复频率和 50：50 的脉冲负载参数打开和关闭。

5．Reversing Light　倒车灯

The reversing light can be activated from terminal 15 when the reverse gear is engaged. Activation takes place after a delay of 0. 3 s in order to prevent flashing during gear changes；deactivation takes place without any delay.

当挂入倒车挡时，倒车灯可以从总线端 Kl. 15 接通位置起接通。为了避免换挡时倒车灯突然闪亮，接通时延迟约 0. 3 秒，关闭时不延迟。

6．Front Fog Lamp　前雾灯

The front **fog lamps** are activated when the front-fog-lamps button is pressed at terminal 15 and with the light switch in the parking-light or low-beam setting.

在总线端 Kl. 15 接通时且灯开关在停车灯或近光灯位置上，如果按动前雾灯按钮可接通前雾灯。

7. Rear Fog Light　后雾灯

The rear fog light is activated when the rear-fog-light button is pressed at terminal 15 and with the light switch in the low-beam setting or when the front fog lamps are activated.

在总线端 Kl. 15 接通时且灯开关在近光灯位置上或接通了前雾灯时，如果按动后雾灯按钮可接通后雾灯。

8. Anti-theft Alarm System Alarm　防盗报警系统报警

The LM responds to an anti-theft alarm-system alarm with hazard-warning flashing and periodic activation of the low-beam or/and high-beam headlights. This function is terminated（停止）by deactivation of the alarm system or after a maximum period of 330 s.

灯光模块通过闪烁报警和周期性开关近光灯或（和）远光灯对防盗报警系统的报警做出反应。防盗报警系统停止工作或最多持续 330 秒后将停止反应。

9.2　Interior Lighting 车内照明

9.2.1　Introduction　引言

The **interior lighting** is controlled by the power module. For this purpose, the power module sets up the corresponding outputs and divides the entire interior lighting into 3 circuits：

— interior lighting；

— consumer deactivation, roof；

— consumer deactivation, body.

车内照明由供电模块控制。为此，供电模块提供相应的输出端，并将整个车内照明分为 3 个回路：

——车内照明；

——断开车顶用电器；

——断开车身用电器。

9.2.2　Functional Description　功能描述

1. Door Warning Light　车门警示灯

The door warning light is integrated in the end face of the door and is visible from the rear when the door is open. The door warning light alerts road traffic behind to that particular car door being open. It is activated/deactivated when the door is opened/closed.

车门警示灯安装在车门端面上，在车门打开时可从后面看到它。车门警示灯用于提醒后面的车辆及行人注意此时车门已开启。车门警示灯随车门的开或关而接通或关闭。

2. Electric Entrance Light 登车照明灯

The electric entrance light is located in the lower front section of the door. It serves to illuminate the ground outside the vehicle in the area of the vehicle door. It is activated/deactivated when the door is opened/closed.

登车照明灯位于车门的前下部区域。它用于照亮车辆外部车门附近区域的地面。登车照明灯随车门的开或关而接通或关闭。

3. Ambient Lighting/Background Lighting 环境照明/背景照明

The **ambient lighting** serves to illuminate the controls in the individual doors and is connected to the **instrument lighting**. The term "ambient lighting" is used to **denote** the **incident lighting** and the switch background lighting. It is controlled by the light module via the K-CAN system. The light is dependent on the position of the **knurl** of the instrument lighting.

环境照明用于照亮各车门上的操作元件，它与仪表照明连在一起。透光照明和开关背景照明称为环境照明。环境照明由灯光模块经过 K-CAN 系统总线控制。此照明亮度取决于仪表照明滚轮的调节位置。

4. Courtesy Light 前部区域照明灯

The **courtesy light** is located in the **door handle** operated from the outside and serves to illuminate the front area of the door. It is controlled by the power module via the K-CAN system.

前部区域照明灯安装在外侧的车门把手内，用于车门前部区域照明。前部区域照明灯由灯光模块经过 K-CAN 系统总线控制。

It is activated by remote control when the door is unlocked. It is deactivated by a **timer** when the door is closed.

在通过遥控器开启车门锁时，前部区域照明灯接通。在关闭车门时通过延时电路关闭。

9.3 Anti-theft Alarm System 防盗报警系统

The **anti-theft alarm system** has the task of indicating attempts to break into the vehicle, or to tamper（操控）with it and to issue acoustic and visual alarms.

防盗报警系统的任务是通过声光报警信号显示强行进入车辆或操控车辆的企图。

The anti-theft alarm system must be differentiated from the electronic immobilizer. The purpose of the anti-theft alarm system is to deter（阻止）a potential intruder（入侵者）or thief and to alert passers-by to the crime.

要区别的是，防盗报警装置与电子禁启动防盗装置不同。防盗报警装置应吓退闯入车辆的人或盗贼，并提醒过路人注意所发生的事。

The new system consists of the following components：

（1）Interior sensor with integrated anti-theft alarm system logic；

（2）Emergency siren（报警器）with integrated tilt sensor；

（3）Anti-theft alarm system LED under the **rear view mirror**；

（4）External switches，e. g. bonnet（发动机罩）or door contacts.

这个新系统由下列部件组成：

（1）带防盗报警装置逻辑电路的车内传感器；

（2）带组合式倾斜度传感器的应急电源报警器；

（3）后视镜下的防盗报警装置 LED 指示灯；

（4）外部开关，例如发动机罩或车门触头。

9. 3. 1　Overview of the Anti-theft Alarm System　防盗报警系统概览

Figure 9 – 1 shows a overview of the anti-theft alarm system.

防盗报警系统的构成如图 9 – 1 所示。

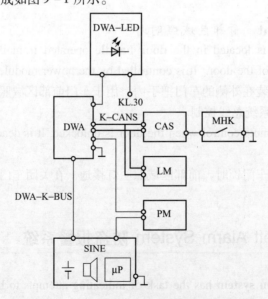

Figure 9 – 1　Overview of the anti-theft alarm system

Index	Description	中文名称	Index	Description	中文名称
MHK	Bonnet contact	发动机罩触点	DWA	anti-theft alarm system	防盗报警系统
CAS	Car Access System	便捷进入及起动系统	DWA-K-BUS	Local data bus of anti-theft alarm system	防盗报警系统本地数据总线
LM	Light module	灯光模块			
K-CAN S	K-CAN System	K-CAN 系统总线	SINE	Emergency siren with integrated tilt sensor	带组合式倾斜度传感器的应急电源报警器
DWA-LED	Anti-theft alarm system LED	防盗报警系统的 LED 指示灯			

9.3.2 Installed Position of the Anti-theft Alarm System
防盗报警系统的安装位置

The anti-theft alarm system interior sensor is located at the centre of the headlining (See Figure 9 – 2). This central location allows the entire vehicle interior to be monitored very effectively.

防盗报警装置车内传感器布置在车顶内衬的中间（见图 9 – 2）。在这一中央位置可以对整个车辆内部进行监控。

The emergency siren with integrated tilt sensor is installed in the left rear **wheel arch** where good protection is provided against tampering with the emergency siren or anti-theft alarm system K bus.

带组合式倾斜度传感器的应急电源报警器安装在左后轮罩内，这样就防止了对应急电源报警器或防盗报警装置车身总线的强行操控。

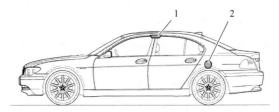

Figure 9 – 2　Installed position of anti-theft alarm system

Index	Description	中文名称
1	Anti-theft alarm system interior sensor	防盗报警系统车内传感器
2	Emergency siren with integrated tilt sensor	带组合式倾斜度传感器的应急电源报警器

9.3.3 Components of the Anti-theft Alarm System 防盗报警系统的组件

1. Interior Sensor with Integrated Anti-theft Alarm System Logic
带防盗报警装置逻辑电路的车内传感器

The interior sensor is an ultrasound-based motion detector（超声波移动信息发射器）which detects all movements inside the vehicle interior and evaluates them via the anti-theft alarm system logic. The anti-theft alarm system issues an alarm if the interior sensor detects a movement which satisfies the triggering criteria（触发条件）, or if alarm triggers are indicated via the K-CAN system or anti-theft alarm system K bus.

车内传感器是超声波移动信息发射器，能识别整个车厢内部的移动情况，并用防盗报警装置逻辑电路进行分析。如果车内传感器识别到符合报警条件的移动情况，或者通过K-CAN 系统总线或防盗报警装置车身总线获得了报警触发信息，就会通过防盗报警装置发出报警。

2. Emergency Siren with Integrated Tilt Sensor
带组合式倾斜度传感器的应急电源报警器

If the alarm is triggered, the emergency siren issues an acoustic signal. In certain countries, an acoustic signal may also be triggered by changes of state（locking/unlocking）.

应急电源报警器在警报情况下发出声音报警信号。某些国家的车辆，在车辆状态发生变化时（联锁或解锁）也会发出声音信号。

The emergency siren communicates with the anti-theft alarm system passenger-compartment sensor（防盗监控传感器）along a bidirectional line（anti-theft alarm system K bus）. The emergency siren is programmable and has diagnostic capability.

应急电源报警器通过双向导线（防盗报警系统车身总线）与防盗报警系统车内防盗监控传感器进行信息交换。应急电源报警器可编程、可诊断。

Detected alarm triggers are initially indicated to the anti-theft alarm system passenger-compartment sensor, which then activates the alarm. However, the independent alarm is an exception. The emergency siren has an independent voltage supply and additionally monitors the voltage supplied by the vehicle battery. It also monitors tampering with any leads.

识别到的报警触发情况首先告知防盗报警系统车内防盗监控传感器，由其再发出报警。在这里有一个例外，就是其独立的电源报警。应急电源报警器独立供电，此外还监控车辆蓄电池的供电情况。此报警器还进一步监控对所有供电线路的强行操控。

3. Tilt Sensor 倾斜度传感器

The tilt sensor monitors the horizontal（水平的）position of the vehicle and also has the task of detecting and indicating tire theft and wheel theft as well as attempts to tow away（拖走）the whole vehicle.

　　倾斜度传感器监控车辆的水平情况，识别轮胎或者车轮被盗或者整辆车被牵引的情况，并发出信息。

The current parked position of the vehicle is stored together with the components "longitudinal angle"（纵向角）and "transverse angle"（横向角）. If a defined change of angle is exceeded in the longitudinal direction and/or the transverse direction, an alarm telegram is sent to the anti-theft alarm system passenger-compartment sensor.

　　车辆当前停放位置与纵向角度和横向角度部分一起存储。如果纵向和（或）横向移动超过规定的角度，就会向防盗报警系统车内防盗监控传感器发出一个报警电码。

4．Anti-theft Alarm System LED　防盗报警系统的 LED 指示灯

The anti-theft alarm system LED is activated directly by the anti-theft alarm system.

防盗报警系统的 LED 指示灯由防盗报警系统直接控制。

5．Anti-theft Alarm System K Bus　防盗报警系统车身总线

The anti-theft alarm system K bus is a local sub-bus to K bus specification. The anti-theft alarm system communicates with the emergency siren or the tilt sensor via the anti-theft alarm system bus.

　　防盗报警系统车身总线是符合车身总线规格的本地子总线。防盗报警系统通过防盗报警系统总线与应急电源报警器或倾斜度传感器进行信息交换。

9.3.4　Functional Description　功能描述

1．Anti-theft Alarm System Alarm　防盗报警系统报警

If a triggering criterion is met when the anti-theft alarm system is armed（打开的）, the alarm is issued both acoustically and visually as per country code.

　　如果防盗报警系统进入戒备状态后满足一个报警标准条件，则会根据车辆的国家编码而发出声光报警。

2．Acoustic Alarm　声音报警

After a triggering criterion is met, the anti-theft alarm system sends the telegram to the anti-theft alarm system K bus. The emergency siren acknowledges the alarm telegram. If the anti-theft alarm system receives no confirmation from the emergency siren with integrated tilt sensor, it repeats the alarm telegram up to 8 times. If it receives no reply, the emergency running horn（喇叭）function is activated.

报警标准条件满足后，防盗报警系统向防盗报警系统总线发出电码。应急电源报警器确认这个报警电码。如果防盗报警系统未收到带组合式倾斜度传感器的应急电源报警器的确认，那么报警电码会重复到最多 8 次。如果未收到答复，则喇叭紧急运行功能会激活。

3. Visual Alarm   视觉报警

After a triggering criterion is met, the anti-theft alarm system outputs the telegram to the K-CAN system. This triggers a visual alarm at the same time as the acoustic alarm for a period of 5 minutes. The visual alarm is indicated by the hazard-warning lights (flashing with low beam or flashing with high beam) as per country code.

在报警标准条件满足后，防盗报警系统向 K-CAN 系统总线发出电码。这时在声音报警的同时会有 5 分钟的视觉报警。根据车辆的国家编码，视觉报警会通过闪烁报警（近光灯闪烁或远光灯闪烁）发出。

9.4   Central Locking 中控锁/自动软关闭装置

9.4.1 Overview   概览

The following assemblies can be operated with the central locking（中控锁）system：
— Door locks；
— Tailgate lock（后行李箱盖锁）；
— Fuel-tank flap（燃油箱盖板）.

通过中控锁可操作下列部分：
——车门锁；
——后行李箱盖锁；
——燃油箱盖板。

In order to improve anti-theft security, the operating location of the lock cylinder（锁芯）in the tailgate for central locking has been omitted（取消）. The lock cylinder in the tailgate is now only still used for mechanical emergency unlocking（机械式紧急解除联锁装置）.

为提高防盗安全性，后行李箱盖锁芯的操作点取消了中控锁功能。后行李箱盖的锁芯只用于机械式紧急解除联锁装置。

The central locking system electronics is incorporated in various components (door modules, power module for tailgate scopes and remote-control-services transceiver).

中控锁电子装置安装在不同部件内（车门模块，用于后行李箱盖范围和遥控功能发射器/接收器的供电模块）。

The individual components communicate with each other via the K-CAN periphery and with the rest of the vehicle via the K-CAN system (e. g. anti-theft alarm system).

各部件之间通过 K-CAN 外围总线进行相互间的信息交换，并通过 K-CAN 系统总线与车辆的其他部件（例如防盗报警系统）之间通信。

9. 4. 2　Central-locking Master　中控锁主控单元

Central-locking master controls all the **higher-level** functions of the central-locking system.

中控锁主控单元控制中控锁的所有高级功能。

It monitors centrally the battery voltage of the central locking system assemblies（构件）. The central locking system assemblies function within a voltage range of 9 V to 16 V.

它对中控锁各构件的蓄电池电压进行中央监控。中控锁构件的工作电压范围为 9～16 伏。

In addition, some central locking system scopes at the rear are activated by the power module：

— Tailgate;

— Fuel-tank flap.

此外，车后的部分中控锁控制范围通过供电模块激活：

——后行李箱盖；

——燃油箱盖板。

9. 4. 3　Functions　功能

1. Central Double Locking　中央保险锁死

When central double locking is engaged, the locking pin（联锁销）in each door is disengaged from the lock by a mechanical coupling（机械联轴节）. It is no longer possible to unlock the vehicle from the inside or from the outside. The fuel-tank flap is locked.

如果设置了中央保险锁死，则车门的联锁销通过一机械联轴节与锁脱开。无论从车内还是车外都无法对车辆解除联锁。燃油箱盖板被闭锁了。

2. Selective Unlocking　选择性解除联锁

Selective unlocking can be activated by means of coding. With selective unlocking, only the driver's door is unlocked on the first unlocking command via the driver's door operating location or radio remote control. The other doors move into the locked position. Only with the second unlocking attempt is the entire vehicle unlocked.

可通过设码激活选择性解除联锁功能。在使用选择性解除联锁功能时，通过驾驶员车门或遥控器的操作点，第一个解除联锁命令只对驾驶员车门解除联锁，其他车门仍处于锁止位置。只有在第二次解除联锁时整个车辆才解除联锁。

3. Electric Lock-out Protection 防止将驾驶员锁在车外的电子装置

With electric lock-out protection, the electronics ensures that the central-locking assembly is unlocked again, e. g. when the locking knob（按钮）is pressed down in the open driver's door. This protects the driver against being inadvertently（无意间）locked out.

该电子装置的用途是确保中控锁构件解除联锁，例如在按动打开的车门上的联锁按钮时，这样可避免无意间将驾驶员锁在车外。

4. Automatic Locking 自动联锁

The central-locking master incorporates the coding option of automatic relocking. If the double-locked（保险锁死）central locking is **accidentally** unlocked with the remote control, automatic relocking（no double locking）is initiated after 2 minutes under the following conditions：

— No further central locking system operator prompt；

— No door/lid, tailgate, bonnet open；

— No auto-remote opening initiated；

— Key not inserted.

在中控锁主控单元中有自动再联锁的设码选项。如果已保险锁死的中控锁无意间用遥控器解除了联锁，则下列条件满足时，2 分钟后中控锁会自动再联锁（非保险锁死）：

——无其他中控锁操作请求；

——无车门/后行李箱盖、后挡板、发动机罩打开；

——未起动便捷开启；

——钥匙未插入。

5. Automatic Locking While Driving 行驶时自动联锁

Automatic locking takes place when the vehicle exceeds a speed of 16 km/h.

当车辆速度超过 16 公里/小时时会进行自动联锁。

6. Reversing with Valid Transponder Key 车辆内有带信号收发器的有效钥匙时的防锁止功能

With a "double lock" command and a valid key in the ignition lock, the central locking is immediately unlocked again（prevention of key being locked in）. The feedback to the customer takes the form of the reversing process of the central locking, i. e. the assemblies are in fact moved to "locked" but then moved back to their initial state.

当命令为保险锁死且点火开关内是有效的钥匙时，中控锁会立即解锁（防止钥匙锁在车内）。中控锁的防锁止过程向客户发出反馈信息，也就是说中控锁构件虽然进入联锁，但立即又重新回到初始状态。

9.5 Power Windows 车窗升降机

9.5.1 Introduction 引言

The power windows are controlled separately（分散控制）by means of the door modules, i. e. one door module locally controls one power window.

车门模块以非中央方式对车窗升降机进行控制，也就是说一个车门模块控制一个本地车窗升降机。

9.5.2 Functional Description 功能描述

1. Closing and Opening of Windows 车窗玻璃的关闭和打开

The power windows can be operated by means of the switch block in the driver's door or a local control button in the **relevant** vehicle door（See Figure 9 – 3）.

车窗升降机可以通过驾驶员侧车门内的开关组或通过相应车门内的一个本地操作按钮操作（见图 9 – 3）。

The power windows are enabled and disabled by the power window master.

车窗升降机主控单元可授权或禁止闭锁车窗升降机动作。

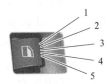

Figure 9 – 3   Power-window switch, door

Index	Description	中文名称
1	Overpressed CLOSED（one-touch）	用力按下关闭（点动）
2	CLOSED（manual）	关闭（手动）
3	Zero position	零位
4	OPEN（manual）	打开（手动）
5	Overpressed OPEN（one-touch）	用力按下打开（点动）

2. Control Options Related to the Switch Positions 操作方法与开关位置有关

Automatic window travel (one-touch) takes place in the closing or opening direction immediately after the switch position "overpressed closed" or "overpressed open" has been reached.

当触动开关位置"用力按下关闭"或"用力按下打开"后，车窗升降机自动向关闭或打开方向运行（点动）。

The power windows are activated in the initial closed/open locking positions (锁止位置) as long as the button is held (保持) in this position.

只要按钮保持在此位置，车窗升降机就会运行到第一个关闭/打开的锁止位置。

Anti-trapping (防夹) protection is active in both automatic and manual operation.

防夹功能不论在自动运行还是在手动操作时都处于工作状态。

3. Emergency Closing 紧急关闭

This function is used for deliberate (有意识地) closing of the windows without anti-trapping protection. Use of this function may be necessary for example in the event of an attack from an outside source or window glass which has frozen solid (冻结).

此功能用于有意识地关闭车窗且无防夹功能。有外部袭击或车窗玻璃冻住时需要使用此功能。

The entire control procedure is divided into two phases (阶段).

整个操作过程分成两个阶段。

1) Phase 1 第 1 阶段

The emergency-close mode is activated after a response time of 0.5 s when the position "overpressed closed" is held. The window is closed at maximum speed and with modified anti-trapping protection. Releasing the button terminates emergency closing, i. e. the window proceeds to be closed with full anti-trapping protection as with automatic operation.

如果按住开关并使之保持在"用力按下关闭"位置，则在 0.5 秒的响应时间后将启用紧急关闭模式。车窗玻璃以最大速度和经过修改的防夹功能关闭。放开按钮紧急关闭结束，此时车窗玻璃同自动运行一样以完全的防夹功能继续向关闭方向运行。

Anti-trapping protection remains activated in modified form even during emergency closing. If trapping is detected, the window travels back (返回) only the short distance of 20 mm. This gives the obstruction (障碍物) or attacker the option of vacating (离开) the danger zone.

即使在紧急关闭时，防夹功能仍以经过修改的形式保持启用状态。如果识别到被夹情况，车窗玻璃仅退回 20 毫米，因此障碍物或袭击者就有机会从危险区中离开。

2）Phase 2　第 2 阶段

The button must now be released（"zero position"）and then **reactuated** in the position "overpressed closed" within 4 s. The window is now closed without anti-trapping protection with full force. In the event of **blocking**, the window is powered until such time that the motor thermal protection（电动机热保护装置）is activated or the window has moved to the upper stop. Releasing the button terminates emergency closing immediately. For safety reasons, it is always possible to open the window independently of（与……无关）the thermal protection.

现在必须松开按钮（零位），然后在 4 秒内重新将按钮按至"用力按下关闭"位置。此时车窗玻璃无防夹功能，以最大的力关闭。在卡住时，车窗玻璃一直通电，直至马达热敏保护装置启动，或车窗玻璃升到最高限位位置。放开按钮紧急关闭立即结束。出于安全方面考虑，不论热保护装置处于何种状态，车窗玻璃总是可以打开的。

If there is no renewed activation of the emergency-close mode within 4 s（overpressing and **holding**）, anti-trapping protection returns to its normal state and is thus fully active.

如果在 4 秒时间内未重新启用紧急关闭模式（用力按下并按住），那么防夹功能重新进入正常状态。

"Emergency close" is not operational from a vehicle speed of ＞ 16 km/h.

车速超过 16 公里/小时时无法启用紧急关闭功能。

When the child Lock（儿童保护功能）is engaged, the emergency-close function cannot be activated by the local switches in the rear doors but only by the switch block in the driver's door.

在设置了儿童保护功能时，紧急关闭功能不能通过后车门上的本地开关启动，只能通过驾驶员车门的开关组启用。

An emergency-closing operation activated by the switch block in the driver's door cannot be interrupted by the local buttons in the front passenger door or the rear doors.

通过驾驶员车门开关组启用的紧急关闭动作无法通过前座乘客侧车门或后车门的本地开关中断。

The emergency-close function can be completely **deactivated** by means of coding. In this way, anti-trapping protection is active in every button position.

紧急关闭功能可通过设码完全关闭，这样防夹功能在任何按钮位置都是激活的。

4. Child Lock　儿童保护功能

Operation of the two rear power-window buttons is disabled by means of the child-lock button in the switch block in the driver's door. When the child lock is engaged, it is only possible to operate the rear power windows from the driver's switch block or via the auto-remote function. An LED in the button indicates the current status of the child lock. The LED is activated by the power-window master.

通过驾驶员侧车门内开关组中的儿童保护功能按钮可闭锁后部两个车窗升降机按钮的操作。在设置了儿童保护功能后，后部车窗升降机的操作只能通过驾驶员开关组或便捷功能进行。按钮内的 LED 指示灯表明了儿童保护装置的当前状态。LED 指示灯通过车窗升降机主控单元控制。

9.6 Seat Heating 座椅加热

The special seat-heating equipment allows the occupants to heat individual seat surfaces and **backrests**.

座椅加热使得乘员可以按个人需要加热椅面和座椅靠背。

The switch block accommodates（提供）the control button and 3 orange LEDs. The LEDs indicate the various heating stages.

开关组内有操作按钮和 3 个橘黄色 LED 指示灯。LED 指示灯显示了不同的加热档。

The signals for operating the **seat heating** are transmitted via the buses.

操作座椅加热的信号通过总线传输。

The seat modules incorporate（包含）activation and control of seat heating. Each seat has 4 heating areas, which are incorporated in the seat cover:

— 1 rapid heating area each in inner（内部的）seat area and in inner backrest area;

— 1 **residual heating area** each in outer seat area and in outer backrest area.

座椅模块包括座椅加热的控制和调节装置。每个座椅的座套内有 4 个加热区:

——在座椅内部区域和靠背内部区域各有 1 个快速加热区;

——在座椅外部区域和靠背外部区域各有 1 个余热区。

Each heating area is monitored by an NTC temperature sensor.

每个加热区由一个温度传感器 NTC 监控。

9.6.1 Schematic Representation of Seat Heating 座椅加热示意图

Figure 9 – 4 shows the backrest.

座椅靠背如图 9 – 4 所示。

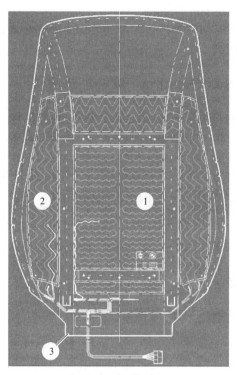

Figure 9 – 4   Backrest

Index	Description	中文名称
1	Rapid heating area	快速加热区
2	Residual heating area	余热区
3	Backrest	座椅靠背

9. 6. 2   Activation of Heating Areas   加热区的控制

When the seat heating is turned on, it is the rapid heating areas which are activated first in order to heat up the seats quickly.

座椅加热接通时，快速加热区首先接通，以便使座椅快速升温。

After the initial rapid heating, the residual heating areas are cut in（接通）in order to ensure a uniform（均匀的）distribution of temperature in the seat.

在首次快速加热后，余热区接通以保证座椅温度均匀分配。

Activation of all the heating fields is timed so that an **established current intensity** is not exceeded during residual heating. The duty factor is dependent on the selected heating stage, the

ON period and the heating-area temperatures.

为了使余热区加热时不会超过规定的电流强度，所有加热区的控制是有节奏地进行的。脉冲负载参数与所选的加热档、接通时间和加热区温度有关。

9.6.3 Operation of Seat Heating 座椅加热操作

Stage 3（maximum temperature）is activated when the button is pressed for the first time. Each subsequent（下一次）pressing of the button selects the next stage lower or "off". The seat heating is turned off if the button is pressed for longer than 1.2 seconds.

第一次按动按钮时接通的是 3 档（最高温度）。以后继续按下按钮选择的是下一档或关闭。如果按下按钮时间超过 1.2 秒钟，座椅加热装置关闭。

The functional status of the heating is maintained（维持）if the ignition is briefly turned off（<15 min）. The heating is switched on again when the ignition is turned on again.

短时断开点火开关时（小于 15 分钟），加热装置的功能状态保持不变。当点火开关重新接通时，加热装置也重新接通。

9.6.4 Balance Control 平衡调节

The operator can use a balance controller to set a temperature differential between the seat surface and the backrest of max +/-3℃. The balance controller can be called up in the control display and is set with the controller. This setting remains permanently（持久的）stored specifically to each remote control key（key memory）.

用户可以通过平衡调节器在椅面和靠背之间设定最多 +/-3℃的温差。平衡调节器可在控制显示中调用，通过控制器进行调整。这一调整将持久存储在相应的遥控钥匙中（钥匙存储器）。

9.7 Exterior Rearview Mirrors 外后视镜

2 electric rearview mirrors are fitted on the driver's and passenger doors of the car. They are activated by the front door modules.

在驾驶员和前座乘客车门上安装了 2 个电动可调外后视镜，由前部车门模块进行控制。

All the mirror functions are served by the control buttons in the switch block in the driver's door. The mirrors are directly connected to the associated door module（via a wiring harness［导线］led out at the mirrors）.

所有后视镜功能都可通过驾驶员侧车门上开关组的操作按钮进行操作。后视镜直接与所属的车门模块连接（通过一根从后视镜上引出的导线）。

The following functions are possible：

— Horizontal and vertical mirror adjustment；

— Mirror heating；

— Mirror pivoting（折起）；

— Mirror memory；

— Under voltage deactivation（低压断电）.

外后视镜可以实现下列功能：

——后视镜的水平和垂直调节；

——后视镜加热；

——后视镜折起；

——后视镜记忆设置；

——低压断电。

9. 7. 1   Horizontal and Vertical Mirror Adjustment 后视镜的水平和垂直调节

Both the exterior mirrors can be moved in the horizontal and vertical directions. However，they can only be adjusted in each case（每次）in one direction（horizontal/vertical）；diagonal（交叉的）adjustment is not possible.

每个外后视镜都能水平和垂直调节。外后视镜每次只能在一个方向上（水平/垂直）进行调节，无法进行交叉调节。

Each exterior mirror accommodates（提供）2 adjusting motors：one motor for each adjusting direction. Potentiometers are fitted for position detection.

在每个外后视镜内都装了 2 个调整马达：对每个调节方向有一个调整马达。为识别位置，各安装了一个电位计。

A common control pad（共同操作区）for both exterior mirrors is located in the driver's door as a separate switch block. The driver uses a slide switch to select between the two mirrors（right/left）.

在驾驶员侧车门上有一个单独的开关组用作对两个外后视镜的共同操作区。驾驶者可通过一个滑动开关选择两个外后视镜（右/左）中的一个。

9. 7. 2   Mirror Heating   后视镜加热

The function of the mirror heating is to keep the mirrors' field of vision free from fog and frost（霜）. The heat output is automatically controlled. The mirror heating is supplied with pulse-width modulated（调制的）power，a sequence controlled by power semiconductors.

后视镜加热装置的任务是使后视镜的镜面区不被水雾冰霜所覆盖。加热功率是自动控制的。后视镜加热装置是按脉冲宽度调制通电的，受功率半导体控制。

The heat output is dependent on outside temperature and **wiper** intensity. The outside temperature and wiper intensity are delivered via the K-CAN system.

加热功率与车外温度和刮水器频率有关。车外温度和刮水器频率通过 K-CAN 系统总线提供。

The heat output is increased in wiper mode in order to make any raindrops（雨点）on the mirrors evaporate（蒸发）. The ON period of the mirror heating is extended（延长）in percentage terms（百分比）.

刮水器运行时加热功率提高，以便使后视镜上可能有的雨滴汽化。后视镜加热的接通持续时间按百分比延长。

When the wiper is deactivated, the higher percentage ON period remains active for a further 5 minutes.

如果刮水器关闭了，按百分比延长的接通时间还会持续 5 分钟。

9.8 Windscreen 风挡玻璃

9.8.1 Components 部件

1. Wiper Drive 刮水器驱动装置

The wiper system（刮水器）used is designed as a two-arm/synchronization（同步）wiper system with a flanged-on（带法兰的）wiper drive.

刮水器设计成双臂同步刮水器，刮水器驱动装置用法兰安装。

The wiper arms are guided by a swinging arm（crank with coupling link 连接拉杆）on the driver's side and by a transverse link（横向连杆）and a four-bar linkage on the front passenger's side.

刮水臂设计成驾驶员侧为一个摆臂（双限位），前座乘客侧为横向连杆和四根杆的形式。

2. Wiper Module 刮水器模块

The wiper module（See Figure 9 – 5）is integrated in the wiper drive. The wiper module controls all wipe/wash functions.

刮水器模块（见图 9 – 5）安装在刮水器驱动装置内。刮水器模块控制所有的刮水功能和清洗功能。

The wiper module **comprises**：

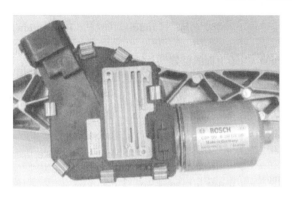

Figure 9 – 5   Wiper module

— output stages for the wiper motor, washer pumps and wet-arm heaters;

— position acquisition（位置测量装置）by 3 Hall sensors;

— CAN interface;

— control unit.

刮水器模块包括:

——刮水器马达、清洗泵和清洗液导管加热器的终端;

——位置测量装置有 3 个霍尔传感器;

——CAN 接口;

——控制装置。

9. 8. 2 Functional Description   功能描述

1. Wiper Positions（See Figure 9 –6） 刮水器位置（见图 9 –6）

Depending on wiper functionality, the wiper moves into various positions on the windscreen.

根据刮水器的功能性,刮水器到达挡风玻璃上的不同位置。

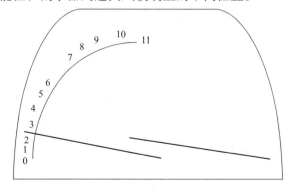

Figure 9 – 6   Wiper positions

Index	Description	中文名称	Index	Description	中文名称
0	Lowest possible position	最下面的位置	6	Blocking limit minimum wiper range, downward stroke	最小刮水区下降行程卡住极限
1	Assembly position	安装位置	7	Rain/driving-light sensor, upward stroke	晴雨/灯光传感器上升行程
2	Park position, moving downward	下降停止位置	8	Rain/driving-light sensor, downward stroke	晴雨/灯光传感器下降行程
3	Park position, moving upwards	上升停止位置	9	Fold-back position	弯折位置
4	Lower reversing position for intermittent wipe	间歇刮水的下部换向位置	10	Blocking limit minimum wiper range, upward stroke	最小刮水区上升行程卡住极限
5	Lower reversing position (wiper stage 1 and 2)	下部换向位置（刮水器挡位1和2）	11	Upper reversing position	上部换向位置

2. Regulated Wiper Speed　刮水器速度调节

Wiping frequency and wiper arm speed are regulated according to:

— wiper stage;

— vehicle speed;

— wiping direction.

刮水频率和刮水臂速度根据下列情况进行调节：

——刮水器档位；

——车辆行驶速度；

——刮水方向。

As a result, system voltage is compensated（补偿）. The **maps** for the wiper speed are stored in the EEPROM（Electrically Erasable Programmable Read-Only Memory，电可擦写可编程只读存储器）.

通过上述情况进行车辆电压补偿。刮水器速度的特性线区存在 EEPROM（电可擦写可编程只读存储器）内。

3. Reverse Wiper Control　刮水器换向控制

Activation of the wiper system by reversing of the wiper motor is implemented in the wiper electronics. This reduces the space required by the wiper linkage（连杆）.

在刮水器电子装置内，刮水器的控制是通过刮水器马达的换向实现的。这样用于刮水器连杆的空间就少了。

Overrun of the wiper positions is prevented, as the wiper is braked in the end position: by changing the polarity of the supply, the wiper motor stops suddenly without running on（继续移动）.

因为刮水器在极限位置停止了：随着电流换向，刮水器马达突然停止，不会再有惯性运行，从而避免了超越刮水器极限位置。

9.9　Tailgate Lift 后行李箱盖提升装置

9.9.1　Introduction　概述

The tailgate lift（后行李箱盖提升装置）controls automatic opening and closing of the vehicle tailgate. The module operates closely in conjunction with the Power module, which is fitted as standard, and the car access system.

后行李箱盖提升装置控制车辆后行李箱盖的自动打开和关闭。该模块与批量安装的供电模块和便捷进入及起动系统紧密协作。

The tailgate lift is active during the **immobilization** period of the vehicle, and not during vehicle operation, on account of its functional content（具体功能）.

后行李箱盖提升装置由于其功能特性，不是在行驶模式下激活，而是在停车状态下激活。

9.9.2　Components　部件

The pump motor, pressure valve, angle of rotation sensor（旋转角传感器）and 3 operating switches belong to the composite system:

—— Tailgate pushbutton on inside of lid（盖子）;

—— Tailgate pushbutton on outside of lid;

—— Tailgate pushbutton in vehicle interior.

Additional operation is possible by remote control.

后行李箱盖提升装置包括调节泵马达、压力阀、旋转角传感器和 3 个操作开关：

——后行李箱盖内部按钮；

——后行李箱盖外部按钮；

——车辆内部后行李箱盖按钮。

另外可以通过遥控器操纵。

9.9.3 Hydraulic System 液压系统

The hydraulic system is operated with a maximum pressure of 100 bar. It is self-venting（自通风的）and **maintenance-free**.

液压系统以最大压力 100 bar 运行。它有自通风功能，无需维护。

The hydraulic components of the system are（See Figure 9 – 7）:

— Hydraulic control unit;

— Hydraulic working cylinder;

— Hydraulic **lines.**

系统液压组件有（见图 9 – 7）:

——液压控制单元；

——液压工作缸；

——液压管路。

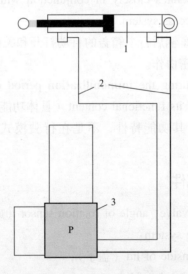

Figure 9 – 7　Diagram of the hydraulic components

Index	Description	中文名称
1	Hydraulic working cylinder	液压缸
2	Hydraulic lines	液压管路
3	Pump	泵

1. Installed Position　安装位置

The hydraulic control unit of the tailgate lift is installed on the right-hand side of the luggage compartment（行李箱）（See Figure 9 – 8）.

Figure 9 – 8　The hydraulic control unit of the tailgate lift

2. Functional Description　功能描述

1）Operation of the TOEHK, TOEHKK and TOEHKI Buttons
按钮 TOEHK、TOEHKK 和 TOEHKI 的操作

The lid can be opened, stopped or closed by operating the exterior tailgate button（TOEHK）or the interior tailgate button（TOEHKK, when lid is open）. It is also possible to stop or activate the lid in any open position. The buttons need only be touched once to move the tailgate into the end position（lid open or closed）. The drive is stopped automatically at the end positions.

通过操纵外部后行李箱盖按钮（TOEHK）或内部后行李箱盖按钮（TOEHKK，在后行李箱盖打开情况下）可以打开、中止或关闭后行李箱。后行李箱盖同样可以在任意打开位置停住或激活。后行李箱盖点按按钮可以控制后行李箱盖直至到达限位（后行李箱盖打开或关闭）。在到达限位时，驱动机构自动停止。

The direction of movement of the lid changes every second time the button is pressed：
Opening — Stop — Closing — Stop — Opening, etc.
再次按动按钮后行李箱盖运动方向改变：
打开—停止—关闭—停止—打开等。

The module assigns equal priority（优先权）to both buttons（TOEHK and TOEHKK）. However, a locked lid can only be opened by operating the TOEHK button.（It is not possible to operate the TOEHKK button.）

两个按钮（TOEHK 和 TOEHKK）由模块同权处理。后行李箱盖锁止时，仅可以通过操纵按钮 TOEHK 打开（无法操纵按钮 TOEHKK 打开）。

The lid can also be opened and stopped from inside the vehicle by means of the inner tailgate button of the central locking system（TOEHKI）. If the lid is in motion（**irrespective of** whether it is opening or closing）, then it is stopped when the button is operated. If the lid is at rest, an actuating mechanism triggers（引发）the opening action.

后行李箱盖还可以通过车厢内部中控锁后行李箱盖按钮（TOEHKI）打开和停止。后行李箱盖运动时（无论打开或关闭），都可以通过操纵按钮停止。当后行李箱盖处于静态时，一个操作就会触发打开动作。

The lid can be **alternately** opened or stopped by operating this button：

Opening — Stop — Opening — Stop, etc.

通过按动该按钮可以交替打开或停止后行李箱盖：

打开—停止—打开—停止等。

2）**Activation via Remote Control Services** 通过遥控器控制

The lid can also be opened, stopped or closed via the remote control services（tailgate button）. Briefly press the button（< 1.6 s）to open or stop the lid；permanently（永久的）press the button（> 1.6 s）, and the lid will be closed as long as the button is held down. Release the button, and the closing operation will be aborted and immediately reversed（reversing time：approx. 300 ms）.

后行李箱盖还可以通过遥控器（后行李箱盖按钮）打开、停止或关闭。快速按下按钮（小于1.6秒）将打开或停止后行李箱盖。持续按住按钮（大于1.6秒）将关闭后行李箱盖。放开按钮将中断关闭过程并立即反向运行（反向时间约300毫秒）。

3. **Operation** 操纵

The control unit recognizes the tailgate position via the angle of rotation sensor attached to the lid hinge（铰链）and the tailgate contact（触点）. The response（反应）of the control unit to the control elements depends on the tailgate position and the last direction of movement.

控制单元通过后行李箱盖铰链上安装的旋转角传感器和后行李箱盖触点识别后行李箱盖处于哪个位置。根据后行李箱盖位置和上次的运动方向，操作元件实现接下来的后行李箱盖运动。

4. **Lid Motion** 后行李箱盖的运行

A lid motion profile（运动轨迹）dependent on lid position can be generated by cycled activation of the pump and valve（See Figure 9 – 9）. Lid speed is reduced and the lid slowly engages in the tailgate lock, shortly before reaching the "lid closed" position（transition from segment 3 to segment 2）. Shortly before reaching the end stop "lid open"（transition from segment 7 to segment 8）, lid speed is also reduced and the lid slowly moves into its end position.

Soft start-up of the lid is also implemented.

借助于控制泵和阀门可以实现后行李箱盖的运行轨迹，它与后行李箱盖位置有关（见图9-9）。在到达位置"后行李箱盖关闭"前（从段3向段2运动），后行李箱盖关闭速度降低，后行李箱盖缓慢进入后行李箱盖锁闭位置。在达到极限位置"后行李箱盖打开"前（从段7向段8运动），同样降低后行李箱盖速度，后行李箱盖缓慢行进到极限位置。其他分段由后行李箱盖的柔顺运行实现。

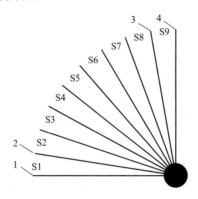

Figure 9-9　Angle sensor with system limits

Index	Description	中文名称	Index	Description	中文名称
1	Lid closed	后行李箱盖已关闭	4	Lid open，upper stop	后行李箱盖打开上部限位
2	Lower switch-off point	下部断开点	S1 - S9	Segment 1 - 9	分段 1～9
3	Upper switch-off point	上部断开点			

The speed of the lid movement is known because the angle sensor is evaluated continuously. This speed is compared with the time-distance curve stored in the module. If the actual speed of movement is less than the nominal value（标准值）by more than 300 ms, the lid is stopped and reverses for 1 s（blockage identification，锁止识别）. This serves as a form of trapping protection.

通过角度传感器的连续运作识别后行李箱盖速度。它与模块中存储的路径-时间曲线进行比较。如果当前运行速度小于标准值的时间超过300毫秒，则后行李箱盖停止运行，并反向运行1秒（锁止识别）。这是一种防夹功能。

9.10 Park Distance Control（PDC）驻车距离报警系统

PDC supports the driver on manoeuvring（操纵）into and out of parking spaces：signal tones and a visual display indicate the current distance to an obstacle（障碍物）.

在驶入和驶出停车位时，PDC 给驾驶员提供帮助，用声音信号和视频显示提示当前障碍物与车辆的距离。

1. PDC Control Unit   PDC 控制单元

The control unit is located in the rear of the luggage compartment on the right. Its main tasks are：

— Activation of transducers（转换器）and reception of echoes；

— Evaluation of the received echo pulses；

— Activation of the function indicator（指示灯）（LED in the switch）；

— Sending messages via K-CAN to audio sound controller and control display equipment；

— Monitoring the inputs and outputs；

— Management of the diagnosis and test functions.

该控制单元安装在行李箱中右后侧。其主要任务包括：

——控制转换器和接收超声波；

——分析接收的超声脉冲；

——控制指示灯（开关中的 LED 指示灯）；

——通过 K-CAN 总线系统发送信息至音频系统控制器和控制显示设备；

——监控输入输出端；

——管理诊断和测试功能。

2. Basis of Calculation   计算原理

PDC uses the echo sounding principle（回波探测法）to calculate the distances between each of the 4 transducers in the front and rear **bumpers** and any obstacle that might be present.

PDC 根据回波探测法原理计算前后保险杠中 4 个转换器和障碍物之间的距离。

In addition，a three-way calculation（三角计算）can be used to calculate the effective distance to the bumper in the case of an obstacle between two sensors. This three-way calculation is enabled by co-sensing（共同监测）of the neighboring sensors.

此外，当障碍物位于两个传感器之间时，采用三角计算得出至保险杠的有效距离。三角计算可以通过相邻传感器的共同监测得出。

An active sensor system in the transducer processes the received echo signals，performs the evaluation and communicates across a bi-directional （双向） data line with the control unit.

通过转换器中的主动式传感器元件处理接收到的超声波信号，做出评估并通过双向的数据导线与控制单元进行通信。

3. Transducer （Ultrasonic Sensor） 转换器（超声波传感器）

The control unit sends a digital signal to set the ultrasonic transducer either in a combined transmit and receive mode or in a pure receive mode.

控制单元通过一个数字信号使超声波转换器转入发射接收模式或纯接收模式。

1）Combined Mode 发射接收模式

The transducer first transmits a packet （信息包） of ultrasonic pulses and then receives the echoes reflected by the obstacle within its sensing range. **On the basis of** the time span between transmission and reception, the control unit calculates the distance to the obstacle.

转换器首先发射一个超声波脉冲包，接着转到接收模式，接收感知范围内障碍物的反射波。根据发射和接收的时间间隔，控制单元计算出车辆至障碍物的距离。

2）Pure Receive Mode 纯接收模式

The transducer receives the pulses deflected by the neighboring transducers. The evaluation of these signals in the control unit improves the certainty （准确性） of detection of the system.

转换器接收相邻转换器发射的脉冲信号。通过在控制单元内评估该信号，提高系统的探测准确性。

The advantages of this round membrane （外膜） shape are the greater detection range and lower **sensitivity** in wet conditions. The transducer is always painted in the car color.

在外膜形状上，转换器的圆形外膜具有更大的探测范围，对潮湿的敏感度也较低。转换器总是与车身同色。

The front and rear transducers only differ in that the installation location requires a different arrangement of the connector exit （接头） （See Figure 9 – 10 and Figure 9 – 11）.

前后转换器只有安装插头不同（见图9 – 10和图9 – 11）。

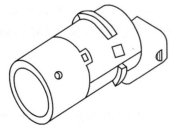

Figure 9 – 10   Transducer, front bumper

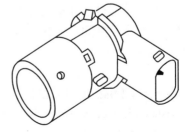

Figure 9 – 11   Transducer, rear bumper

4. PDC Button   PDC 按钮

The PDC button (See Figure 9 – 12) is to the left of the start/stop key and it consists of the following components：

— Button；

— Function indicator (LED)；

— Locating light (LED).

PDC 按钮（见图 9 – 12）在起动/停止按钮左侧，由下列组件组成：

——按钮；

——功能指示灯（LED）；

——查寻照明灯（LED）。

The button can be used to activate or deactivate the parking aid manually.

通过该按钮可以手动激活或退出驻车。

Figure 9 – 12   PDC button

5. Audio System Controller (ASK)   音频系统控制器

The acoustic distance warning is output through the front midrange speaker of the audio system in the doors and in the rear parcel shelf （衣帽架）. The signal tones for all 4 speakers as well as their intervals are processed in the ASK and they overlay （覆盖） the audio sound. The PDC control unit only provides the distance indications between the ultrasonic transducers and the obstacle.

声音车距报警通过前部车门音频系统的中音喇叭和后部衣帽架的中音喇叭发出。所有 4 个扬声器的信号音及其间歇音在 ASK 中预制并转存。PDC 控制单元仅提供转换器和障碍物之间的距离信息。

6. Control Display (CD)   控制显示

The visual distance warning is displayed in the CD if the configuration is selected. The graphic is generated in the CD. The PDC control unit only provides the distance indications between the transducers and the obstacle. In addition, extended Check Control messages are displayed in the CD.

在选择配置后，车距视觉报警在控制显示中显示。图像显示在控制显示中。PDC 控制单元仅提供转换器和障碍物之间的距离信息。另外，控制显示中还显示其他的检查控制信息。

7. Instrument Cluster   组合仪表

The instrument cluster serves as a display of Check Control messages and provides the outside temperature as well as the mileage/km reading（里程数）.

组合仪表用于显示检查控制信息，并提供车外温度和里程数。

Ice and dew（露水）can lead to activation of the ultrasonic transducers where it is not required. In order to reduce the effect of this phenomenon（现象）, the response characteristics are adapted via software as of $+6\text{℃}$ and colder.

结冰和露水会使转换器产生错误的回应。为了避免这些现象，$+6\text{℃}$ 或更冷时通过软件来调整回应性能。

8. PDC Acoustic Warning   PDC 声音报警

The distance to an obstacle can also be indicated by an intermittent（间歇的）tone according to the position. If, for example, an obstacle is detected to the front left of the vehicle, the sound signal is issued at the front left. The closer the vehicle comes to the object, the shorter the intervals become.

根据障碍物的位置，车辆与障碍物的距离通过相应的间歇鸣响信号音提示。例如，如果识别到车辆前方左侧有障碍物，则信号音在左前方鸣响。车辆距离障碍物越近，间歇信号音就越急促。

The maximum acoustic detection range of PDC acoustic warning is shown in Figure 9 – 13.

PDC 声音报警的最大声音监测范围如图 9 – 13 所示。

Figure 9 – 13   PDC acoustic warning

If the distance to a detected object is smaller than approx. 30 cm, a continuous tone sounds.

如果与障碍物距离小于约 30 厘米，则系统持续鸣响。

The sound signal is interrupted after approx. 3 seconds if the vehicle is driven **parallel to** a wall. This interruption does not occur in the continuous tone mode (distance smaller than 30 cm).

当平行于墙壁行驶时，信号音在约 3 秒钟后中断。在持续鸣响情况下，不会发生中断（距离小于 30 厘米）。

Key Words

exterior lighting　外部照明	reactuate　再次开动
headlight　汽车大灯	block　卡住
clearance light　示宽灯	hold　保持
duty factor　负载参数	deactivate　使无效
fog lamp　雾灯	backrest　靠背
interior lighting　车内照明	seat heating　座椅加热
ambient lighting　环境照明	residual heating area　余热区
instrument lighting　仪表照明	established current intensity　规定的电流强度
denote　表示	wiper　刮水器
incident lighting　透光照明	comprise　包含
knurl　滚花轮	map　特性曲线
courtesy light　前部区域照明灯	immobilization　停车
door handle　车门把手	maintenance-free　免维护的
timer　延时电路	line　管路
anti-theft alarm system　防盗报警系统	irrespective of　不考虑
rear view mirror　后视镜	alternately　交替地
wheel arch　轮罩	bumper　保险杠
higher-level　高级的	on the basis of　以……为基础
accidentally　偶然地	sensitivity　灵敏度
relevant　相关的	parallel to　平行于

Exercises

1. The load currents are switched by means of _____, thus resulting in high service-life reliability.

2. From terminal R ON and with the turn-signal/dipping switch in the flashing left/right position, the turn-signal lamps on the corresponding side are switched on and off with a pulse rate of 640 ms and _____ .

3. The LM responds to an anti-theft alarm-system alarm with _____ and periodic activation of the low-beam or/and high-beam headlights.

4. _____ alerts road traffic behind to that particular car door being open.

5. _____ is used to denote the incident light and the switch background lighting.

6. The courtesy lighting is controlled by the power module via _____ .

7. The purpose of _____ is to deter a potential intruder or thief and to alert passers-by to the crime.

8. The emergency siren with integrated tilt sensor is installed in _____ where good protection is provided against tampering with the emergency siren or anti-theft alarm system K bus.

9. If a defined change of angle is exceeded in the longitudinal direction and/or the transverse direction, _____ is sent to the anti-theft alarm system passenger-compartment sensor.

10. The visual alarm is indicated by _____ (flashing with low beam or flashing with high beam) as per country-specific coding.

11. _____ is now only still used for mechanical emergency unlocking.

12. When central double locking is engaged, the locking pin in each door is _____ from the lock by a mechanical coupling.

13. With electric lock-out protection, the electronics ensures that the central-locking assembly is _____ again, e. g. when the locking knob is pressed down in the open driver's door.

14. With a "double lock" command and a valid key in the CAS/ignition lock, the central locking is immediately _____ again (prevention of key being locked in).

15. The power windows can be operated by means of _____ in the driver's door or a local control button in the relevant vehicle door.

16. _____ is used for deliberate closing of the windows without anti-trapping protection.

17. If _____ is detected, the window travels back only the short distance of 20 mm.

18. For safety reasons, it is always possible to _____ independently of the thermal protection.

19. When the child lock is engaged, it is only possible to operate the rear power windows from _____ or via the auto-remote function.

20. When the seat heating is turned on, it is _____ areas which are activated first in order to heat up the seats quickly.

21. _____ is activated when the button is pressed for the first time.

22. The operator can use _____ to set a temperature differential between the seat surface and the backrest of max $+/-3°C$.

23. All the mirror functions are served by _____ in the switch block in the driver's door.

24. The driver uses _____ to select between the two mirrors (right/left).

25. The heat output of the mirror heating is dependent on _____ and wiper intensity.

26. _____ controls all wipe/wash functions.

27. The maps for the wiper speed are stored in the _____.

28. Activation of the wiper system by _____ is implemented in the wiper electronics.

29. The tailgate lift is active during the immobilization period of the vehicle, and not during vehicle operation, on account of _____ .

30. The buttons need only be _____ to move the tailgate into the end position (lid open or closed).

31. If the lid is in motion (irrespective of whether it is opening or closing), then it is _____ when the inner tailgate button of the central locking system is operated.

32. The control unit recognizes the tailgate position via _____ attached to the lid hinge and the tailgate contact.

33. If the actual speed of movement is less than the nominal value by more than 300 ms, the lid is _____ and reverses for 1 s.

34. PDC uses the echo sounding principle to calculate _____ between each of the 4 transducers in the front and rear bumpers and any obstacle that might be present.

35. On the basis of _____ between transmission and reception, the control unit calculates the distance to the obstacle.

36. The evaluation of these signals in the control unit improves the _____ of detection of the system.

37. _____ serves as a display of Check Control (CC) messages and provides the outside temperature as well as the mileage/km reading.

38. The sound signal is interrupted after approx. 3 seconds if the vehicle is driven _____ a wall.

Unit 10
Body 车身结构

10.1　Requirements of Body Structure 对车身结构的要求

The body structure is designed in accordance with the following standpoints：
— Static performance（静力学特性）;
— Dynamic performance（动力学特性）;
— Crash performance（防撞性能）;
— Weight optimization.
在进行车身结构设计时考虑了下列要素：
——静力学特性；
——动力学特性；
——防撞性能；
——重量优化。

1. Static Performance　*静力学特性*

Good static **rigidity** serves as the basic prerequisite（先决条件）for good dynamic performance. The flexural **strength**, torsional resistance（抗扭刚度）and transversal rigidity（横向刚度）of the body are all determined by the design. The strength is determined by the choice of materials used（high-tensile steels）and by the additional bonding（粘结）of welding flanges.
　　静刚度良好是动力学特性良好的基本条件。车身的抗弯刚度、抗扭刚度和横向刚度由其结构而定。其强度则是通过选择所用材料（高强度钢材）及焊接翼缘的附加粘结来实现的。

2. Dynamic Performance　*动力学特性*

The aim of dynamic configuration of the body structure is to achieve the vibrational（振动）and acoustic（噪声）comfort objectives.
　　车身结构动力学设计的目标是在振动和噪音方面满足舒适性要求。

3. Crash Performance 防撞性能

Static and dynamic performance forms an outstanding basis for **crash** optimization, which in turn serves to improve passive passenger protection（被动安全性）.

防撞性能的优化主要以静力学和动力学特性为基础，它用于改善对乘客的被动保护能力。

4. Weight Optimization 重量优化

Next to aerodynamics（空气动力学）, vehicle weight is the most important factor in reducing fuel consumption and improving handling performance（操控性能）.

除空气动力学特性外，车辆重量是减小耗油量及改善操控性能的最重要因素。

10.2 Body Structure 车身结构

A panel is a steel or plastic sheet（板材）stamped or molded into a body part. Various panels are used in a vehicle. Usually, the name of the panel is self-explanatory：hood panel, fender panel, trunk lid panel, or roof panel.

车身面板是钢质或塑料的板材，通过（模具）冲压或铸造成车身的一个零件。在汽车上使用多种面板。通常，面板的名称是不需要解释的，如引擎罩面板、挡泥板面板、行李箱盖面板或车顶面板。

The major outer panels of a vehicle are shown in Figure 10 – 1. Study the names and locations of each part or panel carefully.

汽车主要的外部面板显示在图 10 – 1 中。仔细研究每个面板或零件的位置和名称。

1. Front End 车身前端

The front bumper cross-member（保险杠横梁）（See Figure 10 – 2）is made from aluminum.

前保险杠横梁（见图 10 – 2）为铝合金制造。

A large part of the impact（碰撞）energy is absorbed by the honeycomb-structured（蜂窝状）aluminum deformation（变形）elements in the profile section which are bolted to the bumper cross-member.

大部分碰撞能量被拧在保险杠横梁上断面为蜂窝状的铝合金变形吸能元件吸收。

The engine carriers are designed in the profile section（断面）as a double hexagon（六角形）. Front-axle attachments are integrated in the engine carrier（发动机支架）. The wheel arch has a diagonal strut（斜支撑）made from an IHPD（internal high-pressure deformation, 内部高

压成型）profile section.

发动机支架的断面为双六角型结构。前桥固定件集成在发动机支架内。轮罩有一个由 IHPD（内部高压成型）型材制成的斜支撑。

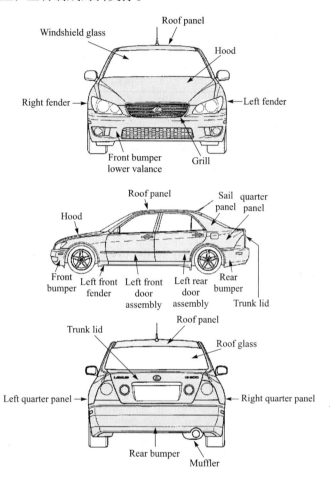

Figure 10 – 1　Structure, body panels

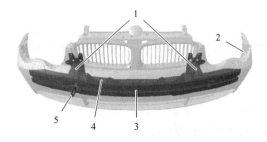

Figure 10 – 2　Structure, front bumper

Index	Description	中文名称
1	Deformation elements	变形吸能元件
2	Bumper trim	保险杠饰板
3	Polystyrene-foam impact absorber	聚苯乙烯泡沫塑料碰撞缓冲器
4	Bumper cross-member	保险杠横梁
5	Tow hook	拖钩

2. Side Carcass　侧车架

The profile section is reinforced（加固）at both sills（门槛）by an additional reinforcement profile section（side-frame attachment）（See Figure 10 – 3）, which also serves to accommodate the sill trim.

两个车门槛上的型材由一个附加加强型材（侧窗框添加件）加固（见图 10 – 3）。该型材还用于固定车门槛饰板。

This profile section offers additional safety in the event of both frontal and side impacts.

在发生正面和侧面碰撞时，这个型材还可提供附加的安全性。

Figure 10 – 3　Reinforcement profile section

3. Rear End　车身后端

Like its front counterpart（副本）, the rear bumper cross-member（See Figure 10 – 4）is made from aluminum. In the event of a rear-end impact, the bumper cross-member together with the bumper trim absorbs the impact energy.

后保险杠横梁（见图 10 – 4）与前部一样，也是由铝合金制成的。在发生尾部碰撞时，保险杠横梁与保险杠饰板一起吸收碰撞能量。

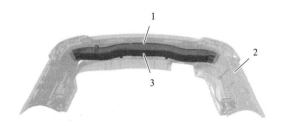

Figure 10 – 4　Structure, rear bumper

Index	Description	中文名称
1	Polystyrene-foam impact absorber	聚苯乙烯泡沫塑料碰撞缓冲器
2	Bumper trim	保险杠饰板
3	Aluminum bumper cross-member	铝合金保险杠横梁

4. **Outer Skin Panel**　*车身面板*

Both the front side panels（面板）and all the individual parts of the bonnet（车盖）are manufactured from aluminum for reasons of weight reduction. For this reason, wing covers（翼子板）with magnetic fastening elements（磁性固定元件）cannot be used as usual.

为减轻重量，两个前侧围板和车前盖所有零件都是由铝合金制成的。出于这个原因，翼子板不能像平常一样用磁性固定元件固定。

The front side panels are bolted to the body.

前部侧围板通过螺栓与车身连接。

The front grille（格栅）is not integrated in the bonnet but rather attached to it by means of screws and clips（螺钉和夹子）.

前装饰格栅没有集成在车前盖内，而是用螺钉和夹子固定在车前盖上。

The **boot lid** consists of sheet steel with a single shackle hinge（弓形铰链）（See Figure 10 – 5）. Because it is attached to the partition between the luggage compartment and the C-pillar （C柱）, it requires a considerable amount of work to replace the shackle hinge. Several add-on parts and trims must be removed for this purpose.

后行李箱盖由钢板制成，带有一个单铰接弓形铰链（见图10 – 5）。由于弓形铰链固定在行李箱与 C 柱之间的隔板上，因此更换时需花费较多的工时。为此要拆下多个安装件和饰板。

To remove the hinge shackles, it is necessary to remove the parcel shelf（置物架）behind the rear window.

拆卸铰链弓形件时，必须先拆下后窗玻璃后面的置物架。

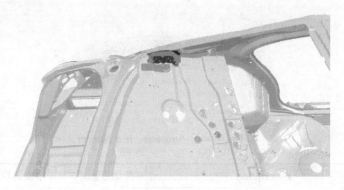

Figure 10 – 5　Attachment, boot-lid hinge

5. Doors　车门

The inner door panel is clearly thicker in the hinge area (tailored blanks). Increased rigidity in the hinge area prevents the doors from "hanging". The doors are thus easier to open after a side impact.

车门内板在铰链区（特制焊接件）明显加厚。因提高了铰链区的刚度，所以避免了车门"下垂"。因此，发生侧面碰撞后车门较易开启。

A side-impact beam made from high-tensile steel is bolted to the inside of the door and safety is increased by a removable plastic "crash pad"（防撞垫块）. Crash safety is positively influenced by spot-weld（点焊）bonding, reinforcement of the inner panel in the hinge area, the side-impact beam and the crash pads.

此外在车门内侧还以螺纹连接方式安装了一个由高强度钢材制成的侧面防撞杆，同时可拆卸的塑料"防撞垫块"提高了安全性。通过点焊粘接、铰链区内板加强件、侧面防撞杆及防撞垫块的使用改善了车辆的碰撞安全性。

Figure 10 – 6 is an exploded view of doors.

图 10 – 6 所示为车门的分解图。

6. Roof　车顶

The outer roof skin is laser-welded at the sides to the side carcass（侧车架）.

用激光将车顶面板的四边焊接在侧车架上。

Figure 10 – 6   Exploded view, doors

Index	Description	中文名称
1	Side-impact beam, front	前部侧面防撞杆
2	Side-impact beam, rear	后部侧面防撞杆
3	Inner door panel, front	前部车门内板
4	Inner door panel, rear	后部车门内板
5	End piece, door, front	前车门封闭饰板
6	Reinforcement rail, door, front	前车门加强导轨
7	Outer door panel, front	前车门面板
8	Outer door panel, rear	后车门面板

continued

Index	Description	中文名称
9	Reinforcement rail, door, rear	后车门加强导轨
10	End piece, door, rear	后车门封闭饰板

10.3 Passive Safety 被动安全性

1. Requirements of Structure 对结构的要求

Denting（翘起）susceptibility in the flange area is reduced by the use of bonding agent（粘结剂）. This results in stabilization（稳定性）of the carrier profile sections and connections. Deformation（变形）of the passenger cell is significantly reduced by the use of bonding agent.

使用高强度粘接剂减少了翼缘区域翘起的可能性，因此保证了架梁型材和连接节点的稳定。使用粘接剂后，乘客区构架变形明显减小。

2. Properties of Engine Carriers 发动机支架的特性

Thanks to the optimal cross-sectional layout, the front engine carriers are designed to absorb the axial forces and thus the energy in the event of a frontal impact. The rear engine carriers serve to support the forces and flexural torques（弯矩）. The crash beads result in a deformation at defined points.

前部发动机支架通过最佳的横断面造型吸收轴向力，并借此吸收正面碰撞时的能量。后部发动机支架用于承受力和弯曲力矩。碰撞用圆槽会使变形发生在规定位置。

Key Words

rigidity 刚度	boot lid 行李箱盖
strength 强度	crash 碰撞

Exercises

1. This profile section offers ＿＿＿＿＿＿＿ in the event of both frontal and side impacts.

2. In the event of a rear-end impact, _____ together with the bumper trim absorbs the impact energy.

3. For _____ , wing covers with magnetic fastening elements cannot be used as usual.

4. Because it is attached to the partition between the luggage compartment and the C-pillar, it requires a considerable amount of work to _____ .

5. The outer roof skin is laser-welded at _____ to the side carcass.

Vehicle Identification
汽车识别

Unit 11
Types of Vehicle 车辆类型

Key Terms

body classification
car size
roof design

Various methods of classifying vehicles exist: engine type (gas or diesel), fuel system type (carburetor [化油器] or injection), drive line type (automatic or manual transmission, front wheel versus rear-wheel drive), and so forth.

有多种方法对汽车进行分类，例如：按发动机类型（汽油或柴油）、按燃料系统类型（化油器或喷油器）、按汽车驱动类型（手动或自动变速器、前轮对后轮驱动），等等。

The body classifications most recognized by consumers are car size, body shape, seat arrangement, number of doors, and so on.

消费者公认的车身分类方法是按汽车尺寸、车身形状、座椅布置、车门数目，等等。

11.1 Car Size 汽车尺寸

A compact car, also called an economy car, is the smallest body classification. It normally uses a small, 4-cylinder engine, is very light in weight, and gets the highest gas mileage （英里里程）.

紧凑型汽车，也称为经济型汽车，具有最小的车身等级。它通常使用小型四缸机，重量很轻，其一加仑汽油所行驶的里程最远。

An intermediate car is medium in size. It often uses a 4-, 6-, or 8-cylinder engine and has average weight and physical dimensions. It usually has unibody （承载式车身）construction, but a few older vehicles have body-over-frame construction.

中级车尺寸中等。它经常使用4、6或8缸发动机，具有平均水平的质量和尺寸。通常采用承载式车身，也有少数早期车辆采用非承载式车身。

A full size car, or luxury car, is the largest classification of passenger car. It is larger and heavier and often uses a high-performance V8 engine. Full-size cars can have either unibody or body-over-frame construction. Full-size cars get lower fuel economy ratings, primarily because of their increased mass（质量）.

全尺寸汽车或豪华车，是乘用车中的最大等级。它更长、更重，经常使用高性能的8缸机。全尺寸汽车或者采用承载式车身，或者采用非承载式车身。全尺寸汽车燃油经济性更低，主要是由于它们增加的质量。

11.2 Roof Design 车顶设计

As shown in Figure 11 – 1, there are several basic body shapes or roof designs in use today.

如图11 – 1所示，今天使用如下几种车身形式或车顶设计。

A sedan refers to a body design with a center **pillar** that supports the roof. Sedans come in both two-door and four-door versions.

私家轿车指的是车身设计有支撑车顶的中柱。私家轿车有两门版和四门版。

A hardtop（硬顶）does not have a center pillar to support the roof, so the roof must be reinforced to provide enough strength. A hardtop is also available in both two- and four-door versions.

硬顶车没有支撑车顶的中柱，因此必须加强车顶以提供足够的强度。硬顶车也有两门版和四门版。

A hatchback（掀背式轿车）has a large third door at the back. This design is commonly found on small compact cars so that more rear storage space is available.

掀背式轿车在后面有一宽大的第三扇门。这一设计常见于小型紧凑型轿车，以便得到更多的后储物空间。

A convertible uses a retractable（可收回的）canvas（帆布）roof with a steel tube framework. The top folds down into an area behind the seat. Some convertibles use a removable hardtop. Some newer vehicles have gone back to the use of retractable hardtops.

敞篷汽车使用可收回的钢构架帆布车顶。车顶向下收入座位后面的存储区。一些敞篷车使用可移动的硬顶。一些较新的汽车又开始使用可收回的硬顶。

A station wagon（旅行车，轿车）extends the roof straight back to the rear of the body. A rear hatch or window and **tailgate** open to allow access to the large storage area.

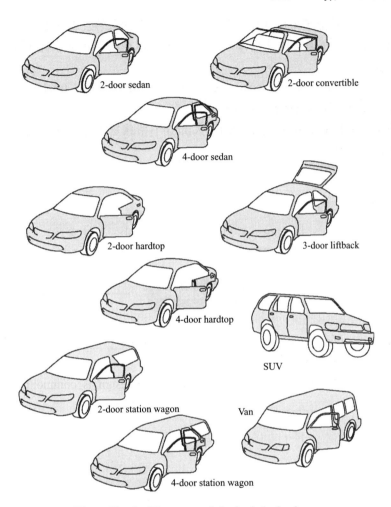

Figure 11 – 1   The names of the basic body shapes

旅行车将车顶延伸到汽车后部。打开后部的舱门或窗户和挡板可以出入宽大的储物区。

A van has a large, box-shaped body to increase interior volume or space. A full-size van normally is front-engine, rear-wheel drive with a full perimeter frame. A minivan is smaller and often uses front-engine, front-wheel drive with unibody construction.

货车有宽大的箱形车身,增大了内部的体积或空间。全尺寸货车通常采用前置发动机,后轮驱动,边梁式车架。小型货车较小,经常采用前置发动机,前轮驱动,承载式车身结构。

An SUV, or sport utility vehicle, has four-wheel drive and room for multiple passengers. This all-weather vehicle generally sits higher than passenger cars for increased ground clearance on rough terrain. Often classified(分类)as an off-road vehicle, the SUV is ideal for driving through snow and mud.

SUV 或运动型多功能车采用四轮驱动，可乘坐更多的乘客。为了提高在粗糙路面上的通过能力，这一全天候车通常比乘用车要高。SUV 适于在淤泥和冰雪路面上行驶，经常被作为越野车一类。

A pickup truck normally has a separate **cab** and bed. Most pickup trucks use a front-engine, rear-wheel drive setup. Some are four-wheel drive.

小型载货卡车有独立的驾驶室和卧铺。大部分小型载货卡车使用前置发动机，后轮驱动，部分采用四轮驱动。

Key Words

pillar　柱子　　　　tailgate　后挡板　　　　cab　驾驶室

Exercises

1. The body classifications most recognized by consumers are _____, body shape, seat arrangement, number of doors, and so on.

2. A hatchback has a large third door at the back. This design is commonly found on small compact cars so that _____ storage space is available.

Unit 12
VIN 车辆识别码

Before starting vehicle repairs, ordering parts, or using service information, you must first record the alphanumeric（文字数字的）code（letters and numbers）that identifies（识别）the vehicle.

在维修车辆、订购零件或使用维护信息之前，你必须首先记录识别这辆车的文字数字编码（字母和数字）

The vehicle identification number（VIN）is used to find out how and when the vehicle was manufactured. The **VIN** denotes（表示）the year, make, model, body style, manufacturing location, engine, trim, and other facts about the vehicle.

车辆识别码（VIN）用于找到汽车是在何时及如何制造出来的。车辆识别码表示汽车的生产年份、构造、类型、车身形式、产地、发动机、装饰件和其他有关事实。

The Vehicle Identification Number was originally described in ISO Standard 3779 in February 1977 and last revised（修订）in 1983. The ISO-VIN was designed to identify motor vehicles, **trailers**, motorcycles（摩托车）and mopeds（机动脚踏两用车）and consists（组成）of three sections.

车辆识别码起源于 1977 年 2 月的 ISO 3779 标准，并在 1983 年进行了修订。设计 ISO-VIN是为了识别汽车、拖车、摩托车和机动脚踏两用车，它由 3 个部分组成。

WMI — World Manufacturer Identifier（标识符）, which uniquely identifies the maker of the vehicle. It occupies（占用）the first three positions of the VIN, except（除了……之外）when a manufacturer builds less than 500 vehicles per year, in which case the third digit is always a 9 and the 12th, 13th and 14th position of the VIN are used for the second part of the WMI. The WMI is described in ISO 3780.

WMI——全球制造商标识符，它唯一确定了车辆的生产商。除了年产量低于 500 台车的制造商，它占用 VIN 的前三位，年产量低于 500 台车的制造商，第三位总是 9，VIN 的第 12、13 和 14 位用于 WMI 的第二部分。ISO 3780 标准对 WMI 进行了描述。

VDS — Vehicle Descriptor（描述符）Section. These 6 characters occupy positions 4 through 9 of the VIN and may be used by the manufacturer to identify attributes（特征）of the vehicle.

VDS——车辆描述符部分，有 6 个字符，占用 VIN 第 4 位到第 9 位，被制造商用来定义车辆特征。

VIS — Vehicle Identifier Section. The last 8 characters of the VIN are used for the identification of specific vehicle. The last four characters shall always be numeric.

VIS——车辆标识符部分。VIN 的最后 8 个字符用于标识特殊车辆。最后 4 位始终是数字。

ISO 3779 makes a provision（规定）for a code for the year in which a vehicle is built. When a manufacturer uses a year code, ISO recommends（推荐）that the 10th position of the VIN is used.

ISO 3779 规定了汽车生产年份编码。当制造商使用年份编码时，ISO 推荐使用 VIN 的第 10 位。

The same applies to the use of a factory code. When a manufacturer uses a factory or plant code, ISO recommends that the 11th position of the VIN is used. In the VIN-code, capital letters（大写字母）A through Z and numbers 1 through 9 may be used, except the letters I, O and Q for obvious reasons. No signs or spaces are allowed in the VIN.

工厂编码的使用与它相似。当制造商使用工厂或车间编码时，ISO 推荐使用 VIN 的第 11 位。在 VIN 编码中，除了字母 I、O 和 Q 由于明显的原因不能被使用外，大写字母 A～Z 和数字 1～9 可以被使用。VIN 中不允许出现符号或空格。

The European Union has issued a directive（命令）to the effect that a VIN must be used for all road vehicles in the EU member states. This directive complies with the ISO Standard but a year digit or factory code is not mandatory（强制的）. Also, it is left to the choice of the manufacturer whether the VDS is actually used for vehicle attributes or not. The system only applies to motor powered（发动机驱动）vehicles with at least four wheels capable of speed above 25 km/h and trailers.

欧盟发布命令，规定在欧盟成员国内所有路上车辆必须使用 VIN。这一命令基本遵循了 ISO 标准，但生产年份和工厂编码的使用是可选择的。它也为生厂商们提供了是否使用 VDS 描述车辆属性的选择。这一系统只用于发动机驱动的，至少四个车轮，时速大于 25 公里/小时的车辆和拖车。

In North America, a system is used that is far more stringent（严厉）than the ISO Standards but is, to use a computer phrase, downward compatible（向下兼容）. Here, the VIN is divided in four sections.

在北美，使用的系统比 ISO 标准更严，但用计算机习语来说，是向下兼容的。在这里，VIN 分成 4 个部分。

The first three characters shall uniquely identify the manufacturer, make and type of vehicle (with the same exception of manufacturers that produce less than 500 vehicles). Effectively, this is the WMI（世界制造厂识别代号）. There are indeed examples of manufacturers who have more than one WMI that use the third character as a code for a vehicle category（种类）(for instance bus or truck). Just as often however this is not the case.

最前面 3 个字符唯一标识生产商、结构和车辆类型（同样不包括年产量在 500 台车以下的生产商）。实际上，这就是 WMI。确实有生产商拥有多个 WMI，该 WMI 使用第 3 个字符代表车辆的种类（例如公共汽车或卡车）。正像经常遇到的一样，这并不常见。

The second section consists of five characters（VIN positions 4 – 8）and identifies the attributes of the vehicle. For each type of vehicle（passenger cars, MPV's, trucks, buses, trailers, motorcycles, incomplete vehicles other than trailers）, different information is required. For cars, MPV's and light trucks it is required that the first two characters of this section are alphabetic, the third and fourth shall be numeric and the fifth alphanumeric. This section is the VDS in ISO 3779 but there it comprises（包含）another position of the VIN.

第 2 部分由 5 个字符组成（VIN 4～8 位），标识车辆属性。对于每一类型的车辆（轿车、MPV、卡车、客车、拖车、摩托车、除了拖车的不完全车辆），要求的信息有所不同。对于轿车、MPV 和轻型卡车，要求前两个字符是字母，第 3 位和第 4 位是数字，第 5 位是字母或数字。这个部分是 ISO 中的 VDS，但在 ISO 标准中要多占 VIN 一位。

The third section consist of one character which is the check digit, calculated over the other 16 characters of the VIN. This character can be numeric or the letter X.

第 3 部分有一个字符，是校验位，由 VIN 的其他 16 个字符计算得到。这个字符可以是数字或字母 X。

The fourth section consists of eight characters on positions 10 – 17 of the VIN. The last five shall be numeric for cars, MPV's and light trucks and the last four shall be numeric for all other vehicles. The first character represents the vehicle model year; the second character represents the plant of manufacture. The third through eighth characters are a sequential（连续的）production number（for manufacturers producing more than 500 vehicles per year）. For other manufacturers, the sixth, seventh and eight position represent the sequential production number. This section confirms to the VIS in ISO 3779.

第 4 部分由 8 个字符组成，位于 VIN 的第 10～17 位。对于轿车、MPV 和轻型卡车，最后 5 位会是数字，对于所有其他车辆最后 4.位会是数字。第 1 个字符代表车型年份，第 2 个字符代表总装工厂、第 3～8 个字符是一个连续的产品顺序号（对于年产量 500 台车以上的制造商）。对于其他制造商，第 6、7、8 位代表产品顺序号。这个部分确认了 ISO 3779 中的 VIS。

The VIN plate（金属板）is a metal tag（标签）with a vehicle identification number stamped（铭刻）on it. Since 1981, the VIN plate has been riveted（用铆钉钉牢的）to the upper left corner of the instrument panel and is visible through the **windshield**（See Figure 12 – 1）.

VIN 金属板是一块铭刻车辆识别码的金属标签。从 1981 年起，VIN 金属板就被铆钉钉在仪表板的左上角，透过挡风玻璃就可以看到（见图 12 – 1）。

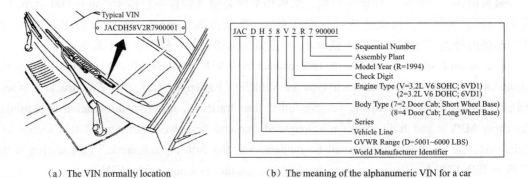

（a）The VIN normally location　　　　（b）The meaning of the alphanumeric VIN for a car

Figure 12 – 1　Vehicle identification number

Check the service information for the location of the VIN, vehicle certification label, or body plate for vehicles made prior to（早于）1981.

对于 1981 年以前制造的车辆，通过维修信息可查找 VIN 的位置、车辆证明标签或车身金属板。

Service manuals and crash-estimating guides（指南）contain all of the necessary VIN decoding information.

维修手册和碰撞评估指南包含全部必要的 VIN 译码信息。

VIN decode（解码）software is a computer program that will automatically look up and convert the vehicle identification number into year, make, model, body style, engine, transmission, **restraint system**, and other vehicle-specific information.

VIN 译码软件是一个计算机程序，能自动查找并将车辆识别码转化为年份、结构、类型、车身形式、发动机、变速器类型、制动系统和其他车辆特有信息。

By typing in the alphanumeric VIN code, the program will automatically decipher and fill in the needed information about the vehicle. The computer screen for VIN decode software is shown in Figure 12 – 2.

通过键入 VIN 码，程序将自动译码并填写车辆的必要信息。VIN 解码软件的计算机界面如图 12 - 2 所示。

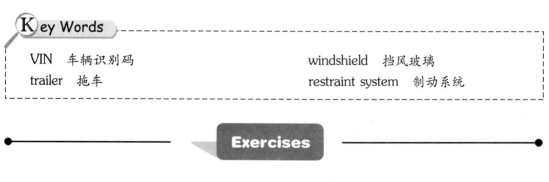

Figure 12 – 2   The computer screen for VIN decode software

Access to（有权使用）VIN information also allows shop personnel, locksmiths（锁匠）, fire departments（消防队）, police departments, and car rental（租用的）agencies to save valuable time and money by having the right tools for lockouts or lock replacements（置换）.

使用 VIN 信息也使商店职员、锁匠、消防队、警察局和轿车租赁中介由于有了正确的工具来决定是否提供服务，从而节约了宝贵的时间和金钱。

Key Words

VIN 车辆识别码	windshield 挡风玻璃
trailer 拖车	restraint system 制动系统

Exercises

1. The vehicle identification number（VIN）is used to find out _____ the vehicle was manufactured.

2. The VIN system only applies to motor powered vehicles with at least four wheels capable of speed above _____ and trailers in Europe.

3. VIN decode software is a computer program that will automatically _____ the vehicle identification number into year, make, model, body style, engine, transmission, restraint system, and other vehicle-specific information.

3

Engine Control Systems
发动机控制系统

Unit 13

Outline of Engine Control System 发动机控制系统概述

Key Terms

EFI	ESA
ISC	diagnostic system

A gasoline engine produces power through the explosion of a mixture of gasoline and air. The three essential elements for a gasoline engine to produce power are the following（See Figure 13 – 1）:

(1) Good air-fuel mixture;

(2) Good compression;

(3) Good spark.

汽油机通过汽油和空气混合物的爆燃产生能量。汽油机做功的 3 个主要因素如下（见图 13 – 1）:

(1) 良好的空气 – 燃料混合物;

(2) 适当的压缩;

(3) 正确的点火。

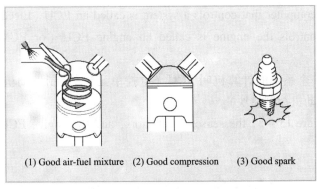

(1) Good air-fuel mixture   (2) Good compression   (3) Good spark

Figure 13 – 1   Three essential elements for a gasoline engine

To achieve these three elements simultaneously, it is important to precisely control the formation of the air-fuel mixture and the timing of the sparks.

为了同时实现这三点，恰当地控制空气－燃料混合物的形成和点火正时很重要。

Before 1981, the only engine control system in existence was the **EFI**（**Electronic Fuel Injection**）, which used a computer to control the fuel injection volume.

在 1981 年前，唯一存在的发动机电控系统是 EFI（电子燃料喷射系统），它采用计算机控制燃料喷射的容积。

In addition to the EFI, there are now various computer-controlled systems, including the **ESA**（**Electronic Spark Advance**）, **ISC**（**Idle Speed Control**）, **diagnostic system**, etc.

除了 EFI，现在有多种计算机控制系统，包括 ESA（电子点火提前系统）、ISC（怠速控制系统）、诊断系统等。

Toyota uses a computer-controlled system called the TCCS（Toyota Computer-Controlled System）to optimally control the fuel injection, ignition timing, drivetrain, brake system, and other systems in accordance with（根据）the operating conditions of the engine and the vehicle.

丰田公司使用的计算机控制系统称为 TCCS（丰田计算机控制系统），可根据发动机和汽车的运行状况优化控制燃料喷射、点火正时、动力传动系统、制动系统和其他系统。

For the computer to function properly, it requires a comprehensive（全面的）system comprised of various input and output devices.

为了使计算机正确工作，需要一个包含各种输入和输出设备的全面系统。

On an automobile, sensors such as a water temperature sensor or an air flow meter correspond to（相当于）the input device. And actuators such as injectors or igniters correspond to the output device.

在汽车上，水温传感器或空气流量计等传感器相当于输入设备，喷油器或点火器等执行器相当于输出设备。

At Toyota, the computer that controls a system is called an ECU（Electronic Control Unit）. The computer that controls the engine is called an engine ECU（or ECM[①]: Engine Control Module）.

在丰田，控制一个系统的计算机叫 ECU（电控单元）。控制发动机的计算机叫发动机 ECU（或 ECM：发动机控制模块）。

As shown in Figure 13 - 2, the sensors, actuators, and the engine ECU are connected with wiring harnesses.

---

① "ECM" is a SAE（Society of Automotive Engineers）terminology（术语）.
　　ECM 是 SAE（汽车工程师协会）的术语。

如图 13 - 2 所示，传感器、执行器和发动机 ECU 通过线束连接。

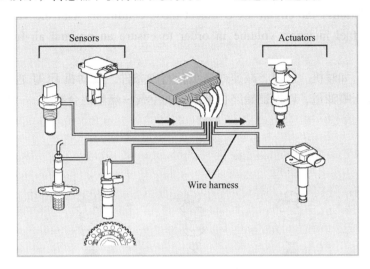

Figure 13 - 2　A computer-controlled system

Only after the engine ECU processes the input signals from the sensors and outputs control signals to the actuators can the entire system operate as a computer-controlled system.

只有当发动机 ECU 处理了来自传感器的输入信号，向执行器发出控制信号后整个系统才能作为计算机控制系统运行。

13.1　Outline of EFI（Electronic Fuel Injection）System
EFI（电控燃料喷射）系统概述

The EFI system（See Figure 13 - 3）uses various sensors to detect the operating conditions of the engine and the vehicle. In accordance with the signals from these sensors, the ECU calculates the optimal fuel injection volume and operates the injectors in order to inject the proper volume of fuel.

EFI 系统（见图 13 - 3）使用各种传感器检测发动机和汽车的运行条件。根据来自传感器的信号，ECU 计算出最佳喷油量，并操纵喷油器喷射正确的燃料量。

During ordinary driving, the engine ECU determines the fuel injection volume for achieving the theoretical（理论的）air-fuel ratio, in order to ensure the proper power, fuel consumption, and exhaust emission levels simultaneously.

在正常驾驶时，发动机 ECU 根据理论空气 - 燃料比决定燃料喷射量，以便同时得到合适的功率、燃油消耗和废气排放物水平。

At other times, such as during warm-up（暖机）, acceleration, deceleration, or high-load driving conditions, the engine ECU detect those conditions with the various sensors and then corrects the fuel injection volume in order to ensure an optimal air-fuel mixture at all times.

在其他时间，如暖机、加速、减速或高负荷行驶条件，发动机 ECU 通过传感器检测这些条件，然后校正喷油量，以保证始终得到最佳的空气 - 燃料混合物。

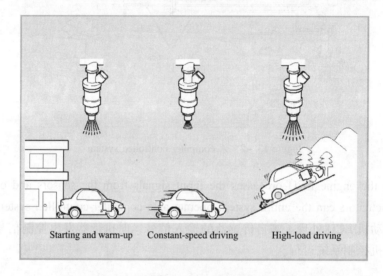

Starting and warm-up   Constant-speed driving   High-load driving

Figure 13 – 3   EFI（Electronic Fuel Injection）system

13.2 Outline of ESA（Electronic Spark Advance）System
ESA（电子点火提前）系统概述

The ESA system（See Figure 13 – 4）detects the conditions of the engine based on the signals provided by various sensors, and controls the spark plugs to generate sparks at the appropriate timing.

ESA 系统（见图 13 – 4）根据各种传感器信号得到发动机运行状况，控制火花塞在合适的时候产生火花。

Based on engine speed and engine load, the ESA precisely controls the ignition timing so that the engine can generate improve power, purify（净化）exhaust gases, and prevent knocking in an effective manner.

基于发动机转速和负荷，ESA 恰当地控制点火正时，以便发动机以有效方式提高功率，净化排气，避免爆震。

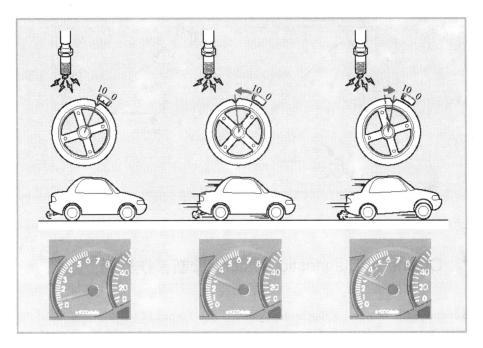

Figure 13 – 4　ESA（Electronic Spark Advance）system

13.3 Outline of ISC（Idle Speed Control） System
ISC（怠速控制）系统概述

The ISC system （See Figure 13 – 5） controls the idle speed so that it is always appropriate （适当的） under varying conditions （warm-up, electrical load, etc. ）.

ISC 系统（见图 13 – 5）控制怠速转速，以使怠速转速在变工况条件（暖机、增加用电器等）下是合适的。

To minimize fuel consumption and noise, an engine must operate at a speed that is as low as possible while maintaining a stable idle. Moreover, the idle speed must be increased to ensure the proper warm-up and drivability （驾驶性能） when the engine is cold or the air conditioner is being used.

为了将燃油消耗和噪音降到最低，发动机在保证怠速稳定的前提下把转速尽可能降低。此外，当发动机处于冷态或使用空调时，怠速转速必须提高，以保证正确的暖机和驾驶性能。

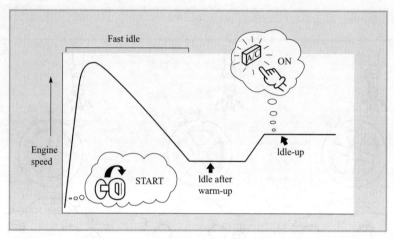

Figure 13 – 5　ISC（Idle Speed Control）system

13.4　Outline of Diagnostic System 诊断系统概述

The engine ECU contains a diagnostic system（See Figure 13 – 6）.
发动机 ECU 包括一个诊断系统（见图 13 – 6）。

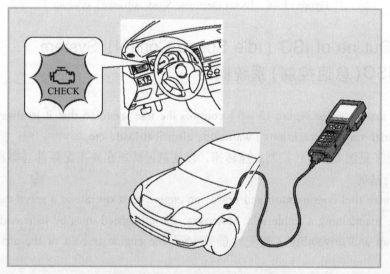

Figure 13 – 6　Diagnostic system

The ECU constantly monitors the signals that are being input by various sensors. If it detects a malfunction（故障）with an input signal, the ECU records the malfunction in the form of DTCs（Diagnostic Trouble Codes，诊断故障码）and illuminates the MIL（Malfunction Indicator

Lamp). If necessary, the ECU can output the DTCs by blinking the MIL or displaying the DTCs or other data on the display panel of a hand-held tester（手持式检测器）.

ECU 不断检测各种传感器正在输入的信号。如果它检测到一个输入信号的故障，ECU 以 DTC（故障诊断码）的形式记录故障，并点亮 MIL（故障指示灯）。如果有必要，ECU 通过使 MIL 闪烁或在手持式检测器的显示面板上显示 DTC 或其他数据来输出 DTC。

The diagnostic functions that output the DTCs and data of a malfunction on a hand-held tester are a highly advanced and complex form of electronics system.

在手持式检测器上输出 DTC 和故障数据的检测功能是电子系统高度先进性和复杂性的表现。

Because a diagnostic system must comply with（遵守）the regulations of each country, its contents vary slightly by destination.

由于诊断系统必须遵守各国的规章，其内容会根据目的地的不同而发生少量的变化。

Key Words

EFI（Electronic Fuel Injection） 电子燃料喷射
ESA（Electronic Spark Advance）   电子点火正时
ISC（Idle Speed Control） 怠速控制
diagnostic system 诊断系统

Exercises

1. _____ the engine ECU detect those conditions with the various sensors and then corrects the fuel injection volume in order to ensure an optimal air-fuel mixture at all times.

2. Based on engine speed and engine load, the ESA precisely controls the ignition timing so that the engine can generate improve power, purify exhaust gases, and prevent _____ in an effective manner.

3. To minimize fuel consumption and noise, an engine must operate at a speed that is as low as possible while maintaining a _____ idle.

4. The diagnostic functions that output the DTCs and data of a malfunction on a hand-held tester are a highly _____ form of electronics system.

Unit 14

Components of Engine Control System 发动机控制系统的组成

14.1 Description 概述

As shown in Figure 14 – 1, the engine control system consists of three groups including sensors (and sensor output signals), engine ECU, and actuators. This unit explains the sensors (signals), power **circuitry** and ground circuitry, and sensor **terminal** voltages.

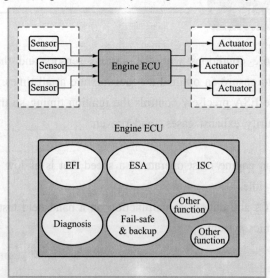

Figure 14 – 1　Description of engine control system

如图 14 – 1 所示，发动机控制系统由 3 个组成部分：传感器（和传感器信号）、发动机 ECU 和执行器。本单元讲述传感器（信号）、供电电路和地线电路、传感器终端电压。

The engine ECU functions are divided into EFI control, ESA control, ISC control, diagnosis function, fail-safe（自动防故障装置的）and backup functions, and other functions. These functions and the actuator functions are explained in separate units.

发动机 ECU 的功能分为 EFI 控制、ESA 控制、ISC 控制、诊断功能、自动防故障和备份功能及其他功能。这些功能和执行器的功能将在其他单元中讲述。

14.2 Power Circuitry 电源电路

The power circuitry is the electrical circuits that supply power to the engine ECU. These electric circuits include the ignition switch, the EFI main relay（继电器）, etc.

电源电路是为发动机 ECU 供电的电路，包括点火开关、EFI 主继电器等。

The power circuitry actually used by the vehicle consists of the following two types.

实际用于车辆的电源电路有以下两种类型。

1. Control by Ignition Switch *点火开关控制型*

As shown in Figure 14 – 2, the diagram shows the type in which the EFI main relay is operated directly from the ignition switch.

图 14 – 2 所示为点火开关操纵 EFI 主继电器的类型。

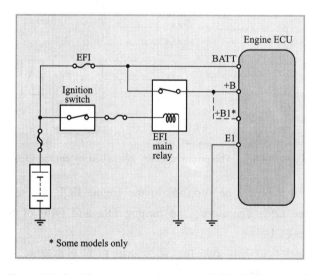

Figure 14 – 2   The power circuitry controlled by ignition switch

When the ignition switch is turned on, **current** flows to the coil（线圈）of the EFI main relay, causing the contacts to close. This supplies power to the ＋B and ＋B1 terminals of the engine ECU. Battery voltage is supplied at all times to the BATT terminal of the engine ECU to prevent the diagnostic codes and other data in its memory from being erased when the ignition switch is turned off.

当点火开关闭合时，电流流向 EFI 主继电器线圈，使触点闭合，向发动机 ECU 的 + B 和 − B 终端供电。电池电压始终加在发动机 ECU 的 BATT 终端，防止诊断码和内存中的其他数据在点火开关断开时被清除。

2. Control by Engine ECU 发动机 ECU 控制型

The power circuitry in Figure 14 – 3 is the type where operation of the EFI main relay is controlled by the engine ECU.

图 14 – 3 所示为发动机 ECU 控制 EFI 主继电器的类型。

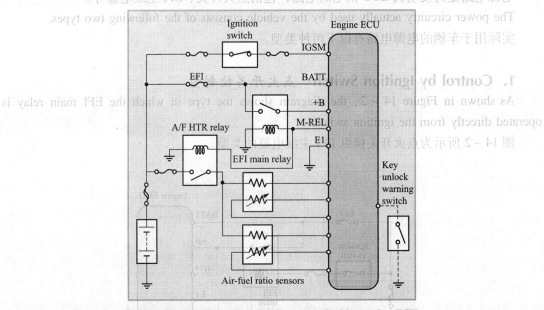

Figure 14 – 3   The power circuitry controlled by engine ECU

This type requires that power be supplied to the engine ECU for several seconds after the ignition switch is turned OFF. Therefore, the turning ON and OFF of the EFI main relay is controlled by the engine ECU.

这种类型的电路要求在点火开关断开后向发动机 ECU 供电数秒。因此，EFI 主继电器的闭合与断开由发动机 ECU 控制。

When the ignition switch is turned ON, battery voltage is supplied to the IGSM terminal of the engine ECU, and the EFI main relay control circuitry in the engine ECU sends a signal to the M-REL terminal of the engine ECU, turning on the EFI main relay. This signal causes current to flow to the coil, closing the contacts of the EFI main relay and supplying power to the + B terminal of the engine ECU.

当点火开关闭合时，电池电压供给发动机 ECU 的 IGSM 终端，发动机 ECU 中的 EFI 主继电器控制电路向发动机 ECU 的 M-REL 终端发送信号，闭合 EFI 主继电器。这个信号导致电流流向线圈，闭合主继电器的触点，并向发动机 ECU 的 +B 终端供电。

Battery voltage is always supplied to the BATT terminal for the same reason as for the control by ignition switch type.

由于和点火开关控制类型同样的原因，电池电压始终供给 BATT 终端。

In addition（另外），some models include a special relay for the air-fuel ratio sensor heater circuitry which is required large amount of current.

另外，部分型号包括一个用于空气–燃料比传感器加热电路的专门继电器，该电路需要大电流。

In models where the engine ECU controls the engine immobilizer（固定）system, the EFI main relay is also controlled by the key unlock warning switch signal.

在发动机 ECU 控制固定发动机系统的类型中，EFI 主继电器也受基本开启警报信号控制。

14.3 Ground Circuitry 地线电路

The engine ECU contains the following three basic ground circuits（地线电路）（See Figure 14 – 4）.

发动机 ECU 包括以下 3 个地线电路（见图 14 –4）。

1. Ground for Engine ECU Operation（E1） 发动机 ECU 操作地线（E1）

The E1 terminal is the engine ECU unit ground terminal, and is normally connected close to the air intake chamber of the engine.

E1 终端是发动机 ECU 单元地线终端，通常连接到发动机空气进气室附近。

2. Grounds for Sensor（E2, E21） 传感器地线（E2,E21）

The E2 and E21 terminals are sensor ground terminals, and these are connected to the E1 terminal in the engine ECU.

E2 和 E21 是传感器地线终端，连接到发动机 ECU 的 E1 终端。

These prevent the sensors from detecting erroneous（错误的）voltage values by keeping the sensor ground potential and engine ECU ground potential at the same level.

通过保持传感器地线电压和发动机 ECU 地线电压相同，它们防止传感器检测到错误的电压值。

3. Grounds for Actuator Operation（E01，E02） 执行器操作地线（E01, E02）

The E01 and E02 terminals are actuator ground terminals，such as for the actuators，ISC valve，and air-fuel ratio sensor heater，and，as with the E1 terminal，they are connected close to the air intake chamber of the engine.

E01 和 E02 终端是执行器地线终端，例如为执行器、ISC 阀和空气 – 燃料比传感器的加热器服务。其与 E1 终端一样，连接到发动机空气进气室附近。

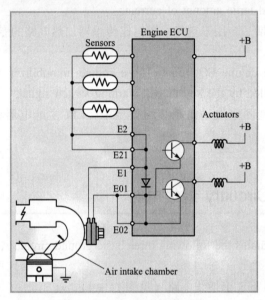

Figure 14 – 4　Ground circuitry

Exercises

1. The engine control system consists of three groups including sensors（and sensor output signals），engine ECU，and _____．
2. The power circuitry actually used by the vehicle consists of two types：control by ignition switch and control by _____．
3. The E2 and E21 terminals are _____，and these are connected to the E1 terminal in the engine ECU.

Unit 15

Sensors and Signals
传感器和信号

Key Terms

air flow meter

manifold pressure sensor

throttle position sensor

accelerator pedal position sensor

G signal and NE signal

water temperature sensor/intake air temperature sensor

oxygen sensor (O_2 sensor)

air-fuel (A/F) ratio sensor

vehicle speed sensor, knock sensor

STA (starter) signal/NSW (neutral start switch) signal

15.1 Air Flow Meter 空气流量计

The air flow meter (流量计) is one of the most important sensors because it is used in L-type EFI to detect the intake air mass (质量) or volume (体积).

因为在 L 型 EFI 中用作进气质量或体积检测，所以空气流量计是最重要的传感器之一。

Signal of the intake air mass or volume is used to calculate the basic **injection duration** and basic ignition advance angle.

进气质量或体积信号用于计算基本喷油持续期和基本点火提前角。

The air flow meter is largely classified (分类) into two types, mass air flow meters that detect the intake air mass, and volume air flow meters, respective types include the following.

(1) Mass air flow meter: Hot-wire type (热线型).

(2) Volume air flow meter：Vane type（文恩式）and optical Karman vortex type（光学卡门涡旋式）．

空气流量计主要分为两种类型，检测进气质量的质量空气流量计和体积空气流量计，各自又包括下面的几种类型（见图 15 – 1）。

(1) 质量空气流量计：热线型。

(2) 体积空气流量计：文恩式和光学卡门涡旋式。

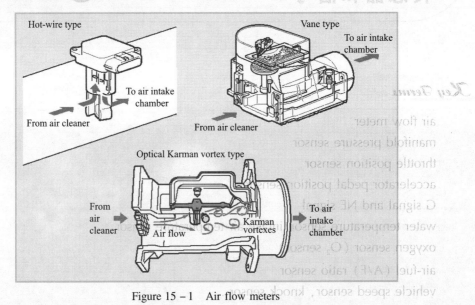

Figure 15 – 1　Air flow meters

Currently, most models use the hot-wire type of air flow meter because it has superior measurement accuracy, lighter weight, and better durability（耐久性）．

目前，大部分类型使用热线式空气流量计，因为它有较高的测量准确性、更小的质量和更好的耐久性。

1. Vane Type　文恩式

The vane type air flow meter is composed of many components, as shown in Figure 15 – 2.

如图 15 – 2 所示，文恩式空气流量计由许多部件组成。

When air passes through the air flow meter from the air cleaner, it pushes open the measuring plate（测量板）until the force acting on the measuring plate is in equilibrium with the return spring（回位弹簧）．

当来自空气滤清器的空气流过空气流量计时，就推动测量板，直到施加在测量板上的力与回位弹簧的力平衡。

The potentiometer, which is connected coaxially with the measuring plate, converts the intake air volume to a voltage signal (VS signal) which is sent to the engine ECU.

与测量板同轴连接的电位计将进气体积转化为一个电压信号（VS 信号），送给发动机 ECU。

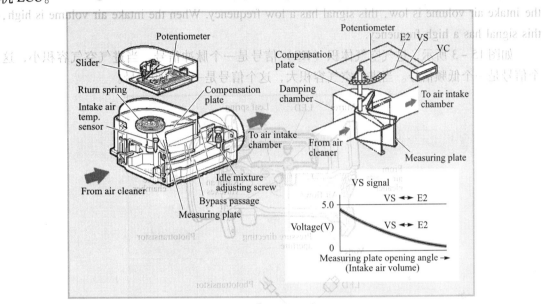

Figure 15 – 2 Vane type of air flow meter

2. Optical Karman Vortex Type 光学卡门涡旋式

This type of air flow meter directly senses the intake air volume optically. Compared to the vane type air flow meter, it can be made smaller and lighter in weight. The simplified construction of the air passage（通道）also reduces intake air resistance（阻力）.

这种流量计通过光学方法直接感知进气体积。与文恩式空气流量计相比，其体积更小，重量更轻。空气通道的简化结构也减少了进气空气阻力。

A pillar（called the "vortex generator"）placed in the middle of a uniform flow of air generates a vortex called a "Karman vortex" down-stream of the pillar. As the generated Karman vortex frequency（频率）is proportional to（成比例的）the air flow speed, the air flow volume can be calculated by measuring the vortex frequency.

一根柱子（称为"涡流发生器"）放置在均匀流动的空气中间，在柱子下游产生了称作"卡门涡旋"的涡旋。由于产生卡门涡旋的频率与空气流动速度成正比，空气流的体积可以通过测量涡旋的频率计算得到。

Vortexes are detected by subjecting the surface of a piece of thin metal foil（金属薄片）（called a "mirror"）to the pressure of the vortexes and optically detecting the vibrations of the mirror by means of a photocoupler（an LED combined with a phototransistor［光电耦合器］）.

通过一片金属薄片（称为"镜子"）承受涡旋的压力检测涡旋，并通过光电耦合器检测镜子的振动。

The intake air volume (KS) signal is a pulse signal like that shown in Figure 15 – 3. When the intake air volume is low, this signal has a low frequency. When the intake air volume is high, this signal has a high frequency.

如图 15 – 3 所示，进气空气体积（KS）信号是一个脉冲信号。当进气空气容积小，这个信号是一个低频信号。当进气空气容积大，这个信号是一个高频信号。

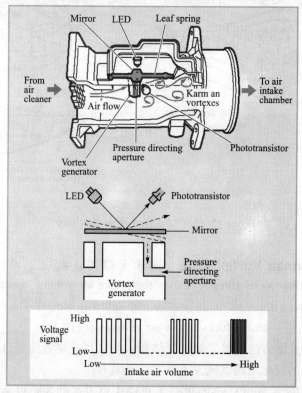

Figure 15 – 3   Optical Karman Vortex Type of air flow meter

3. Hot-wire Type   热线型

As shown in Figure 15 – 4, the construction of the hot-wire type of air flow meter is very simple.

如图 15 – 4 所示，热线型空气流量计的结构非常简单。

The compact and lightweight mass air flow meter shown in Figure 15 – 4 is a plug-in（插入）type that is installed onto the air passage, and causes part of the intake air to flow through the detection area. As shown in Figure 15 – 4, a hot-wire and thermistor（电热调节器），which are used as a sensor, are installed in the detection area.

图 15 – 4 所示的紧凑轻巧的质量空气流量计是插入到空气流当中的插入类型，使部分进气流过检测区域。如图 15 – 4 所示，一根热线和一个电热调节器作为传感器安装在检测区域。

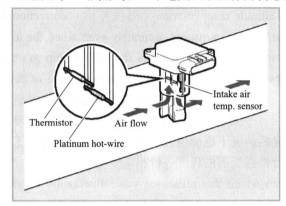

Figure 15 – 4   Hot-wire type of air flow meter

By directly measuring the intake air mass, detection precision （精度）is improved and there is almost no intake air resistance. In addition, since there are no special **mechanisms**, this meter has excellent durability.

直接测量进气质量，提高了检测精度，几乎不产生进气阻力。另外，由于没有特殊的机构，该流量计非常耐用。

The air flow meter shown in Figure 15 – 4 also has a built-in （安装）intake air temperature sensor.

图 15 – 4 所示的空气流量计也安装了一个进气温度传感器。

4. Manifold Pressure Sensor（Vacuum Sensor）
歧管压力传感器（真空传感器）

The manifold pressure sensor （歧管压力传感器）（See Figure 15 – 5）is used with D-type EFI for sensing the intake manifold pressure. This is one of the most important sensors in D-type EFI.

歧管压力传感器（见图 15 – 5）在 D 型 EFI 中用来感知进气歧管压力。这是 D 型 EFI 中最重要的传感器之一。

By means of an IC built into this sensor, the manifold pressure sensor senses the intake manifold pressure as a PIM **signal**. The engine ECU then determines the basic injection duration and basic ignition advance angle on the basis of this PIM signal.

通过在传感器中装入一块 IC（集成电路），歧管压力传感器将进气歧管压力转化为一个 PIM 信号。发动机 ECU 在 PIM 信号的基础上确定基本喷油持续期和基本点火提前角。

As shown in Figure 15 – 5, a silicon chip（硅芯片）combined with a vacuum chamber maintained at a predetermined（预定的）vacuum is incorporated into the sensor unit. One side of the chip is exposed to intake manifold pressure and the other side is exposed to the internal vacuum chamber. Therefore, high-altitude compensation（海拔补偿）correction is not required because the intake manifold pressure can be measured accurately even when the altitude changes. A change in the intake manifold pressure causes the shape of the silicon chip to change, and the resistance value of the chip fluctuates（变动）in accordance with the degree of deformation.

如图 15 – 5 所示，一块带有一个预定压力的真空室的硅芯片被装入传感器本体。芯片的一面承受进气歧管压力，另一面连接内部的真空室。这样，就不需要海拔补偿校正了，因为进气歧管压力在海拔变化的情况下也能得到准确的测量。进气歧管压力的变化改变了硅芯片的形状，而芯片的阻值会根据变形的程度进行相应变化。

The voltage signal into which this resistance value fluctuation is converted by the IC is the PIM signal.

阻值的波动被 IC 转化为电压信号，这个电压信号就是 PIM 信号。

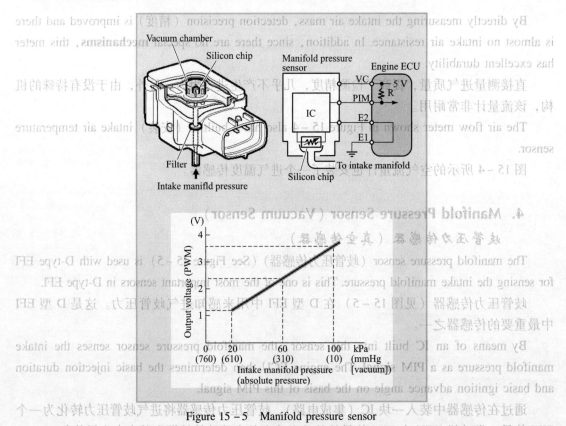

Figure 15 – 5　Manifold pressure sensor

15.2 Throttle Position Sensor 节气门位置传感器

The throttle（节气门）position sensor（See Figure 15 – 6）is installed on the throttle body. The sensor converts the throttle opening angle to voltage, which is sent to the engine ECU as the throttle opening signal（VTA）. In addition, some devices output an individual IDL signal. Others determine it at idle when the throttle opening signal voltage is below the standard value.

　　节气门位置传感器（见图 15 – 6）安装在节气门体上。传感器把节气门开启的角度转化为电压送往发动机 ECU，作为节气门开启信号（VTA）。另外，一些设备输出一个单独的 IDL 信号。当节气门开启信号电压值低于标准值时，其他设备就认为发动机处于怠速状态。

Currently, two types, the linear type and hall element type, are used. In addition, 2-system output is used to improve reliability.

　　目前使用两种型号的传感器：线性输出型和霍尔元件型。另外，为提高可靠性，采用了双系统输出。

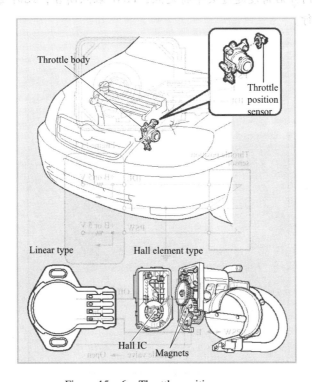

Figure 15 – 6 Throttle position sensor

--- **REFERENCE · 参考** ---

On-Off Type

As shown in Figure 15 – 7, this type of throttle position sensor uses an idle (IDL) contact and power (PSW) contact to detect whether the engine is idling or is running under a heavy load. When the throttle valve is completely closed, the IDL contact is ON and the PSW contact is OFF. The engine ECU determines that the engine is idling. When the accelerator pedal（踏板）is depressed（踩下）, the IDL contact turns OFF, and when the throttle valve opens beyond a certain point, the PSW contact turns ON, at which time the engine ECU determines that the engine is running under a heavy load.

开 – 关型

如图 15 – 7 所示，这种类型的节气门位置传感器采用一个怠速（IDL）触点和一个动力（PSW）触点来检测发动机是正在怠速还是在大负荷下运转。当节气门完全关闭，IDL 触点闭合，PSW 触点打开，发动机 ECU 断定发动机怠速运转。当加速踏板被踩下，IDL 触点断开。当节气门开启角度超过某个特定点，PSW 触点闭合，此时发动机 ECU 断定发动机在大负荷下运行。

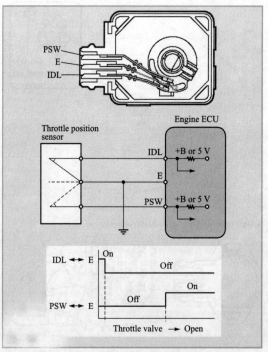

Figure 15 – 7　On-off type of throttle position sensor

1. Linear Type　线性输出型

As shown in Figure 15 – 8, this sensor consists of two sliders and a resistor, and contacts for the IDL and throttle opening signals are provided on the ends of each.

如图 15 – 8 所示，这种传感器包括两个滑片和一个电阻器。在滑片末端各有一个触点，分别表示 IDL 和节气门开启信号。

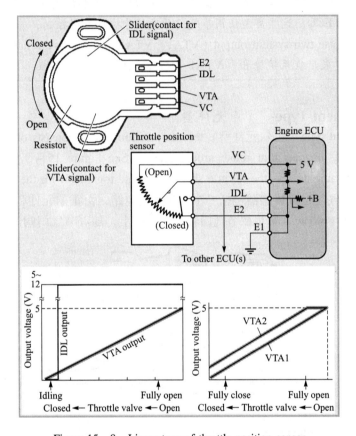

Figure 15 – 8　Linear type of throttle position sensor

When the contact slides along the resistor in sync（同步）with the throttle valve opening angle, the voltage is applied to the throttle opening signal terminal proportionally to the throttle opening angle.

当触点沿着电阻器与节气门开启角度同步移动时，对应节气门开启信号终端的电压值与节气门开启角度成正比。

When the throttle valve is completely closed, the IDL signal contact is connected to the IDL and E2 terminals.

当节气门完全关闭，IDL 信号触点接通 IDL 和 E2 终端。

HINT · 提示

Recent linear type throttle position sensors include models without an IDL contact or models that have an IDL contact, but it is not connected to the engine ECU. These models use the throttle opening signal to perform learned control and detect idling condition.

近期的线性输出型节气门位置传感器包括具有 IDL 触点和没有 IDL 触点的类型，但没有连接到发动机的 ECU。这些类型使用节气门开度信号执行习得控制，并监测怠速条件。

Some models use two-system output (VTA1, VTA2) to improve reliability.

还有一些类型采用双系统输出（VTA1、VTA2），以提高可靠性。

---

2. Hall Element Type 霍尔元件型

The hall element type（霍尔元件型）throttle position sensor consists of a hall ICs made of hall elements and of magnets that rotate around them (See Figure 15 – 9). The magnets are installed above the same axis as the throttle shaft and rotate together with the throttle valve.

霍尔元件型节气门位置传感器包括一个霍尔集成电路，由霍尔元件和绕其旋转的磁铁组组成（见图 15 – 9）。磁铁组安装在节气门轴的延伸线上，随着节气门阀门一起转动。

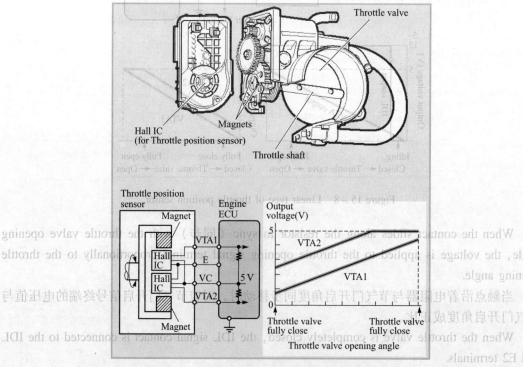

Figure 15 – 9　Hall element type of throttle position sensor

When the throttle valve opens, the magnets rotate at the same time, and the magnets change their position.

当节气门阀门打开，磁铁组同时转动，并改变了自己的位置。

At this time, the hall IC detects a change in the magnetic flux（磁通量）caused by the change in the magnet's position, and the resulting hall effect outputs voltage from the VTA1 and VTA2 terminals in accordance with the amount of change. This signal is sent to the engine ECU as the throttle valve opening signal.

此时，霍尔集成电路检测到由于磁铁组位置变化而产生的磁通量变化，霍尔效应根据变化的数量从 VTA1 和 VTA2 终端输出电压。这一信号送给发动机 ECU 作为节气门开度信号。

This sensor not only accurately detects the throttle valve opening, but it also uses a non-contact（非接触式）method and has a simple construction, so it does not break down easily. In addition, to maintain the reliability of this sensor, it outputs signals from two systems with different output characteristics.

这种传感器不但能够准确检测节气门的开度，而且采用非接触的方法，结构简单，因此不容易损坏。另外，为了保持这种传感器的可靠性，采用不同输出特性的两个系统输出信号。

REFERENCE · 参考

Hall Effect

The hall effect is the electrical potential difference that occurs perpendicular to the current and magnetic field when a magnetic field is applied perpendicular to the current flowing in a conductor（See Figure 15 – 10）. In addition, the voltage generated by this electrical potential difference changes proportionally to the applied magnetic flux density. The hall element type throttle position sensor utilizes this principle to convert the change in throttle valve position（opening）to a change in flux density to accurately measure the change in throttle valve position.

霍 尔 效 应

如果磁场中的导体有电流流过，该磁场的方向垂直于电流流动的方向，那么则在既与磁场垂直又与所施加电流方向垂直的方向上会产生一个电势差，产生这种现象被称为霍尔效应（见图 15 – 10）。此外，这个电势差产生的电压与施加磁场的磁通密度成比例。霍尔元件型节气门位置传感器应用这一原理把节气门位置（开度）的变化转变为磁通密度的变化，从而准确测量节气门位置的变化。

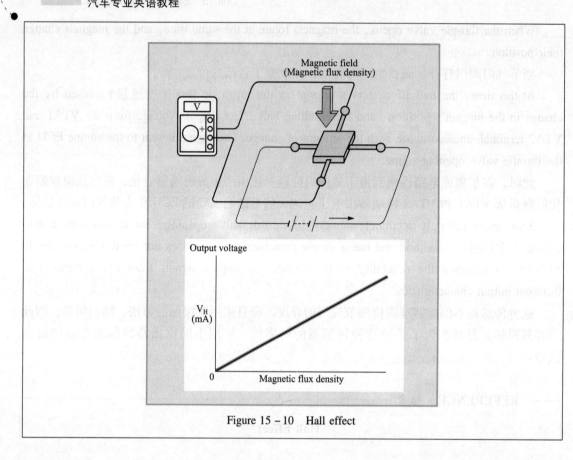

Figure 15 – 10　Hall effect

15.3 Accelerator Pedal Position Sensor 加速踏板位置传感器

The accelerator pedal position sensor（加速踏板位置传感器）converts the amount that the accelerator pedal is depressed（angle）to an electrical signal that is sent to the engine ECU.

加速踏板位置传感器将踏下加速踏板的程度（角度）转化为电信号，传给发动机 ECU。

In addition, to ensure reliability, this sensor outputs signals from two systems with differing output characteristics.

另外，为了保证可靠性，传感器输出的信号来自具有不同输出特性的两个系统。

There are two types of accelerator pedal position sensors, the linear type and the hall element type.

共有两种类型的加速踏板位置传感器：线性输出型和霍尔元件型。

1. Linear Type   线性输出型

The construction and operation of this sensor is basically the same as the linear type throttle position sensor（See Figure 15 – 11）.

这种传感器的结构和操作基本和线性输出节气门位置传感器一样（见图 15 – 11）。

Of the signals from the two systems, one is a VPA signal that linearly outputs the voltage within the entire range of the accelerator pedal depression. The other is the VPA2 signal, which outputs the offset voltage from the VPA signal.

来自两个系统的信号，一个是在加速踏板被踩下的整个过程中线性输出电压值的 VPA 信号，另一个是 VPA2 信号，它输出 VPA 信号的偏移电压。

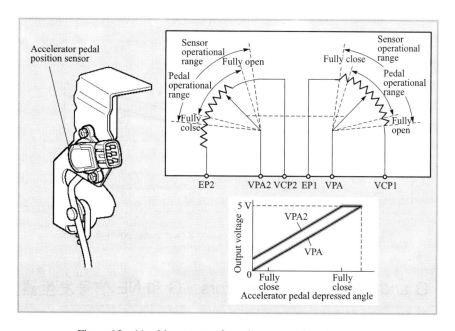

Figure 15 – 11   Linear type of accelerator pedal position sensor

2. Hall Element Type   霍尔元件型

The construction and operation of this sensor is basically the same as the hall element type throttle position sensor（See Figure 15 – 12）.

这种传感器的结构和操作基本和霍尔元件型节气门位置传感器一样（见图 15 – 12）。

To ensure better reliability, an independent electrical circuit is provided for each of the two systems.

为了得到更好的可靠性，为双系统中的每一个提供了一个独立的电路。

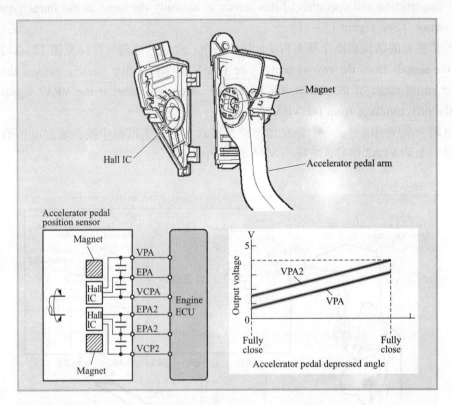

Figure 15 – 12　Hall element type of accelerator pedal position sensor

15.4 G and NE Signal Generators　G 和 NE 信号发生器

The G signal and NE signal are generated by the pickup coil（耦合线圈）. The information from these two signals is combined by the engine ECU to comprehensively detect the crankshaft angle and engine speed.

G 信号和 NE 信号由耦合线圈产生，发动机 ECU 把这两个信号结合起来检测曲轴角度和发动机转速。

These two signals are not only very important to the EFI systems but to the ESA system as well.

这两个信号对 EFI 系统和 ESA 系统都很重要。

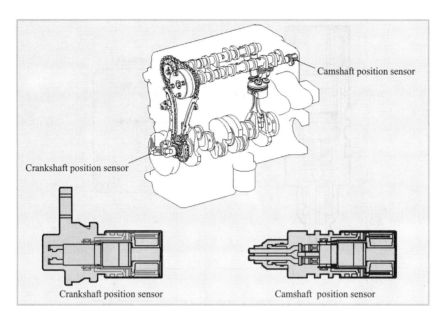

Figure 15 – 13　Camshaft position sensor and crankshaft position sensor

1. Camshaft Position Sensor（**G Signal Generator**）
凸轮轴位置传感器（**G** 信号发生器）

As shown in Figure 15 – 14, on the camshaft opposite the camshaft position sensor is a G signal plate with a protrusion(s)（凸起）. The numbers of protrusions are 1, 3, or another number depending on the engine model. (There are 3 protrusions in Figure 15 – 14.) When the camshaft rotates, the air gap（间隙）between the protrusions on the camshaft and the sensor changes. This change in gap generates a voltage in the pickup coil built into the sensor, resulting in the G signal. This G signal is sent as the information of the standard crankshaft angle to the engine ECU, which combines it with the NE signal from the crankshaft position sensor to determine the compression **TDC**（**Top Dead Center**）of each cylinder for ignition and detect the crankshaft angle. The engine ECU uses this to determine the injection duration and the ignition timing.

如图 15 – 14 所示，在凸轮轴上，凸轮轴位置传感器的对面是一个带凸起的 G 信号金属盘。凸起的数目是 1、3 或其他，由发动机类型决定。（图 15 – 14 中所示的金属盘有 3 个凸起。）当凸轮轴旋转时，凸轮轴上的凸起与传感器之间的空气间隙发生变化。间隙的变化在传感器内部的线圈产生了一个电压，导致 G 信号。这一 G 信号作为标准曲轴角度信息送到发动机 ECU，与来自曲轴位置传感器的 NE 信号结合，从而判定各缸压缩 TDC（上死点），以决定何时点火，并检测当前的曲轴转角。发动机 ECU 用这一信息确定喷射持续期和点火正时。

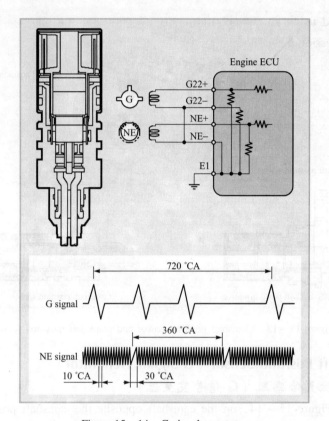

Figure 15 – 14　G signal generator

2. Crankshaft Position Sensor（NE Signal Generator）

曲轴位置传感器（NE 信号发生器）

NE signal is used by the engine ECU to detect the crankshaft angle and engine speed. The engine ECU uses the NE signal and G signal to calculate the basic injection duration and basic ignition advance angle.

发动机 ECU 使用 NE 信号检测曲轴转角和发动机转速。发动机 ECU 使用 NE 信号和 G 信号计算基本的喷射持续期和基本的点火提前角。

As with the G signal, the NE signal is generated by the air gap between the crankshaft position sensor and the protrusions on the NE timing rotor periphery（外围）installed on the crankshaft.

和 G 信号一样，曲轴位置传感器和安装在曲轴上的 NE 定时转子边缘的凸起之间有间隙，NE 信号由间隙产生。

Figure 15 – 15 shows a type of signal generator（信号发生器）with 34 protrusions on the NE timing rotor periphery and an area with two teeth missing（缺失）. The area with two teeth missing can be used to detect the crankshaft angle, but it cannot determine whether it is at the TDC of the compression cycle or the TDC of the exhaust cycle.

图 15－15 显示了 NE 定时转子边缘是一种有 34 个凸起的信号发生器，并在某处缺失了两个齿。可使用缺失两个齿的位置来检测曲轴转角，但无法断定它是压缩 TDC，还是排气循环 TDC。

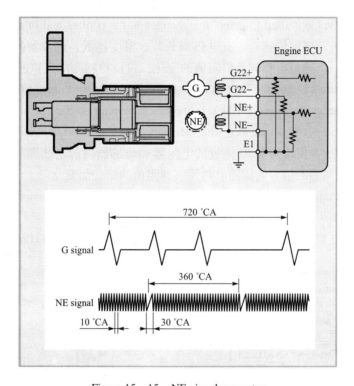

Figure 15－15   NE signal generator

The engine ECU combines the NE signal and G signal to accurately determine the crankshaft angle. In addition to this, some signal generators have 12, 24, or another number of protrusions, but the crankshaft angle detection accuracy（检测精度）varies depending on the number of protrusions. For example, types with 12 protrusions have a crankshaft angle detection accuracy of 30 CA.

发动机 ECU 将 NE 信号和 G 信号结合起来，准确地判定曲轴转角。另外，一些信号发生器带有 12、24 或其他数目的凸起，但曲轴转角的检测精度随着凸起的数目而变化。例如，带有 12 个凸起的类型曲轴转角检测精度为 30 度曲轴转角。

15.5 Water Temperature Sensor/Intake Air Temperature Sensor 水温传感器/进气温度传感器

The water temperature sensor and intake air temperature sensor have built in thermistors（电热调节器）for which the lower the temperature, the larger the resistance value（阻值）and, conversely, the higher the temperature, the lower the resistance value. And this change of the thermistor resistance value is used to detect the changes in the coolant and intake air temperatures.

水温传感器和进气温度传感器带有电热调节器。温度越低，调节器的阻值越大；相反，温度越高，阻值越低。通过电热调节器阻值的变化，可以检测冷却液和进气空气的温度。

As shown in Figure 15 – 16, the built-in resistor（电阻器）in the engine ECU and the thermistor in the sensor are connected in series（串联）in the electric circuit so that the signal voltage detected by the engine ECU changes in accordance with the changes in the thermistor resistance.

如图 15 – 16 所示，发动机 ECU 内置的电阻器和传感器内的电热调节器串联在电路中，因此发动机 ECU 检测到的信号电压随电热调节器阻值的变化而变化。

When the temperature of the coolant or intake air is low, the thermistor resistance becomes large, creating a high voltage in the THW and THA signals.

当冷却液或进气空气的温度低时，电热调节器的阻值变大，在 THW 和 THA 信号端产生高电压。

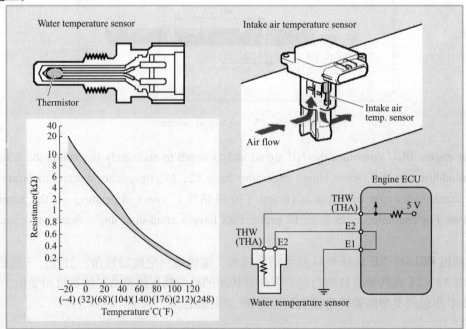

Figure 15 – 16　Water temperature sensor and intake air temperature sensor

1. Water Temperature Sensor　水温传感器

The water temperature sensor measures the temperature of the engine coolant. When the engine coolant temperature is low, the idling must be increased, the injection duration increased, the ignition timing angle advanced, etc., to improve drivability and to warm up. For this reason, the water temperature sensor is indispensable（不可缺少的）for the engine control system.

水温传感器测量发动机冷却液的温度。当发动机冷却液的温度低时，怠速转速必须提高，喷油持续期延长，点火提前角增大等，以提高驾驶性能和暖机。为此，发动机控制系统必须安装水温传感器。

2. Intake Air Temperature Sensor　进气温度传感器

The intake air temperature sensor measures the temperature of the intake air. The air amount and density change according to the air temperature. Therefore, even if the air amount detected by the air flow meter is the same, the amount of fuel that is injected must be corrected.

进气温度传感器测量进气温度。进气数量和密度随进气温度而变化。因此，即使空气流量计检测到的空气量相等，喷油量也必须（根据进气温度）进行修正。

However, hot-wire type air flow meter directly measures the air mass. Therefore, the correction is not required.

然而，热线型空气流量计直接测量空气质量，因此不需要修正。

15.6 Oxygen Sensor（O_2 Sensor）氧气传感器

To maximum the exhaust purification（净化）function of the engine with **TWC**（Three-Way Catalytic Converter）, the air-fuel ratio must be kept within a narrow range around the **theoretical air-fuel ratio**. The oxygen sensor detects whether the oxygen concentration in the exhaust gas is richer or leaner than the theoretical air-fuel ratio. The sensor is mainly installed in the exhaust manifold, but the location and number that are installed differ depending on the engine.

为了使带有三元催化转化器的发动机达到最佳的排气净化功能，空气－燃料比必须保持在理论空气－燃料比附近一个狭窄的范围内。氧传感器检测排气中氧气的浓度是比理论空气－燃料比稀还是浓。该传感器主要安装在排气歧管，但安装位置和数量根据发动机而变化。

The oxygen sensor（See Figure 15 – 17）contains an element made of zirconium oxide（ZrO_2）, which is a type of ceramic. The inside and outside of this element is covered with a thin coating of platinum（铂）. The ambient（周围环境的）air is guided into the inside of the sensor and the outside of the sensor is exposed to the exhaust gas.

氧传感器（见图 15 – 17）包括一个由二氧化锆（ZrO$_2$）制成的元件，这是一种陶瓷。元件的内外覆盖一层薄金属铂。环境空气被引入传感器内，传感器外部暴露在排气中。

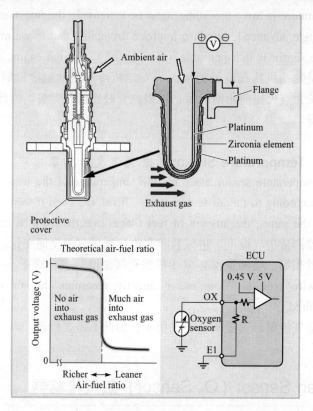

Figure 15 – 17 Oxygen sensor（O$_2$ sensor）

At high temperatures（400 ℃［752 ℉］and higher），the zirconium element generates a voltage as a result of the large difference between the oxygen concentrations on the inside and outside of the zirconium element.

在高温下（400 ℃［752 ℉］或更高），由于锆元件内部和外部氧气浓度的较大差别，锆元件产生一个电压。

In addition，the platinum acts as a catalyst（催化剂）to cause a chemical reaction between the oxygen and carbon monoxide（CO）in the exhaust gas. Therefore，this reduces the amount of oxygen and increases sensor sensitivity.

另外，铂作为催化剂引起排气中氧气和一氧化碳（CO）的化学反应，因此减少了氧气的数量，提高了传感器的灵敏度。

When the air-fuel mixture is lean，there is much oxygen in the exhaust gas so that there is only a little difference in the oxygen concentration between the inside and outside of the zirconium element. Therefore, the zirconium element will only generate a low voltage (nearly 0 V). Conversely (相反的), when the air-fuel mixture is rich (浓), there is almost no oxygen in the exhaust gas. For this reason, there is a large difference in the oxygen concentration between the inside and outside of the sensor so that the zirconium element generates a relatively large voltage (approx. 1 V).

当空气 – 燃料混合物浓度低时, 排气中的氧气就多, 所以锆元件内部和外部的氧气浓度差别很小。因此, 锆元件将会产生一个较低的电压（接近 0 伏）。相反, 当空气 – 燃料混合物浓度高时, 排气中的氧气几乎没有。由于这个原因, 传感器内部和外部的氧气浓度差别较大, 所以锆元件将会产生一个较高的电压（接近 1 伏）。

Based on the OX signal output by the sensor, the engine ECU increases or decreases the fuel injection volume so that the average air-fuel ratio is maintained at the theoretical air-fuel ratio.

根据传感器输出的 OX 信号, 发动机 ECU 增大或减小燃料喷射量, 使平均空气 – 燃料比保持在理论空气 – 燃料比。

Some zirconium oxygen sensors have heaters (加热器) to heat the zirconia element. This heater is also controlled by the engine ECU. When the amount of the intake air is low (in other words, when the exhaust gas temperature is low), current is sent to the heater to heat the sensor.

一些锆氧传感器带有加热器, 用来加热锆元件。该加热器也受发动机 ECU 控制。当进气量少时（换句话说, 当排气温度低时）, 电流流向加热器, 对传感器加热。

15.7 Air-fuel (A/F) Ratio Sensor 空气 – 燃料比传感器

As with the oxygen sensor, the air-fuel ratio sensor detects the oxygen concentration in the exhaust gas.

和氧传感器一样, 空气 – 燃料比传感器检测排气中的氧气浓度。

Conventional oxygen sensors are such that the output voltage tends to change drastically (剧烈地) at the boundary (分界线) of the theoretical air-fuel ratio. In comparison, the air-fuel ratio sensor (See Figure 15 – 18) applies a constant voltage to obtain a voltage that is nearly proportional to the oxygen concentration. This improves the air-fuel ratio detection accuracy.

对于常规的氧产感器, 输出电压在理论空气 – 燃料比处发生剧烈的变化。与之相比, 空气 – 燃料比传感器（见图 15 – 18）产生的电压几乎和氧气浓度成正比。这就提高了空气 – 燃料比的检测精度。

The output illustration shows an air-fuel ratio sensor displayed in a hand-held tester. A circuit that maintains a constant voltage on the AF + and AF-terminals of the engine ECU is built in. Therefore, the output condition of the air-fuel ratio sensor cannot be detected by a voltmeter. Please use the hand-held tester.

输出曲线显示的是空气－燃料比传感器在手持式检测仪上的显示情况。安装了一个电路，在发动机 ECU 的 AF＋和 AF－终端维持恒定电压。因此，不能使用电压表检测空气－燃料传感器的输出。请使用手持式检测仪。

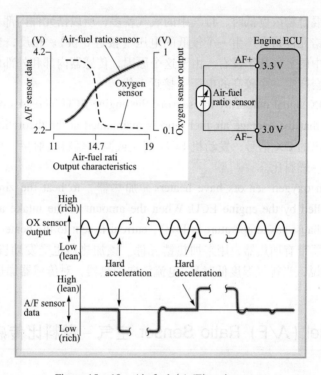

Figure 15 - 18   Air-fuel（A/F）ratio sensor

The output characteristics of the air-fuel ratio sensor make it possible to correct as soon as there is a change in the air-fuel ratio, which makes the air-fuel ratio feedback correction faster and more accurate.

由于空气－燃料传感器的线性输出特性，当空气－燃料比发生变化时，就可能进行修正，这使空气－燃料比的反馈修正更快、更准确。

As with some oxygen sensors, the air-fuel ratio sensor also has a heater for maintaining detection performance when the exhaust temperature is low. However, the air-fuel ratio sensor heater requires much more current than the heaters in the oxygen sensors.

与一些氧气传感器一样，为了保持检测性能，空气－燃料比传感器也有一个加热器，在排气温度低的时候进行加热。然而，与氧传感器的加热器相比，空气－燃料比传感器的加热器需要的电流要大得多。

15.8 Vehicle Speed Sensor 车速传感器

The speed sensor（See Figure 15 – 19）detects the actual speed at which the vehicle is running.

车速传感器（见图 15 – 19）检测汽车行驶的实际速度。

The sensor outputs the SPD signal, and the engine ECU uses this signal mainly to control the ISC system and the air-fuel ratio during acceleration or deceleration as well as other uses.

传感器输出 SPD 信号，发动机 ECU 使用这个信号主要是为了控制 ISC 系统和加速或减速时的空气 – 燃料比。

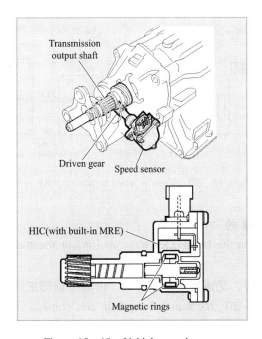

Figure 15 – 19   Vehicle speed sensor

The MRE（Magnetic Resistance Element）types（See Figure 15 – 20）are the main type of speed sensor used, but recently many models use the SPD signal from the ABS ECU.

MRE（磁阻元件）型（传感器）（见图 15 – 20）是主要使用的速度传感器，但是近来许多型号采用来自 ABS ECU 的 SPD 信号。

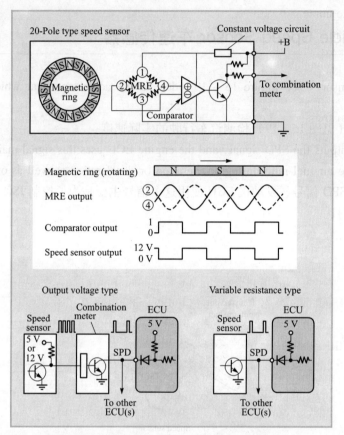

Figure 15 – 20　Vehicle speed sensor of MRE type

1. Construction　结构

This sensor is installed on the **transaxle**, transmission, or transfer, and is driven by the drive gear of the output shaft.

该传感器安装在驱动桥、变速器或分动器上，由输出轴的主动齿轮驱动。

As shown in Figure 15 – 20, the sensor is built-in and consists of a HIC (Hybrid Integrated Circuit) with a MRE and magnetic rings.

如图 15 – 20 所示，传感器是嵌入式的，由带有 MRE 的 HIC（混合集成电路）和磁性圆环组成。

2. Operation　操作

The MRE resistance changes depending on the direction of the magnetic force applied to the MRE. When the direction of the magnetic force changes according to the rotation of the magnet attached to the magnetic ring, the MRE output becomes an AC waveform（波形） as shown in

Figure 15 – 20. The comparator（比较器）in the sensor converts this AC waveform into a digital signal and outputs it.

　　MRE 的阻抗随作用在 MRE 上的磁力的方向变化而变化。当该磁力的方向由于连接在磁性圆环上的磁铁的旋转而发生变化时，MRE 的输出变成如图 15 – 20 所示的交流波形。传感器中的比较器将该交流波形转化为数字信号输出。

The waveform frequency is determined by the number of poles of the magnets attached to the magnetic ring.

　　该波形的频率由连接在磁性圆环上的磁铁磁极的数目决定。

There are two types of magnetic rings, 20-pole type and 4-pole type, depending on the vehicle model. The 20-pole type generates a 20-cycle waveform (in other words, twenty pulses for each rotation of the magnetic ring), and the 4-pole type generates a 4-cycle waveform.

　　有两种类型的磁性圆环，即 20-磁极型和 4-磁极型，这取决于汽车的类型。20-磁极型产生 20 个周波波形（换句话说，磁性圆环每转一圈产生 20 个脉冲），4-磁极类型产生 4 个周波波形。

In some models, the signal from the speed sensor passes through the combination meter before arriving at the engine ECU, and in the other models, the signal from the speed sensor arrives directly at the engine ECU.

　　在某些类型上，来自速度传感器的信号在到达发动机 ECU 之前要经过组合仪表；在其他类型上，来自速度传感器的信号直接到达发动机 ECU。

The output circuits of the speed sensor consist of the output voltage type and the variable resistance type.

　　速度传感器的输出电路由输出电压型和可变阻抗型组成。

15.9　Knock Sensor 爆震传感器

　　The **knock sensor** is attached to the cylinder block, and sends a KNK signal to the engine ECU when engine knocking is detected. The engine ECU receives the KNK signal and retards（延迟）the ignition timing to suppress the knocking.

　　爆震传感器与气缸体相连，当检测到发动机爆震时向发动机 ECU 发送 KNK 信号。发动机 ECU 收到 KNK 信号，推迟点火正时以避免爆震。

This sensor contains a piezoelectric（压电的）element, which generates an AC voltage when knocking causes vibration in the cylinder block and deforms the element.

　　该传感器包括一个压电元件，当爆震引起气缸体振动，使该元件变形，该元件就产生一个交流电压。

The engine knock frequency is in the range of 6 to 13 kHz depending on the engine model. The proper knock sensor is used in accordance with the knocking generated by each engine.

根据发动机类型的不同，发动机爆震的频率在 6 ~ 13 千赫兹之间变化。应根据每一发动机产生的爆震采用正确的爆震传感器。

There are two types of knock sensors. As can be seen from Figure 15 – 21, one type generates a high voltage in a narrow vibration frequency range, and the other generates a high voltage in a wide vibration frequency range.

共有两种类型的爆震传感器。如图 15 – 21 所示，一种类型在一个狭窄的频率范围内产生一个高电压，另一种类型在一个较宽的频率范围内产生一个高电压。

Recently some sensors that detect open and short circuits, as shown in Figure 15 – 21, have come into use. In this type of circuit, 2. 5 V is constantly supplied so the KNK signal is also output with a 2. 5 V base frequency.

如图 15 – 21 所示，近期一些能够检测开路和短路的传感器已投入使用。在这种类型的电路中，持续供给 2. 5V 电压，因此 KNK 信号也以 2. 5V 为基准输出。

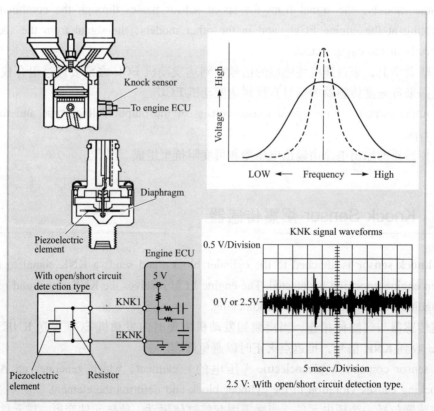

Figure 15 – 21   Knock sensor

15.10 STA (Starter) Signal/NSW (Neutral Start Switch) Signal
STA (启动) 信号/NSW (空挡启动开关) 信号

1. STA (Starter) Signal STA (启动) 信号

The STA signal is used to detect whether or not the engine is cranking (开动).

使用 STA 信号检测发动机是否启动。

The main role of the signal is to gain approval (批准) from the engine ECU to increase the fuel injection volume during cranking.

信号的主要任务是获得 ECU 的批准，在启动过程中增加燃料喷射量。

As can be seen from the circuit diagram (See Figure 15 – 22), the STA signal detects in the engine ECU the same voltage that is supplied to the starter.

如图 15 – 22 中的电路图所示，STA 信号检测的发动机 ECU 电压与供给起动机的电压相同。

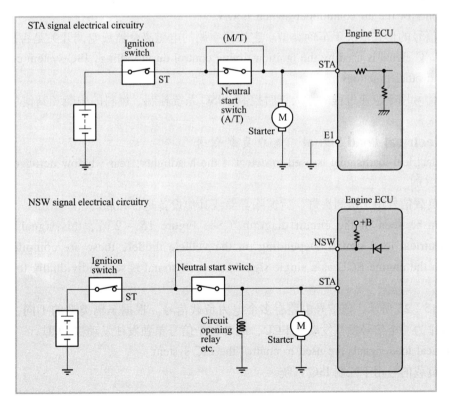

Figure 15 – 22　STA (starter) signal/NSW (neutral start switch) signal electrical circuitry

2. NSW（Neutral Start Switch）Signal　NSW（空挡启动开关）信号

This signal is only used in vehicles with an automatic transaxle, and is used to detect the shift lever position. The engine ECU uses this signal to determine if the shift lever is in the "P" or "N" position, or other position. The NSW signal is mainly used to control the ISC system.

该信号只用于自动驱动桥的车辆，用来检测换挡杆位置。发动机 ECU 用该信号决定换挡杆是在 "P" 或 "N" 位置，还是在其他位置。NSW 信号主要用来控制 ISC 系统。

15.11　A/C（Air Conditioner）Signal/Electrical Load Signal A/C（空调）信号/电力负载信号

1. A/C（Air Conditioner）Signal　A/C（空调）信号

The A/C signal differs depending on the vehicle model. It detects if the magnetic clutch of the air conditioner or the air conditioner switch is ON.

A/C 信号的形式取决于车辆类型。它检测空调的电磁离合器或空调开关是否打开。

The A/C signal is used by the ignition timing control during idling, ISC system control, fuel cut-off, and other functions.

A/C 信号用于怠速过程的点火正时控制、ISC 系统控制、燃料的中断和其他功能。

2. Electrical Load Signal　电力负载信号

The electrical load signal is used to detect if the headlights, rear window defogger, or other devices are ON.

电力负载信号用于检测头灯、后窗除雾器或其他设备是否开启。

As can be seen in the circuit diagram（See Figure 15 – 23）, this signal circuit has several electrical load signals. Depending on the vehicle model, these are compiled together and sent to the engine ECU as a single signal, or each signal is sent individually to the engine ECU.

如图 15 – 23 所示，该信号电路有多个电力负载信号。根据车辆类型的不同，它们被组合在一起作为一个信号发往发动机 ECU，或者每个信号单独发往发动机 ECU。

Electrical load signals are used to control the ISC system.

电力负载信号用于控制 ISC 系统。

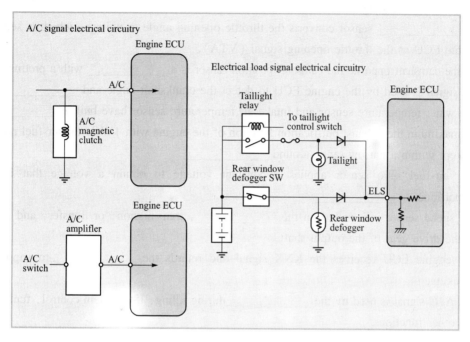

Figure 15 – 23   A/C (air conditioner) signal/electrical load signal electrical circuitry

Key Words

injection duration   喷油持续期
mechanism   机构
signal   信号
TDC (Top Dead Center)   上死点
TWC (Three-Way Catalytic Converter)   三元催化转化器
theoretical air-fuel ratio   理论空气 – 燃料比
transaxle   驱动桥
knock sensor   爆震传感器

Exercises

1. Signal of the intake air mass or volume is used to calculate _____ and basic ignition advance angle.

2. By means of an IC built into this sensor, the _____ sensor senses the intake manifold

pressure as a PIM signal.

3. The _____ sensor converts the throttle opening angle to voltage, which is sent to the engine ECU as the throttle opening signal (VTA).

4. On the camshaft opposite the camshaft position sensor is a _____ with a protrusion(s).

5. NE signal is used by the engine ECU to detect the crankshaft angle and _____.

6. The water temperature sensor and intake air temperature sensor have built in _____.

7. To maximum the exhaust purification function of the engine with TWC, the air-fuel ratio must be kept within a narrow range around _____.

8. The air-fuel ratio sensor applies a constant voltage to obtain a voltage that is nearly proportional to _____.

9. The speed sensor is installed on the _____, transmission, or transfer, and is driven by the drive gear of the output shaft.

10. The engine ECU receives the KNK signal and retards the _____ to suppress the knocking.

11. The A/C signal is used by the _____ during idling, ISC system control, fuel cut-off, and other functions.

Unit 16

EFI（Electronic Fuel Injection）
电子燃料喷射系统

EFI	fuel pump
ESA	pressure regulator
ISC	injector
diagnostic system	

16.1 Description 概述

The EFI system uses various sensors to detect the engine condition and vehicle running condition. And the engine ECU calculates the optimum fuel injection volume, and causes the **injectors** to inject the fuel. Figure 16 - 1 shows the basic EFI configuration.

EFI 系统使用各种传感器检测发动机运行条件和汽车行驶条件。发动机 ECU 计算最佳燃料喷射量，控制喷油器喷射燃料。图 16 - 1 显示了 EFI 的基本配置。

1. Engine ECU 发动机 ECU
This calculates the optimum fuel injection duration based on the signals from the sensors.
用于根据传感器的信号计算最佳喷油持续期。

2. Air Flow Meter or Manifold Pressure Sensor
空气流量计或进气歧管压力传感器
This detects the intake air mass or manifold pressure.
用于检测进气空气质量或进气歧管压力。

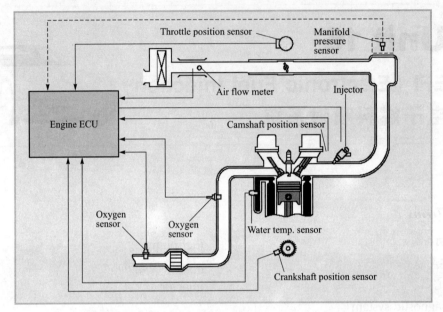

Figure 16 – 1   Electronic fuel injection system configuration

3. Crankshaft Position Sensor   曲轴位置传感器

This detects the crank angle and engine speed.

用于检测曲轴转角和发动机速度。

4. Camshaft Position Sensor   凸轮轴位置传感器

This detects the standard crank angle and the camshaft timing.

用于检测标准曲轴转角和凸轮轴定时。

5. Water Temperature Sensor   水温传感器

This detects the coolant temperature.

用于检测冷却液温度。

6. Throttle Position Sensor   节气门位置传感器

This detects the throttle valve opening angle.

用于检测节气门开启角度。

7. Oxygen Sensor   氧传感器

This detects the oxygen concentration in the exhaust gas.

用于检测排气中氧的浓度。

16.2　Types of EFI　EFI 的类型

There are two types of EFI system classified by the amount of the intake air detection method （See Figure 16 – 2）.

根据进气空气量的检测方法，可以将 EFI 系统分成两种类型（见图 16 – 2）。

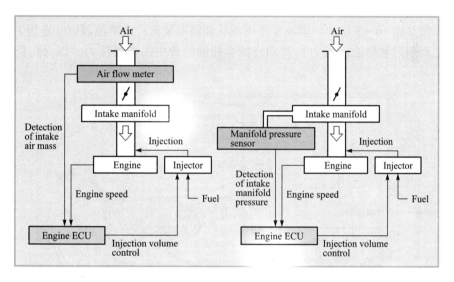

Figure 16 – 2　Types of EFI

1. L-EFI（Air-flow Control Type）　L 型 EFI（空气流量控制型）

This type uses an air flow meter to detect the amount of the air flowing in the intake manifold.

该类型使用空气流量计检测进气歧管内的空气流量。

There are two types of detection methods: One directly measures the intake air mass, and one makes corrections based on the air volume.

有两种检测方法：一种直接测量进气空气质量，另一种根据进气空气体积进行修正。

2. D-EFI（Manifold Pressure Control Type）　D 型 EFI（进气歧管压力控制型）

This type measures the pressure in the intake manifold to detect the amount of the intake air using the intake air density.

该类型测量进气歧管内的压力，使用进气密度推算出进气流量。

16.3 Fuel System 燃油系统

The fuel system is shown in Figure 16－3. The fuel is taken from the fuel tank by the fuel pump and sprayed（喷射）under pressure by an injector. The fuel pressure in the fuel line must be regulated（控制）to maintain stable fuel injection by the pressure regulator（调节器）and pulsation damper.

燃油系统如图 16－3 所示。燃油泵将燃油从油箱中泵出，由喷油器以一定压力喷射。必须通过压力调节器和燃油（压力）脉动衰减器控制油管中的燃油压力，以保持稳定的燃油喷射。

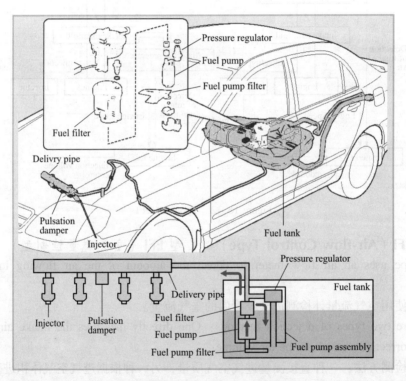

Figure 16－3 Fuel system

16. 3. 1 Fuel Pump 燃油泵

The fuel pump is installed in the fuel tank and is integrated with the fuel filter, pressure regulator, fuel sender gauge, etc.（See Figure 16－4）.

燃油泵安装在油箱内，和燃油滤清器、压力调节器、感应塞等零件集成在一起（见图 16－4）。

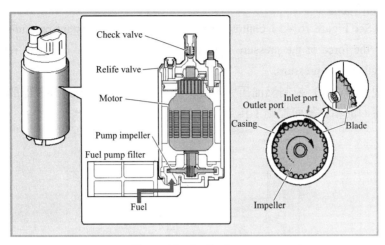

Figure 16 – 4   Fuel pump

The pump impeller (叶轮) is turned by the motor to compress the fuel.

发动机驱动油泵叶轮压缩燃油。

The check valve (控制阀) closes when the fuel pump is stopped to maintain the pressure in the fuel line and make it easier to restart the engine.

当然油泵停止时，控制阀关闭，保持油管中的压力稳定，使发动机的再次起动更容易。

If there is no residual pressure, vapor lock (蒸汽阻塞) can easily occur at high temperatures, making restarting difficult.

如果没有残余压力的存在，高温时就会发生蒸汽阻塞现象，重新起动会变得困难。

The relief valve (减压阀) opens when the pressure on the outlet side becomes too high in order to prevent the fuel pressure from becoming too high.

当出口压力过高时减压阀打开，防止燃油压力过高。

16.3.2 Pressure Regulator   压力调节器

The pressure regulator controls the fuel pressure to the injector at 324 kPa (3.3 kgf/cm^2). (Values may differ depending on engine models.)

压力调节器控制到达喷油器的燃油压力为 324 千帕（3.3 千克力/平方厘米）。（该值会随着发动机的类型而变化。）

In addition, the pressure regulator maintains the residual pressure in the fuel line in the same way as the fuel pump check valve.

另外，压力调节器采用和燃油泵控制阀同样的方法保持油管中的残余压力。

There are two types of fuel regulation methods.

共有两种控制燃油压力的方法。

1. Type 1　类型1

This type（See Figure 16 – 5）controls the fuel pressure at a constant pressure. When the fuel pressure exceeds the force of the pressure regulator's spring, the valve opens to return fuel to the fuel tank and regulate the pressure.

该类型（见图 16 – 5）控制燃油压力不变。当燃油压力超过压力调节器的弹簧力时，阀门打开，燃油流回油箱，从而控制了压力。

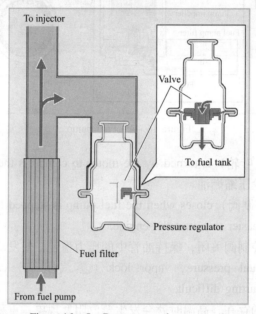

To injector

Valve

To fuel tank

Pressure regulator

Fuel filter

From fuel pump

Figure 16 – 5　Pressure regulator, type 1

2. Type 2　类型2

This type（See Figure 16 – 6）is equipped with a delivery pipe that continually regulates the fuel pressure to keep the fuel pressure higher than a determined pressure from the manifold pressure.

该类型（见图 16 – 6）安装有一根传输管，持续控制燃油压力，保持燃油压力比进气歧管内的压力高。

The basic operation is the same as type 1, but because the manifold vacuum is applied to the diaphragm's upper chamber（上腔室），the fuel pressure is controlled by changing the fuel pressure when the valve is opened in accordance with the manifold vacuum.

其基本的操作和类型 1 相同，但是由于进气歧管真空度作用在膜片的上腔室，当阀门根据进气歧管真空度而相应开启一定角度时，燃油压力发生变化。

The fuel is returned to the fuel tank via the fuel return pipe（回油管）.

燃油通过回油管回到燃油箱。

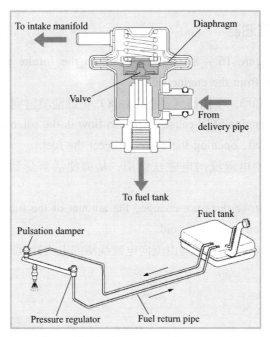

Figure 16-6   Pressure regulator, type 2

16.3.3   Pulsation Damper   燃油（压力）脉动衰减器

The pulsation damper (See Figure 16-7) uses a diaphragm (薄膜) to absorb a slight amount of fuel pressure pulsation generated by the fuel injection and the compression of the fuel pump.

燃油（压力）脉动衰减器（见图 16-7）使用一块薄膜来吸收燃料喷射和燃油泵的压缩产生的少量燃油压力脉动。

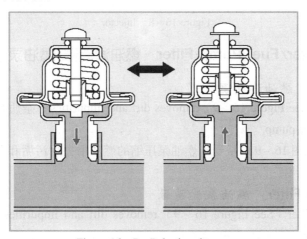

Figure 16-7   Pulsation damper

16. 3. 4　Injector　喷油器

The injector（See Figure 16 – 8）injects fuel into the **intake ports** of the cylinders in accordance with the signal from the engine ECU.

根据发动机 ECU 的信号，喷油器（见图 16 – 8）把燃油喷射到气缸的进气口。

The signals from the engine ECU cause current to flow in the solenoid coil, which causes the plunger（活塞）to be pulled, opening the valve to inject the fuel.

发动机 ECU 的信号使电流流向电磁铁线圈，从而使活塞受到吸引，阀门打开，喷射燃油。

Because the plunger stroke does not change, the amount of the fuel injection is controlled at the time the current is flowed to the solenoid.

由于活塞行程不变，燃料喷射数量由流向电磁线圈的电流持续时间控制。

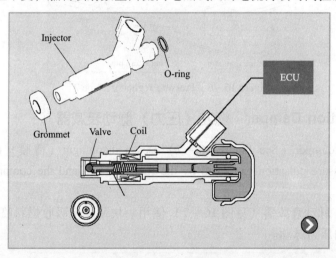

Figure 16 – 8　Injector

16. 3. 5　Fuel Filter/Fuel Pump Filter　燃油滤清器/燃油泵滤清器

1.　Fuel Filter　*燃油滤清器*
The fuel filter（See Figure 16 – 9）removes dirt and impurities（杂质）from the fuel that is compressed by the fuel pump.

燃油滤清器（见图 16 – 9）从受到燃油泵压缩的燃油中去除污垢和杂质。

2.　Fuel Pump Filter　*燃油泵滤清器*
The fuel pump filter（See Figure 16 – 9）removes dirt and impurities from the fuel before entering the fuel pump.

在燃油进入燃油泵之前，燃油泵滤清器（见图 16 – 9）从燃油中去除污垢和杂质。

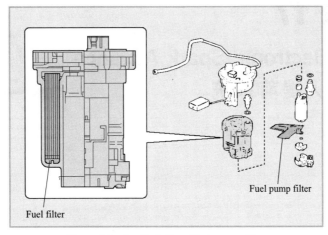

Figure 16 – 9　Fuel filter/fuel pump filter

K ey Words

injector　喷油器　　　　　　intake port　进气口

Exercises

1. The fuel pressure in the fuel line must be _____ to maintain stable fuel injection by the pressure regulator and pulsation damper.

2. When the fuel pressure exceeds the force of the pressure regulator's spring, _____ opens to return fuel to the fuel tank and regulate the pressure.

3. Because _____ , the amount of the fuel injection is controlled at the time the current is flowed to the solenoid.

Unit 17
ESA (Electronic Spark Advance)
电子点火提前系统

ESA

IGT signal and IGF signal

The ESA (Electronic Spark Advance) system (See Figure 17 – 1) is a system that uses the engine ECU to determine the ignition timing based on the signals from the various sensors.

ESA（电子点火提前）系统（见图 17 – 1）使用发动机 ECU 根据各种传感器的信号决定点火正时。

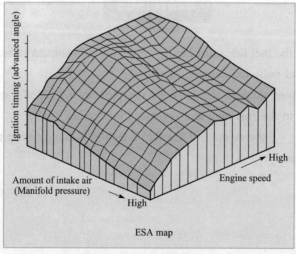

Figure 17 – 1   ESA map

The engine ECU calculates the ignition timing from the optimum ignition timing stored in memory to match the engine conditions, and then sends the ignition signal to the igniter.

发动机 ECU 从存储在内存中的最佳点火定时计算实际点火定时，与发动机运行条件相匹配，然后向点火器发出点火控制信号。

The optimum ignition timing is basically determined using engine speed and intake air mass（manifold pressure）.

最佳点火定时主要由发动机转速和进气空气质量（进气歧管压力）决定。

As shown in Figure 17 – 2, the ESA system consists of the various sensors, engine ECU, igniters, ignition coil, and spark plugs.

如图 17 – 2 所示，ESA 系统由各种传感器、发动机 ECU、点火器、点火线圈和火花塞组成。

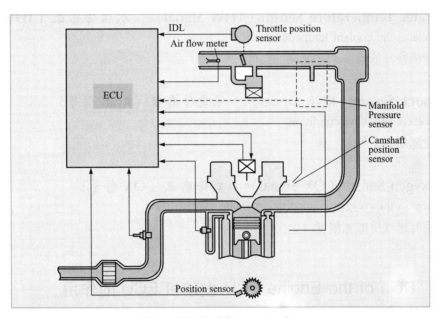

Figure 17 – 2　ESA construction

17.1　Role of the Sensors 传感器的作用

1. Camshaft Position Sensor（G Signal）　凸轮轴位置传感器（G 信号）
This detects the standard crank angle and the camshaft timing.
用于检测标准曲轴转角和凸轮轴定时。

2. Crankshaft Position Sensor（NE Signal）　曲轴位置传感器（NE 信号）
This detects the crank angle and engine speed.
用于检测曲轴转角和发动机速度。

3. Air Flow Meter or Manifold Pressure Sensor（VG or PIM Signal）
空气流量计或进气歧管压力传感器（VG 或 PIM 信号）

This detects the intake air mass or manifold pressure.

用于检测进气空气质量或进气歧管压力。

4. Throttle Position Sensor（IDL Signal）　节气门位置传感器（IDL 信号）

This detects the idling condition.

用于检测怠速条件。

5. Water Temperature Sensor（THW Signal）　水温传感器（THW 信号）

This detects the coolant temperature.

用于检测冷却液温度。

6. Knock Sensor（KNK Signal）　爆震传感器（KNK 信号）

This detects knocking condition.

用于检测爆震条件。

7. Oxygen Sensor（OX Signal）　氧传感器（OX 信号）

This detects the oxygen concentration in the exhaust gas.

用于检测排气中的氧浓度。

17.2　Role of the Engine ECU 发动机 ECU 的作用

The engine ECU receives the signals from the sensors, calculates the optimum ignition timing for the engine conditions, and sends the ignition signal to the igniter.

发动机 ECU 接收传感器的信号，计算与发动机工况相符的最佳点火定时，向点火器发出点火信号。

17.3　Role of the Igniter 点火器的作用

The igniter responds to the ignition signal（IGT）output by the engine ECU to intermittently apply the **primary current** to the ignition coil. It also sends the ignition confirmation signal（IGF） to the engine ECU.

点火器对发动机 ECU 输出的点火信号（IGT）立刻做出反应，在点火线圈中产生初级电流。它也向发动机 ECU 发出一个点火确认信号（IGF）。

17.4 Ignition Circuitry 点火电路

The ignition circuitry is shown in Figure 17 – 3.

点火电路如图 17 – 3 所示。

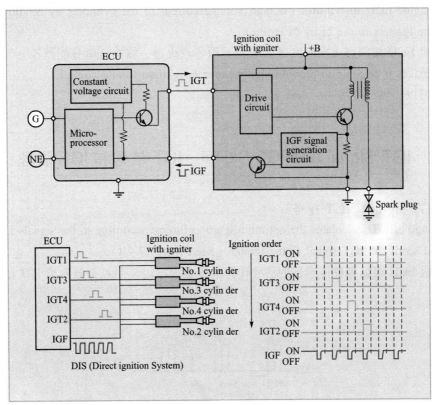

Figure 17 – 3   Ignition circuitry

The engine ECU determines the ignition timing based on the G signal, NE signal and the signals from other various sensors.

发动机 ECU 根据 G 信号、NE 信号和其他各种传感器的信号确定点火定时。

When the ignition timing has been determined, the engine ECU sends the IGT signal to the igniter.

当点火定时确定后，发动机 ECU 向点火器发出 IGT 信号。

While the IGT signal sent to the igniter is ON, the primary current flows to the ignition coil. While the IGT signal turns OFF, the primary current to the ignition coil is shut off.

当送往点火器的 IGT 信号启动，初级电流流向点火线圈。当 IGT 信号关闭，流向点火线圈的初级电流被切断。

At the same time, the IGF signal is sent to the engine ECU.

同时，IGF 信号被送往发动机 ECU。

Currently, the main ignition circuitry used is the DIS (Direct Ignition System).

目前，主要使用的点火电路是 DIS（直接点火系统）。

The engine ECU **distributes** the high voltage current to the cylinders by sending each IGT signal to the igniters in the order of ignition.

发动机 ECU 按照点火次序发送 IGT 信号给各点火器，将高压电分配到各个气缸。

This makes it possible to provide highly accurate ignition timing control.

这就可以提供高度准确的点火定时控制。

17.5　IGT Signal and IGF Signal　IGT 信号和 IGF 信号

1. IGT Signal　IGT 信号

The engine ECU calculates the optimum ignition timing according to the signals from various sensors and sends the IGT signal to the igniter (See Figure 17 – 4).

发动机 ECU 根据各种传感器的信号计算最佳点火定时，向点火器发出 IGT 信号（见图 17 – 4）。

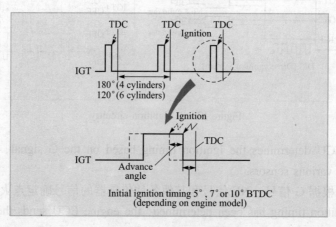

Figure 17 – 4　IGT signal

The IGT signal is turned ON immediately before the ignition timing calculated by the microprocessor（微处理器）in the engine ECU, and then is turned OFF. When the IGT signal is turned OFF, the spark plug sparks.

在发动机 ECU 中的微处理器计算的点火定时之前，IGT 信号立刻开启，然后关闭。当 IGT 信号关闭，火花塞点火。

2. IGF Signal   IGF 信号

The igniter sends an IGF signal（See Figure 17 – 5）to the engine ECU by using the counter-electromotive force that is generated when the primary current to the ignition coil is shut off or by using the primary current volume. When the engine ECU receives the IGF signal, it determines that ignition occurred.（This does not mean, however, that there was actually a spark.）

点火器使用流向点火线圈的初级电流被切断时产生的反电动势或者初级电流量向发动机 ECU 发出 IGF 信号（见图 17 – 5）。当发动机 ECU 接收到 IGF 信号，它推断点火发生了（然而，这并不意味着一个事实上的火花）。

If the engine ECU does not receive an IGF signal, the diagnosis function operates and a DTC（Diagnostic Trouble Code 故障诊断码）is stored in the engine ECU and the fail-safe function operates and stops injecting fuel.

如果发动机 ECU 没有收到 IGF 信号，诊断功能启动，DTC（故障诊断码）被存储在发动机 ECU 中，而且自动防故障功能启动，喷油停止。

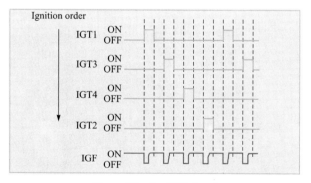

Figure 17 – 5   IGF signal

 ey Words

| primary current   初级电流 | distribute   分配 |

Exercises

1. The engine ECU calculates _____ to match the engine conditions by receiving signals from various sensors.

2. The engine ECU sends _____ to the igniter.

3. The igniter responds to the IGT signal output by the engine ECU to intermittently apply the primary current to _____ .

4. The igniter sends the ignition confirmation signal (IGF) to the engine ECU when the spark plug sparks. (True/False)

Unit 18

ISC (Idle Speed Control)
怠速控制系统

Key Terms

ISC (Idle Speed Control)
ISCV (Idle Speed Control Valve)

18.1 Description 概述

The ISC (Idle Speed Control) system is provided with a circuit that bypasses (设旁路) the throttle valve, and the air volume drawn in from the bypass circuit is controlled by the ISCV (Idle Speed Control Valve).

怠速控制系统提供了一个节气门旁路，从旁路进入的空气体积由 ISCV（怠速控制阀）控制。

The ISCV uses the signal from the engine ECU to control the engine at the optimum idling speed at all times.

ISCV 使用发动机 ECU 发出的信号控制发动机始终在最佳怠速转速下运行。

As shown in Figure 18 – 1, the ISC system consists of the ISCV, engine ECU, and various sensors and switches.

如图 18 – 1 所示，ISC 系统由 ISCV、发动机 ECU、各种传感器和开关组成。

1. When Starting 启动时

The bypass circuit is opened to improve start ability (启动性能).

旁路管路打开，以提高启动性能。

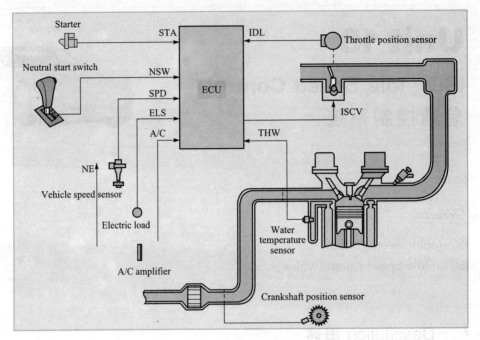

Figure 18 – 1   Idle speed control system

2. When Warming-up the Engine   暖机时

When the coolant temperature is low, the idling speed is increased so that the engine runs smoothly (fast idle).

当冷却液温度降低时，急速转速提高，使发动机运行稳定（快急速）。

As the coolant temperature rises, the idling speed is decreased.

当冷却液温度升高时，急速转速下降。

3. Feedback Control and Estimate Control   反馈控制和估计控制

In the following cases, if the load increases or changes, the idle speed is increased or prevented from changing.

(1) When A/C is used.

(2) When headlights are used.

(3) When the shift lever is shifted from N to D or from D to N while the vehicle is stopped.

在下述情况下，如果负荷增加或变化，急速转速增加或保持不变。

(1) 当使用空调时。

(2) 当头灯打开时。

(3) 在停车的情况下换挡杆由 N 挡换到 D 挡或由 D 挡换到 N 挡时。

18.2 Types of ISCV   ISCV 的类型

The ISCV (See Figure 18 - 2) is a device that controls the amount of the intake air during idling using the signal from the engine ECU and controls the idling speed.

ISCV（见图 18 - 2）是控制怠速期间进气量的设备，它使用发动机 ECU 提供的信号控制怠速转速。

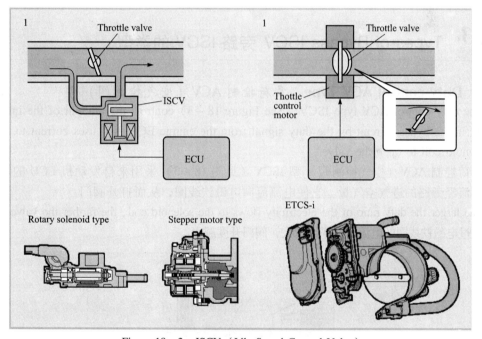

Figure 18 - 2   ISCV (Idle Speed Control Valve)

There are two types of ISCV as follows.

共有以下两种类型的 ISCV。

1. Type That Bypasses the Throttle Valve and Controls the Amount of the Intake Air 旁路节气门控制进气量型

Because the throttle valve is completely closed during idling, the ISCV bypasses the required air volume during idling.

由于节气门在怠速期间完全关闭，ISCV 在怠速期间设旁路得到所需的空气量。

2. Type That Controls the Amount of the Intake Air Using the Throttle Valve 使用节气门控制进气量型

With this type, the throttle valve proper controls the amount of the intake air during idling.
该类型的节气门控制怠速期间的进气量。

This system is called ETCS-i (Electronic Throttle Control System-intelligent), and conducts other control functions in addition to amount of the intake air control during idling.
该系统被称为 ETCS-i（电子节气门控制系统 - 智能型），除了控制怠速期间的进气量，还有其他控制功能。

18.3 Types of Bypass ISCV 旁路 ISCV 的类型

1. Duty-control ACV Type 负荷控制 ACV（空气控制阀）型

The duty-control ACV type ISCV (See Figure 18 - 3) controls the amount of the intake air flowing in the bypass circuit by the duty signal from the engine ECU. It causes current to flow to the solenoid coil to open the valve.
负荷控制 ACV（空气控制阀）型 ISCV（见图 18 - 3）采用来自发动机 ECU 的负荷信号控制流经旁路的进气空气量。它使电流流向电磁铁线圈，从而打开阀门。

The larger the duty ratio of the electricity flows to the solenoid coil, the farther the valve opens.
流过电磁铁线圈的电流的能率比越大，阀门开度越大。

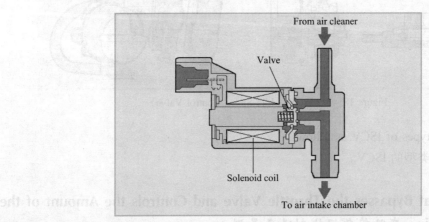

Figure 18 - 3   Duty-control ACV type of bypass ISCV

2. ON-OFF Control VSV Type 开关控制 VSV 型

The ON-OFF control VSV type ISCV (See Figure 18 - 4) controls the amount of the intake air flowing in the bypass circuit by the ON/OFF signal from the engine ECU. It causes current to flow to the solenoid coil to open the valve.

开关控制 VSV 型 ISCV（见图 18 - 4）采用来自发动机 ECU 的开/关信号控制流经旁路的进气空气量。它使电流流向电磁铁线圈，从而打开阀门。

When current flows to the solenoid coil, the idling speed is increased in increments of approx. 100 rpm.

当电流流向电磁铁线圈时，怠速转速以大约 100 转/分的增量增加。

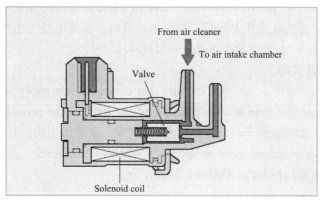

Figure 18 - 4   ON-OFF control VSV type of bypass ISCV

3. Rotary Solenoid Type   旋转螺线管型

The rotary solenoid type ISCV (See Figure 18 - 5) consists of a coil, IC, permanent magnet, valve, and is attached to the throttle body.

旋转螺线管型 ISCV（见图 18 - 5）由线圈、集成电路、永磁体、阀门组成，连接在节气门体上。

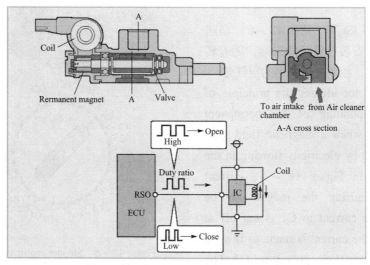

Figure 18 - 5   Rotary solenoid type ISCV

The IC uses the **duty** signal from the engine ECU to control the direction and amount of current that flows in the coil and control the amount of air that bypasses the throttle valve, rotating the valve.

集成电路使用发动机 ECU 提供的负荷信号控制流经线圈的电流的方向和数量，转动阀门，控制从节气门旁路流入的空气量。

When the duty ratio（能率比）is high, the IC moves the valve in the opening direction, and when the duty ratio is low, the IC moves the valve in the closing direction.

当能率比高时，集成电路开大阀门；当能率比低时，集成电路关小阀门。

The ISCV performs opening and closing in this way.

ISCV 就是这样开关的。

If there is trouble, such as an open circuit, that causes the electricity to stop flowing to the ISCV, the valve is made to open at a set position by the force of the permanent magnet.

如果有问题，比如电路断开，电流停止流向 ISCV，永磁体使阀门开启到特定位置。

This will maintain an idling speed of approx. 1, 000 to 1, 200 rpm.

这将使怠速转速维持在大约 1 000 ~1 200 转/分。

4. Stepper Motor Type 步进电机型

The stepper motor（步进电机）type ISCV（See Figure 18 – 6）is attached to the intake chamber. The valve installed at the end of the rotor is in or out by the rotation of the rotor to control the air volume flowing in the bypass circuit.

步进电机型 ISCV（见图 18 – 6）与进气室相连。阀门安装在转子的末端，随着转子的转动而进出，控制流经旁路的空气量。

The step motor utilizes the principle of pulling and rebounding of the permanent magnet (rotor) when a magnetic field（磁场）is generated by electricity flowing in the coil. As shown in Figure 18 – 6, current flows at C1 causing the magnet to be pulled. When the current to C1 is cut off at the same time, the current is made to flow to C2, and the magnet is pulled to C2. The

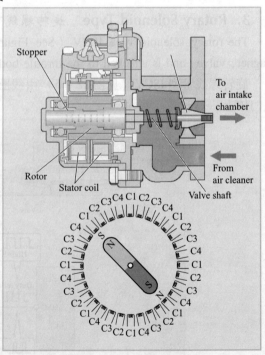

Figure 18 – 6 Stepper motor type ISCV

subsequent switching the current to in order of C3 and C4 in the same manner is used to rotate the magnet.

步进电机应用如下理论：当电流在线圈中流动时，就会产生磁场，永磁体（转子）受到牵引和回弹。如图 18 - 6 所示，电流在 C1 端流动，磁铁受到牵引。当 C1 端电流被切断，电流流向 C2，向 C2 端牵引磁铁。随后按 C3 和 C4 的顺序以同样模式通断电流，使磁铁旋转。

The magnet can also rotate in the opposite direction by switching the current in the direction from C4 to C3, C2, and C1.

按照从 C4 到 C3、C2、C1 的方向通断电流，使磁铁反方向旋转。

This arrangement is used to move the magnet to predetermined（预定）positions.

这种安排可以将磁铁移动到预定位置。

As shown in Figure 18 - 7 and Figure 18 - 8, an actual step motor uses 4 coils to create 32 steps for 1 rotation of the magnet（rotor）.（Some motors have 24 steps per rotation.）

如图 18 - 7 和图 18 - 8 所示，一个实际的步进电机使用 4 个线圈使磁铁（转子）转一圈产生 32 步。（一些转子转一圈有 24 步。）

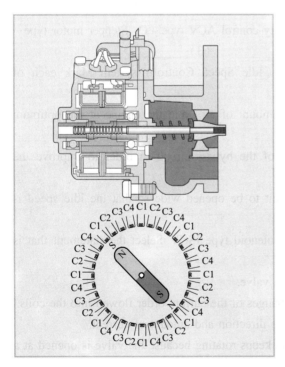

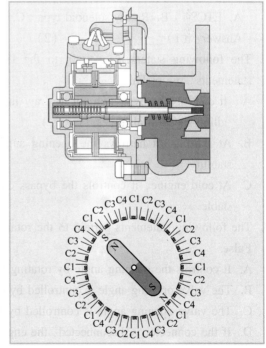

Figure 18 - 7　Stepper motor type ISCV, valve open　　Figure 18 - 8　Stepper motor type ISCV, valve close

Ⓚ ey Words

duty 负荷

Exercises

1. The following illustrations show the ISCV (Idle Speed Control Valve) types. From the following word group, select the type that correspond to each illustration.

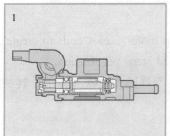
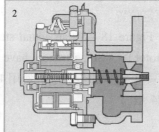
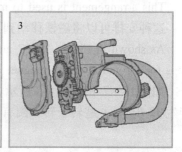

A. ETCS-i   B. Rotary solenoid type   C. Duty-control ACV type   D. Stepper motor type

Answer: (1) _____   (2) _____   (3) _____

2. The following statements pertain to the ISC (Idle Speed Control) system. Mark each of statements True or False.

A. It controls the bypass circuit to draw in (amount of air) and the engine at the optimum idling speed at all times. (   )

B. At starting, it narrows the opening angle of the bypass circuit in order to improve the stability. (   )

C. At cold engine, it controls the bypass circuit to be opened wide so that the idle speed is stable. (   )

3. The following statements pertain to the rotary solenoid type ISCV. Select the statement that is **False**.

A. It controls the opening angle by rotating the valve.

B. The valve opening angle is controlled by changes of the current order flowed into the coils.

C. The valve opening angle is controlled by the direction and amount of current.

D. If the connector is disconnected, the engine keeps rotating because the valve is opened at a constant opening angle.

Unit 19

Diagnosis System 诊断系统

Key Terms

diagnosis
MIL（Malfunction Indicator Lamp）
DTC（Diagnostic Trouble Code）
fail-safe and back-up function

The diagnosis system is shown in Figure 19 – 1.

诊断系统如图 19 – 1 所示。

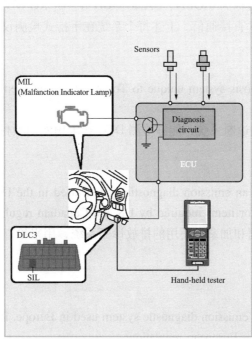

Figure 19 – 1　Diagnosis system

19.1 Description 概述

The engine ECU possesses an OBD（On-Board Diagnostic）function that constantly monitors each sensor and actuator. If it detects a malfunction, the malfunction is recorded as a **DTC** （**Diagnostic Trouble Code**）and the **MIL**（**Malfunction Indicator Lamp**）on the combination meter lights up to inform the driver.

发动机 ECU 具有车载诊断功能，一直监控着每个传感器和执行器。如果检测到一个故障，故障作为 DTC（故障诊断码）被记录，组合式仪表上的 MIL（故障指示灯）点亮，通知驾驶员。

By connecting the hand-held tester to DLC3（Data Link Connector 3）, direct communication with the engine ECU can be performed via terminal SIL to confirm the DTC.

通过将手持式检测仪连接到接口 DLC3（数据链路接口 3），终端 SIL 直接与发动机 ECU 通信，确认 DTC。

The DTC can also be confirmed by causing the MIL to blink, then checking the blinking pattern. To confirm the DTC or data recorded by the engine ECU, a diagnosis system called MOBD, CARB OBD II, EURO OBD or ENHANCED OBD II is used to communicate directly with the engine ECU. Each of these systems displays a 5-digit DTC on the hand-held tester.

通过引发 MIL 闪烁也可以确认 DTC，然后检查闪光方式。为了确认 DTC 或记录在发动机 ECU 中的数据，使用被称为 MOBD、CARB OBD II、EURO OBD 或 ENHANCED OBD II 的诊断系统与发动机 ECU 直接通信。上述每个系统在手持式检测仪上显示 5 位的 DTC。

1. MOBD

The MOBD is a diagnosis system unique to Toyota. It can be used to check the DTC or data for Toyota own items.

MOBD 是丰田专用的诊断系统，能够检测 DTC 或丰田专用项目的数据。

2. CARB OBD II

The CARB OBD II is an emission diagnostic system used in the USA and Canada. It is used to check the DTC or data for items required by US and Canadian regulations.

CARB OBD II 是美国和加拿大使用的排放诊断系统，用来检查 DTC 或美国和加拿大法规要求项目的数据。

3. EURO OBD

The EURO OBD is an emission diagnostic system used in Europe. It is used to check the DTC or data for items required by European regulations.

EURO OBD 是欧洲使用的排放诊断系统，用来检查 DTC 或欧洲法规要求项目的数据。

4. ENHANCED OBD II

The ENHANCED OBD II is a diagnostic system used in the USA and Canada. It is used to check items required by US and Canadian regulations, and check the DTC or data for Toyota own items.

ENHANCED OBD II 是美国和加拿大使用的一种诊断系统，用来检查美国和加拿大法规要求的项目，同时也用来检查 DTC 或丰田专有项目的数据。

19.2 Functions of MIL   MIL 的功能

The MIL has the following functions.

MIL 具有如下功能。

1. Lamp Check Function（Engine Stopped） 灯泡检查功能（发动机停止）

The MIL is turned on when the ignition switch is turned to ON, and it turns off when the engine speed reaches 400 rpm or more, to check whether the bulb is functioning or not（See Figure 19 – 2）.

当点火开关开启时，MIL 打开；当发动机转速达到 400 转/分或更高时关闭，检查灯泡是否能够工作（见图 19 – 2）。

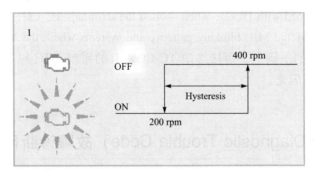

Figure 19 – 2   Lamp check function of MIL

2. Malfunction Indicator Function（Engine Running）

故障指示功能（发动机运行）

If the engine ECU detects a malfunction in a circuit, it turns on the MIL to inform the driver of a malfunction（See Figure 19 – 3）.

如果发动机 ECU 检测到电路中有故障，它便打开 MIL 通知驾驶员存在故障（见图 19 - 3）。

When the malfunction has returned to normal, the lamp goes off after 5 seconds. For CARB OBD II and EURO OBD, when a malfunction returns to normal, the MIL turns off if no malfunction is detected in three continuous driving cycles.

当故障恢复正常，5 秒后该灯关闭。对于 CARB OBD II 和 EURO OBD，当故障恢复正常时，如果在连续三个行驶循环中未检测到故障，MIL 关闭。

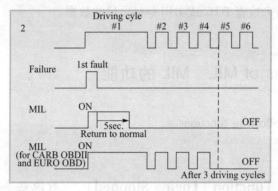

Figure 19 - 3   Malfunction indicator function of MIL

3. Diagnostic Code Display Function   诊断码显示功能

When shorted the terminals TE1-E1 on vehicles equipped with only DLC1 and DLC2, the DTC is displayed by the MIL blinking pattern.

在只有 DLC1 和 DLC2 接口的车辆上，短接终端 TE1-E1，DTC 以 MIL 闪光码的形式显示。

On vehicles equipped with DLC3, when shorted the terminals TC-CG, there are systems where the DTC is displayed by the MIL blinking pattern, and systems where the MIL does not blink.

在有 DLC3 接口的车辆上，短接终端 TC-CG，有的系统 DTC 以 MIL 闪光码的形式显示，有的系统 MIL 不闪光。

19.3 DTC（Diagnostic Trouble Code）故障诊断码

19. 3. 1   The Output of DTC   DTC 的输出

DTCs are output as either 5-digit or 2-digit codes.

故障诊断码以 2 位码或 5 位码输出。

In the Repair Manual, the detection item, detecting condition and trouble area are included for each DTC, so refer to the Repair Manual when troubleshooting.

在维修手册中，包含了故障码对应的检测项目、检测条件和故障位置，维修故障时请参考维修手册。

1. 5-digit DTCs 5位故障诊断码

For 5-digit DTCs (See Figure 19 – 4), connect the hand-held tester to DLC3 to communicate directly with the engine ECU and display the DTC on the tester screen for confirmation.

对于5位故障诊断码（见图 19 – 4），将手持式测试仪连接到 DLC3 接口，直接和发动机 ECU 通信，在测试仪屏幕上显示 DTC。

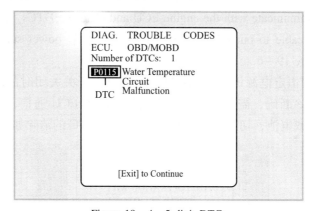

Figure 19 – 4 5-digit DTCs

2. 2-digit DTCs 2位故障诊断码

Confirm 2-digit DTCs (See Figure 19 – 5) by observing the MIL blinking pattern.

通过观察 MIL 闪光码可确认 2 位故障诊断码（见图 19 – 5）。

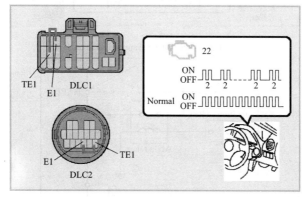

Figure 19 – 5 2-digit DTCs

Short between terminals TE1（Tc）– E1（CG）of DLC1, DLC2 or DLC3 to make the MIL blink and output the DTC.

短接 DLC1、DLC2 或 DLC3 接口的终端 TE1(Tc)– E1（CG），使 MIL 闪光输出 DTC。

Confirm the DTC using the blinking pattern of the lamp.

使用故障指示灯的闪光码可确认 DTC。

19.3.2 The Clearance of DTC DTC 的清除

The engine ECU records DTCs using a constant power supply, so DTCs are not cleared when the ignition switch is turned to off. Accordingly, in order to clear DTCs, it is necessary to use a hand-held tester to communicate with the engine ECU and clear the DTCs, or remove the EFI fuse（保险丝）or battery cable to cut off the constant engine ECU power supply. The clearance of DTC is shown in Figure 19 – 6.

发动机 ECU 使用恒定电源记录故障诊断码，当点火开关关闭时故障诊断码不会消失。因此，为了清除故障诊断码，需要手持式检测仪与发动机 ECU 通信，并清除故障诊断码，或者取下 EFI 保险丝或电池，切断发动机 ECU 的电源。DTC 的清除如图 19 – 6 所示。

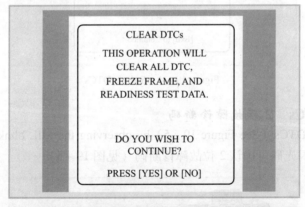

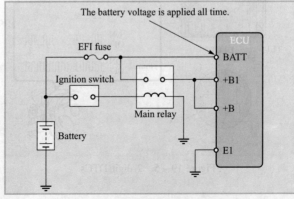

Figure 19 – 6   The Clearance of DTC

However, care is required, because cutting off the constant engine ECU power supply also clears the learning values recorded in the engine ECU memory.

然而，必须注意的是，切断发动机 ECU 的电源也会清除记录在发动机 ECU 存储器中的（与发动机控制有关的）学习数据。

19.4 Diagnostic Mode Selection Function 诊断模式选择功能

The diagnostic system has two modes: normal mode and check mode (See Figure 19 – 7).

诊断系统有两种模式：常规模式和检查模式（见图 19 – 7）。

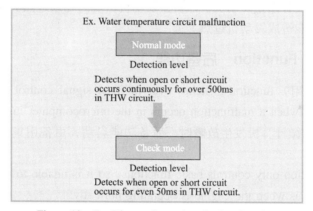

Figure 19 – 7　Diagnostic mode selection function

1. Normal Mode　正常模式

Use this mode for normal diagnosis.

使用该模式进行常规诊断。

2. Check Mode　检查模式

This mode provides higher diagnostic detection sensitivity than normal mode and makes it easier to detect malfunctions.

该模式提供比常规模式灵敏度更高的诊断检测，使故障检测更容易。

It is easier to detect DTCs in this mode when performing malfunction reproduction（再现）tests on the vehicle.

在车辆上进行故障重现检测时，在该模式下更容易检测故障诊断码。

All DTCs and the freeze frame data will be cleared at this mode.

在该模式下，所有的故障诊断码和冻结画面数据将被清除。

19.5 Fail-safe and Back-up Function 自动防故障和后备功能

19.5.1 Fail-safe Function 自动防故障功能

If the ECU detects a malfunction in any of the input signal systems, the fail-safe function controls the engine using standard values contained in the engine ECU, or stops the engine to prevent engine problems or catalytic overheating（过热）which might occur if control continued based on the circuitry with abnormal（反常）signals.

如果 ECU 在任何输出信号中检测到一个故障，自动防故障功能使用发动机 ECU 中的标准参数控制发动机，或者停止发动机，以防止发动机出现问题或过热。如果继续根据反常信号控制发动机，就可能造成发动机过热。

19.5.2 Back-up Function 后备功能

The back-up（备用）function switches over to fixed signal control by the back-up IC to permit driving in cases when a malfunction occurs in the microcomputer inside the engine ECU.

在发动机 ECU 的微计算机发生故障时，后备功能启动，由备用集成电路按固定信号进行控制。

The back-up function only controls basic functions, so it is unable to provide the same level of engine performance as when the engine is operating normally.

后备功能仅控制基本功能，因此不能保证发动机性能与正常运行时相当。

The engine ECU switches to back-up mode if the microcomputer is unable to output the ignition timing（IGT）signal.

如果微计算机不能输出点火定时（IGT）信号，发动机 ECU 启动备用功能。

When back-up mode is executed, the fuel injection duration and ignition timing are activated at their respective（独立的）fixed values in response to the starter signal（STA）and IDL signal.

执行备用模式时，喷油持续期和点火定时根据启动信号（STA）和 IDL 信号采用不相关的固定值。

The MIL also lights up to inform the driver of a malfunction. （The engine ECU does not record a DTC.）

MIL 也会点亮通知驾驶员有故障。（发动机 ECU 不记录 DTC。）

Key Words

DTC (Diagnostic Trouble Code)　　故障诊断码

MIL (Malfunction Indicator Lamp)　　故障指示灯

Exercises

1. Mark each of the following statements True or False.

   A. 5-digit DTCs can be read by connecting the hand-held tester to the DLC 3 (Data Link Connector 3) to communicate directly with the engine ECU. (　　)

   B. 2-digit DTCs can be read with the MIL (Malfunction Indicator Light) blinking pattern by shorting between terminals TE1 (TC) – E1 (CG) of DLC (Data Link Connector). (　　)

   C. The check mode of the diagnosis system provides sensitive diagnostic detection and makes it easier to detect malfunction. (　　)

2. If the engine ECU detects a malfunction, the malfunction is recorded as a DTC (Diagnostic Trouble Code) and _____ on the combination meter lights up to inform the driver.

3. When the malfunction has returned to normal, the lamp goes off after _____ seconds.

4. In order to clear DTCs, it is necessary to use a hand-held tester to communicate with the engine ECU and clear the DTCs, or remove the EFI fuse or battery cable to _____ the constant engine ECU power supply.

5. The engine ECU switches to _____ if the microcomputer is unable to output the ignition timing (IGT) signal.

4

Part

Vehicle Maintenance
汽车维修

Unit 20

Maintenance Schedule
维修计划

maintenance schedule interval	owner checks and services
engine oil viscosity	periodic maintenance inspection
chassis lubrication	tire and wheel inspection and rotation

20.1 Normal Vehicle Use 车辆的日常使用

The maintenance instructions contained in this Maintenance Schedule are based on the assumption（假设）that the vehicle will be used as designed：

- Carry passengers and cargo（货物）within the recommended limitations as indicated on the Tire Placard located on the edge（边缘）of the driver's door.
- Are driven on reasonable road surfaces within legal（合法的）driving limits.
- Driven **off-road** in the recommended manner. For information on the recommended driving manners, refer to the Owner's Manual
- On unleaded（无铅的）gasoline of the recommended type. For information on the proper type of fuel to use, refer to the Owner's Manual.

本维修计划中的保养守则基于车辆将按照设计条件使用。

- 装载的乘客和货物不超过位于驾驶员一侧车门边缘的轮胎标签上注明的推荐限制。
- 在合法的驾驶限制下在合理的路面上驾驶。
- 按推荐方式驾驶汽车越野。关于推荐的驾驶方式的信息，请参考用户手册。
- 使用推荐品牌的无铅汽油。关于合适的燃料型号情况，请参考用户手册。

20.2 Maintenance Schedule Intervals 保养计划的间隔时间

The services shown in this schedule up to 166,000 km (100,000 mi) should be performed after 166,000 km (100,000 mi) at the same intervals （间隔）. The services shown in this schedule to be performed at 240,000 km (150,000 mi) should be performed after 240,000 km (150,000 mi) at the same intervals.

计划中 166 000 km（100 000 mi）以上的服务项目在行驶 166 000 km（100 000 mi）后以相同的间隔时间执行。计划中 240 000 km（150 000 mi）以上的服务项目在行驶 240 000 km（150 000 mi）后以相同的间隔时间执行。

20.3 Engine Oil Change Intervals 发动机机油更换间隔时间

The vehicle is equipped with an Oil Life System. The Oil Life System will show when to change the engine oil and oil filter. This will usually occur between 5,000 km (3,000 mi) and 16,000 km (10,000 mi) since the last oil change. Under severe （严酷） conditions, the indicator （指示灯） may come on before 5,000 km (3,000 mi).

汽车装备了机油寿命系统。机油寿命系统将会显示何时更换发动机机油和机油滤清器。通常在最后一次更换机油后行驶 5 000 km（3 000 mi）到 16 000 km（10 000 mi）之间更换。在严酷条件下指示灯会在行驶 5 000 km（3 000 mi）之前亮起。

Never drive the vehicle more than 16,000 km (10,000 mi) or 12months without an oil and oil filter change. The system will not detect dust （灰尘） in the oil. If the vehicle is driven in a dusty area, be sure to change the oil and oil filter every 5,000 km (3,000 mi) or sooner if the CHANGE OIL SOON indicator comes on. Reset the Oil Life System when the oil and filter have been changed.

从不驾驶车辆行驶超过 16 000 km（10 000 mi）或 12 个月而没有更换机油和机油滤清器。该系统将不检测机油中的灰尘。如果车辆在满是灰尘的地区行驶，保证每 5 000 km（3 000 mi）更换机油和机油滤清器。如果"尽快更换机油"指示灯亮起，立刻更换机油和机油滤清器。更换机油和机油滤清器后重置机油寿命系统。

20.3.1 Engine Oil Quality 发动机机油品质

Oils of the proper quality for the vehicle can be identified by looking for the STARBURST symbol （See Figure 20 – 1）. The STARBURST symbol indicates that the oil has been certified by the American Petroleum （石油） Institute （API）, and is preferred for use in gasoline engines.

通过找到"STARBURST"标签（见图 20 - 1），确认用于车辆的合适品质的机油。"STARBURST"标签表示该机油经过美国石油学会认证，首选用于汽油机。

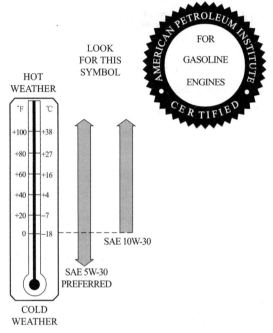

RECOMMENOED SAE VISCOSITY GRADE ENGINE OILS

FOR BEST FUEL ECONOMY AND COLD STARTING, SELECT THE LOWEST SAE VISCQSITY GRADE OIL FOR THE EXPECTED TEMPERATURE RANGE.

LOOK FOR THIS SYMBOL

AMERICAN PETROLEUM INSTITUTE

FOR GASOLINE ENGINES

CER TIFIED

HOT WEATHER

SAE 10W-30

SAE 5W-30 PREFERRED

COLD WEATHER

DO NOT USE SAE 20W-50 OR ANY OTHER GRADE OIL NOT RECOMMENDED

Figure 20 - 1　The STARBURST symbol

20. 3. 2　Engine Oil Viscosity　发动机机油黏度

The recommended oil viscosity（黏度）is SAE 5W – 30. Engine oil viscosity, or thickness, has an effect on the fuel economy and on the cold-weather operation, such as starting and oil flow. Lower viscosity engine oils can provide better fuel economy and cold-weather performance. However, higher temperature weather conditions require higher viscosity engine oils for satisfactory lubrication. Use SAE 10W-30 when the temperature is consistently above − 18℃ (0 ℉). SAE 20W-50 or oils of other viscosity rating or quality designations are NOT recommended for use in any trucks at any time.

推荐的机油黏度是 SAE 5W-30。发动机机油黏度或浓度，对燃料经济性和寒冷季节的运行，例如起动和机油的流动有影响。较低黏度的发动机机油能提供更好的燃油经济性和寒冷气候下的性能。然而，高温气候条件要求更高黏度的发动机机油，以满足润滑要求。当温度始终在 −18℃（0 ℉）以上时，使用 SAE 10W‑30。SAE 20W‑50 或者其他黏度或品质的机油在任何时候在任何卡车上均不推荐使用。

20.4 Chassis Lubrication 底盘润滑

Lubricate（加润滑油）the chassis components with each engine oil and filter change. Lubricate the front suspension, ball joints（接合处）, steering linkage（连接）, transmission shift linkage, transfer case shift linkage, parking brake cable guides, and brake front axle. Ball joints should not be lubricated unless（除非）their temperature is −12℃（10 ℉）or higher, or they could be damaged.

每次更换发动机机油和滤清器时要为底盘部件加润滑油。为前悬、球窝接头、转向联动装置、变速器杆连接处、分动器杆连接处、停车制动闸线导轮和制动前轴加润滑油。除非温度达到 −12℃（10 ℉）或更高，球窝接头不应该加润滑油，否则会被损坏。

Refer to the illustration shown in Figure 20 − 2 and Figure 20 − 3 for the location of the lubrication points for the chassis. Lubricate the following components:

- The transmission shift linkage;
- The park brake guides;
- The underbody contact points;
- The underbody linkage.

参照图 20 − 2 和图 20 − 3 中的示意图找到底盘润滑点的位置，并润滑下列部件:

- 变速器杆连接处；
- 停车制动闸线导轮；
- 底部的接触点；
- 底部的连接。

When lubricating joints that have grease fittings, refer to Figure 20 − 4 for the location of the grease fittings.

当向带有油嘴的结合处加润滑油时，可参照图 20 − 4 找到油嘴的位置。

Apply grease（油脂）slowly while watching the grease seal. Apply the grease until the grease is seen bleeding（流出）from the seal. If the seal expands（张开）but you do not see any grease, do not apply any more grease. Allow time for the grease to bleed from the seal.

一边慢慢加入油脂，一边观察油封。加入油脂，直到看见油脂从密封件里流出。如果油封张开，但没有看到油脂，不要再加入油脂，要等待油脂从油封里流出。

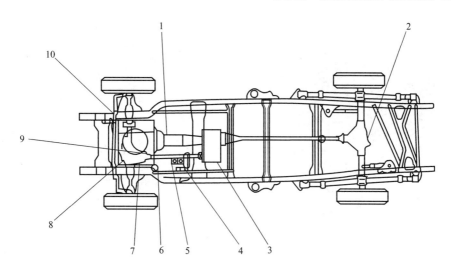

Figure 20 – 2　Lubrication points（4WD）

1. Transmission	变速器	2. Rear Axle Differential	后轴差速器
3. Transfer Case	分动器	4. Clutch Actuator	离合执行器
5. Brake Master Cylinder	制动主缸	6. Oil Filter	燃油滤清器
7. Engine	发动机	8. Front Axle Differential	前轴差速器
9. Front Propeller Shaft	前驱动轴	10. Steering Linkage	转向拉杆

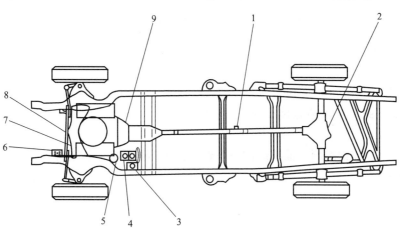

Figure 20 – 3　Lubrication points（rear-wheel drive）

1. Propeller Shaft Slip Joint	传动轴接头	2. Rear Axle Differential	后轴差速器
3. Clutch Actuator	离合执行器	4. Master Cylinder	主缸
5. Oil Filter	燃油滤清器	6. Steering Gear	转向器
7. Engine	发动机	8. Steering Linkage	转向拉杆
9. Transmission	变速器		

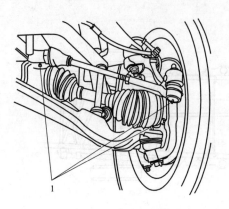

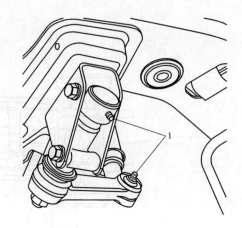

Figure 20 – 4   Lubrication fittings-ball joints
1. Lubrication Fittings   润滑油嘴

Figure 20 – 5   Lubrication fittings-steering linkage
1. Lubrication Fittings   润滑油嘴

Lubricate the steering linkage, the upper ball joint, and the lower ball joint (See Figure 20 – 5).

向转向联动装置、上球窝接头和下球窝接头加润滑油（见图 20 – 5）。

20.5 Scheduled Maintenance 定期保养

12,500 km (7,500 mi)

- Inspect rear/front axle fluid level and add fluid as needed. Check Constant velocity joints and axle seals（车轴油封）for leaking.
- Rotate tires.
- 检查后轴/前轴的润滑油液面，如果需要，添加润滑油。检查等速接头和车轴油封是否漏油。
- 旋转轮胎。

25,000 km (15,000 mi)

- Inspect engine air cleaner filter if you are driving in dusty conditions. Replace filter if necessary. This is an Emission Control Service.
- Inspect rear/front axle fluid level. Add fluid as needed. Inspect the constant velocity joints and the axle seals for leaking.
- Rotate the tires.
- 如果在满是灰尘的环境中驾驶，检查发动机空气滤清器。如果需要，更换滤清器。

这是一种排放控制服务。

- 检查后轴/前轴的润滑油液面，如果需要，添加润滑油。检查等速接头和车轴油封是否漏油。
- 旋转轮胎。

37,500 km (22,500 mi)

- Inspect the rear/front axle fluid level. Add fluid as needed. Inspect the constant velocity joints and the axle seals for leaking.
- Rotate the tires.
- 检查后轴/前轴的润滑油液面，如果需要，添加润滑油。检查等速接头和车轴油封是否漏油。
- 旋转轮胎。

50,000 km (30,000 mi)

- Inspect the rear/front axle fluid level. Add fluid as needed. Inspect the constant velocity joints and the axle seals for leaking.
- Rotate the tires.
- Replace the fuel filter. This is an Emission Control Service.
- Replace engine air cleaner filter. This is an Emission Control Service.
- 检查后轴/前轴的润滑油液面，如果需要，添加润滑油。检查等速接头和车轴油封是否漏油。
- 旋转轮胎。
- 更换燃油滤清器。这是一种排放控制服务。
- 更换发动机空气滤清器。这是一种排放控制服务。

62,500 km (37,500 mi)

- Inspect the rear/front axle fluid level. Add fluid as needed. Inspect the constant velocity joints and the axle seals for leaking.
- Rotate the tires.
- 检查后轴/前轴的润滑油液面，如果需要，添加润滑油。检查等速接头和车轴油封是否漏油。
- 旋转轮胎。

75,000 km (45,000 mi)

- Inspect engine air cleaner filter if you are driving in dusty conditions. Replace if necessary.

- Inspect the rear/front axle fluid level. Add fluid as needed. Inspect the constant velocity joints and the axle seals for leaking.
- Rotate the tires.
- 如果在满是灰尘的环境中驾驶，检查空气滤清器。如果需要，进行更换。
- 检查后轴/前轴的润滑油液面，如果需要，添加润滑油。检查等速接头和车轴油封是否漏油。
- 旋转轮胎。

83,000 km (50,000 mi)

- Change the automatic transmission fluid and filter if the vehicle is mainly driven under one or more of the following conditions：
  ○ In heavy city traffic where the outside temperature regularly reaches 32℃ (90 ℉) or higher；
  ○ In hilly (多坡的) or mountainous terrain；
  ○ When doing frequent trailer towing (拖车牵引)；
  ○ Uses such as found in taxi, police or delivery service.
- Automatic Transfer Case Only：Change transfer case fluid.
- 如果汽车主要在下列一种或一种以上条件下行驶，更换自动变速器油和滤清器：
  ○ 在繁忙城市运输中，那里的外界温度经常达到32℃ (90 ℉) 或更高；
  ○ 在多坡或多山地区；
  ○ 经常牵引拖车；
  ○ 用于出租车、警车或递送服务。
- 仅对于自动分动器：更换分动器油。

87,500 km (52,500 mi)

- Inspect the rear/front axle fluid level. Add fluid as needed. Inspect the constant velocity joints and the axle seals for leaking.
- Rotate the tires.
- 检查后轴/前轴的润滑油液面，如果需要，添加润滑油。检查等速接头和车轴油封是否漏油。
- 旋转轮胎。

100,000 km (60,000 mi)

- Inspect rear/front axle fluid level and add fluid as needed. Inspect constant velocity joints and axle seals for leaking.

- Rotate the tires.
- Replace fuel filter. This is an Emission Control Service.
- Replace engine air cleaner filter. This is an Emission Control Service.
- Inspect the Evaporative Control System. Inspect all the fuel and vapor lines and the hoses （软管）for proper hook-up, routing and condition. Ensure that the purge valve （［碳罐］清污阀）works properly, if equipped. Replace the components as needed. This is an Emission Control Service.
- 检查后轴/前轴的润滑油液面，如果需要，添加润滑油。检查等速接头和车轴油封是否漏油。
- 旋转轮胎。
- 更换燃油滤清器。这是一种排放控制服务。
- 更换发动机空气滤清器。这是一种排放控制服务。
- 检查蒸汽控制系统。检查所有的燃油和蒸汽管路和软管的接头和状况。如果配备了（碳罐）清污阀，确保它工作正常。如果需要，更换部件。这是一种排放控制服务。

112,500 km（67,500 mi）

- Inspect the rear/front axle fluid level. Add fluid as needed. Inspect the constant velocity joints and the axle seals for leaking.
- Rotate the tires.
- 检查后轴/前轴的润滑油液面，如果需要，添加润滑油。检查等速接头和车轴油封是否漏油。
- 旋转轮胎。

125,000 km（75,000 mi ）

- Inspect engine air cleaner filter if you are driving in dusty conditions. Replace filter if necessary. This is an Emission Control Service.
- Inspect the rear/front axle fluid level. Add fluid as needed. Inspect the constant velocity joints and the axle seals for leaking.
- Rotate the tires.
- 如果在满是灰尘的环境中驾驶，检查空气滤清器。如果需要，进行更换。这是一种排放控制服务。
- 检查后轴/前轴的润滑油液面，如果需要，添加润滑油。检查等速接头和车轴油封是否漏油。
- 旋转轮胎。

137, 500 km（82, 500 mi）

- Inspect the rear/front axle fluid level. Add fluid as needed. Inspect the constant velocity joints and the axle seals for leaking.
- Rotate the tires.
- 检查后轴/前轴的润滑油液面，如果需要，添加润滑油。检查等速接头和车轴油封是否漏油。
- 旋转轮胎。

150, 000 km（90, 000 mi）

- Inspect the rear/front axle fluid level. Add fluid as needed. Inspect the constant velocity joints and the axle seals for leaking.
- Replace the fuel filter. This is an Emission Control Service.
- Replace engine air cleaner filter. This is an Emission Control Service.
- Rotate the tires.
- 检查后轴/前轴的润滑油液面，如果需要，添加润滑油。检查等速接头和车轴油封是否漏油。
- 更换燃油滤清器。这是一种排放控制服务。
- 更换发动机空气滤清器。这是一种排放控制服务。
- 旋转轮胎。

162, 500 km（97, 500 mi）

- Inspect the rear/front axle fluid level. Add fluid as needed. Inspect the constant velocity joints and the axle seals for leaking.
- Rotate the tires.
- 检查后轴/前轴的润滑油液面，如果需要，添加润滑油。检查等速接头和车轴油封是否漏油。
- 旋转轮胎。

166, 000 km（100, 000 mi）

- Inspect the spark plug wires. This is an Emission Control Service.
- Replace the spark plugs. This is an Emission Control Service.
- Change the automatic transmission fluid and the filter if the vehicle is mainly driven under one or more of these conditions：
  - In heavy city traffic where the outside temperature regularly reaches 32℃（90 ℉）or higher;

    ○ In hilly or mountainous terrain;

    ○ When doing frequent trailer towing;

    ○ Uses such as found in taxi, police or delivery service.

- If vehicle has not been used under severe service conditions listed previously and, therefore, the automatic transmission fluid has not been changed, change both the fluid and filter.

- Automatic Transfer Case Only: Change transfer case fluid.

- Inspect the positive crankcase ventilation（PCV 强制曲轴箱通风）valve. This is an Emission Control Service.

- 检查火花塞导线。这是一种排放控制服务。

- 更换火花塞。这是一种排放控制服务。

- 如果汽车主要在下列一种或一种以上条件下行驶，更换自动变速器油和滤清器：

    ○ 在繁忙城市运输中，那里的外界温度经常达到32℃（90 °F）或更高；

    ○ 在多坡或多山地区；

    ○ 经常牵引拖车；

    ○ 用于出租车、警车或递送服务。

- 如果汽车没有在前面所列的严酷条件下使用，那么自动变速器油还没有更换过，同时更换自动变速器油和滤清器。

- 仅对于自动分动器：更换分动器油。

- 检查强制曲轴箱通风（PCV）阀。这是一种排放控制服务。

240,000 km（150,000 mi）

- **Drain**, flush and refill the cooling system（or every 60 months since the last service, whichever comes first）.

- Inspect the hoses.

- Clean the following components:

    ○ The radiator;

    ○ The condenser;

    ○ The pressure cap（压力阀）;

    ○ The neck.

- Pressure test the cooling system and the pressure cap. This is an Emission Control Service.

- Inspect engine accessory drive belt（驱动皮带）. This is an Emission Control Service.

- 排空、清洗冷却系统并加入冷却液（或者从上次服务后满60个月进行，按先满足的条件执行）。

- 检查软管。

- 清洗下列部件：
  - 散热器；
  - 冷凝器；
  - 压力阀；
  - 喉部。
- 对冷却系统和压力阀进行压力测试。这是一种排放控制服务。
- 检查发动机附件驱动皮带。这是一种排放控制服务。

20.6 Owner Checks and Services 车主检查和服务

20.6.1 At Each Fuel Fill 每次加油时

It is important to perform these underhood（发动机舱内）check at each fuel fill. The following information covers the checks and services required to retain the safety, dependability（可靠性）, and emission control performance of the vehicle.

每次加油时进行发动机舱内检查很重要。下面的信息涵盖了保持汽车安全性、可靠性和排放控制性能所要求的检查和服务。

Make sure any necessary repairs are completed on time. Whenever any fluids or lubricants are added to the vehicle, make sure that they are the proper ones.

确保按时完成任何必需的维修。当向汽车添加任何液体或润滑剂时，确保它们是合适的。

1. Engine Oil Level 发动机机油液面

Check the engine oil level and add the proper oil if necessary.

检查发动机机油液面，如果需要，加入正确的机油。

2. Engine Coolant Level 发动机冷却剂液面

Check the engine coolant levels and add coolant mixture if necessary.

检查发动机冷却剂液面，如果需要，加入冷却剂混合物。

3. Windshield Washer Fluid Level 挡风玻璃清洗液液面

Check the windshield washer fluid level in the windshield washer tank and add the proper fluid if necessary.

检查挡风玻璃洗涤器储液罐中挡风玻璃清洗液液面，如果需要，加入正确的液体。

20. 6. 2   At Least Once a Month   至少每月一次

1. Tire Inflation   轮胎充气压力

Check tire inflation（轮胎充气压力）. Make sure the tires are inflated to the pressures specified on the Certification/Tire label located on the driver door lock pillar.

检查轮胎充气压力。确保轮胎充气后的压力达到位于驾驶员侧车门装门锁的立柱上的证明或轮胎标签上的指定压力。

2. Cassette Deck   盒式磁带走带机构

Clean the playback heads and capstan on the cassette deck（盒式磁带走带机构）. Cleaning should be done every 50 hours of tape play.

清洗放音磁头和盒式磁带走带机构的绞盘。播放 50 小时磁带应该清洗一次。

20. 6. 3   At Least Twice a Year   至少一年两次

1. Restraint System Check   约束保护系统检查

Make sure the seat belt reminder light and all the belts, buckles, latch plates, retractors and anchorages are working properly. Look for any other loose or damaged safety belt system parts. If you see anything that might keep a safety belt system from doing its job, have it repaired. Have any torn or frayed（磨损的）safety belts replaced.

确保安全带提醒灯和所有安全带、带扣、（安全带）带扣插片、（安全带）卷收器和固定支座工作正常。查找任何其他松弛或损坏的安全带系统零件。如果发现可能阻止安全带系统发挥作用的任何故障，要修好它。更换任何撕破或磨损的安全带。

Also look for any opened or broken Supplemental Inflatable Restraint（SIR 辅助充气约束装置）covers. （The SIR system does not need regular maintenance.）

查找打开或损坏的辅助充气约束装置（SIR）外罩盖。（SIR 系统不需要定期维护。）

2. Wiper Blade Check   刮水片检查

Inspect wiper blades（刮水器刮片总成）for **wear** or cracking（破裂）. Replace blade inserts（橡胶刮片）that appear worn, cracked, damaged or that streak or miss areas of the windshield.

检查刮水器刮片总成是否有磨损或破裂。更换出现磨损、破裂或是在挡风玻璃区域出现裂纹或缺失的橡胶刮片。

3. Spare Tire Check   备胎检查

At least twice a year, after the monthly inflation check of the spare tire determines that the spare is inflated to the correct tire inflation pressure, make sure that the spare tire is stored securely. Push, pull, and then try to rotate or turn the tire. If it moves, use the wheel wrench（扳手）to tighten the cable.

最少一年两次，经过每月的备胎胎压检查，以保证备胎胎压为正确的轮胎充气气压后，确保备胎被安全地保存。推、拉备胎，试着旋转或翻转它。如果备胎移动，使用车轮扳手紧固拉索。

4. Engine Air Cleaner Filter Restriction Indicator Check
发动机空气滤清器限制指示灯检查

The vehicle has an indicator located on the air cleaner in the engine compartment that lets you know when the air cleaner filter is dirty and needs to be changed. Check the indicator at least twice a year or when you engine oil is changed, whichever occurs first. Inspect your air cleaner filter restriction indicator（限制指示灯）more often if the vehicle is used in dusty areas or under off road conditions.

发动机舱空气滤清器的滤芯上有一个指示灯，当空气滤清器的滤芯脏了，需要更换时可以通知你。至少一年两次或者在更换发动机机油时检查指示灯，按照先满足的条件检查。如果汽车经常在满是灰尘的地区或非道路上行驶，则要更频繁地检查空气滤清器限制指示灯。

5. Weatherstrip Lubrication （车身/玻璃）密封条润滑

Silicone grease on weatherstrips（［车身/玻璃］密封条）will make them last longer, seal better, and not stick or squeak（尖叫）. Apply silicone grease with a clean cloth.

（车身/玻璃）密封条上的硅润滑脂使密封条的寿命更长、密封得更严、不会变粘或发出尖叫。使用干净的布涂抹硅润滑脂。

During very cold, damp（潮湿的）weather more frequent application may be required.

在非常寒冷潮湿的气候需要更频繁地进行涂抹。

6. Automatic Transmission Check 自动变速器检查

Check the transmission axle fluid level; add if needed. A fluid loss may indicate a problem. Check the system and repair if needed.

检查变速器轴液体高度，如果需要，就添加。液体的流失可能表示出了问题。检查系统，如果需要，就进行修理。

20.6.4 At Least Once a Year 至少一年一次

1. Body Lubrication 车身润滑

Lubricate all of the following areas:
- Body door hinges;

- Body hood, safety lever, and prop rod pivot;
- Fuel door;
- Rear compartment hinges;
- Rear compartment latches and locks;
- Instrument panel compartment hinges, latch, and lock cylinder;
- Console cover hinges and latch;
- Seat hardware.

润滑下列所有区域：

- 车门铰链；
- 车身引擎罩、安全（保险）杠杆和支撑杆支点；
- 加油口盖；
- 客厢后部铰链；
- 客厢后部车门插销和车锁；
- 座椅金属器件。

More frequent lubrication may be required when exposed to a corrosive（腐蚀的）environment.

当暴露在腐蚀性的环境中时，需要更频繁地润滑。

2. Starter Switch Check　起动开关检查

- Before you start, ensure that you have enough room around the vehicle in case the vehicle jumps suddenly.
- On automatic transmission vehicles, try to start the engine in each gear. The starter should work only in PARK（P）or NEUTRAL（N）. If the starter works in any other position, the vehicle needs service.
- 在起动前，确保在汽车突然跳起的情况下汽车周围有足够的空间。
- 在装有自动变速器的车辆上，试着用各个挡启动发动机。起动机应该只能在停车挡（P）或空挡（N）工作。如果在其他挡位工作，汽车需要修理。

On manual transmission vehicles, put the shift lever in NEUTRAL（N）, push the **clutch** down halfway and try to start the engine. The starter should work only when the clutch is pushed down all the way to the floor. If the starter works when the clutch is not pushed all the way down, the vehicle needs service.

在手动变速器汽车上，把换挡杆置于空挡（N），踩下离合器踏板达到中间位置，试着启动发动机。启动机应该只能在完全踩下离合器踏板时工作。如果启动机在离合器没有完全踩下时工作，汽车需要修理。

3. Automatic Transmission Shift Lock Control Check

自动变速器杆锁止控制检查

- Before you start, be sure you have enough room around the vehicle. It should be parked on a level surface.
- Firmly apply the parking brake.
- With the engine off, turn the key to the RUN position, but don't start the engine.
- Without applying the regular brake, try to move the shift lever out of PARK (P) with normal effort.
- If the shift lever moves out of PARK (P), the vehicle needs service.
- 在开车之前，确保汽车周围有足够的空间。汽车应该停放在水平面上。
- 拉紧驻车制动器。
- 在关闭发动机的情况下，把钥匙转动到起动位置，但不要启动发动机。
- 不使用常规制动器，试着向平常一样用力将换挡杆从停车挡（P）移出。
- 如果换挡杆从停车挡（P）移出，车辆需要修理。

4. Ignition Transmission Lock Check   点火时变速器锁止装置检查

- With the vehicle parked, set the parking brake.
- Try to turn the ignition key to LOCK in each shift lever position.
- With an automatic transmission, the key should turn to LOCK only when the shift lever is in PARK (P).
- With a manual transmission, the key should turn to LOCK only when you press the key release button.
- On all vehicles, the key should come out only in LOCK.
- 在汽车停止时，使用驻车制动器。
- 在每一挡位试着向锁闭位置转动点火开关。
- 对于自动变速器汽车，钥匙应该只能在换挡杆在停车挡（P）时转动到锁闭位置。
- 对于手动变速器汽车，钥匙应该只能在按住钥匙释放按钮时转动到锁闭位置。
- 在所有汽车上，钥匙只有在锁闭位置才能拔出。

5. Park Brake and Automatic Transmission PARK (P) Mechanism Check

驻车制动和自动变速器停车机构检查

Follow this procedure to test the park brake and automatic transmission PARK mechanism.

- Park on a fairly steep （陡峭的）hill, with the vehicle facing downhill.
- Keep your foot on the hydraulic brake pedal.

- Set the park brake.
- Check the park brake.
  - Start the engine.
  - Place the transmission in NEUTRAL.
  - Slowly remove foot pressure from the regular brake pedal. If the vehicle moves, the park brake needs adjustment.
- In order to check the PARK (P) mechanism of an automatic transmission, follow steps 1 – 3 above then do the following.
  - Shift to PARK (P).
  - Release all brakes.

遵循这一过程，检查驻车制动和自动变速器停车机构。
- 车头向下停放在一个相当陡峭的坡上。
- 把脚放在液压制动踏板上。
- 使用驻车制动器。
- 检查驻车制动器。
  - 启动发动机。
  - 把变速器置于空挡。
  - 慢慢减少施加在制动踏板上脚的压力。如果汽车移动，驻车制动器需要调整。
- 为了检查停车机构，遵循上面的第 1 ～ 3 步，然后做下面的事情。
  - 换挡到停车挡（P）。
  - 释放所有制动器。

6. Underbody Flushing   用水冲洗汽车底部

Use plain water to flush any corrosive materials from the underbody at least every spring. Take care to clean thoroughly any areas where mud and other debris can collect.

至少在每年春天使用清水冲洗汽车底部，清除一切腐蚀性物质。小心清洁所有聚集泥巴和其他碎片的地方。

20.7 Periodic Maintenance Inspection 定期养护检查

1. Steering, Suspension, and Front Drive Axle Boot and Seal Inspection
转向系、悬架和前驱动轴罩和密封检查

Inspect the front and the rear suspension for the following:

- Damaged parts;
- Loose or missing parts;
- Signs of wear or lack of lubrication.

检查前后悬架的以下问题：

- 损坏的零件；
- 松动或丢失的零件；
- 磨损或者缺少润滑油的迹象。

Inspect the power steering lines and the hoses for the following：

- Proper hookup;
- Binding;
- Leaks;
- Cracks（裂缝）；
- Chafing, etc.

检查动力转向的管路和软管，确认以下情况：

- 正确的连接；
- 粘结；
- 泄漏；
- 裂缝；
- 表面损伤，等等。

Clean and inspect the drive axle boot seals for the following：

- Damage;
- Tears;
- Leakage（泄漏）.

清洁并检查驱动轴罩密封是否存在以下问题：

- 损坏；
- 破损；
- 泄漏。

2. Exhaust System Inspection 排放系统检查

Inspect the complete system. Inspect the body near the exhaust system. Look for broken, damaged, missing or out-of-position parts as well as open seams（接缝）, holes, loose connections or other conditions which could cause a heat build-up in the floor pan or could let exhaust fumes（排气）into the vehicle.

检查整个系统。检查靠近排气系统的车身。查找断掉的、损坏的、缺失的或离开原来位置的零件，还有裂开的接缝、破洞、不牢固的连接或者其他问题。这些问题会造成地板发热或排气进入汽车内部。

3. Fuel System Inspection   燃料系统检查

Inspect the complete fuel system for damage or leaks.

在整个燃料系统中查找损坏或泄漏。

4. Engine Cooling System Inspection   发动机冷却系统检查

- Inspect the hoses and replace if they are cracked, swollen（膨胀）or deteriorated.
- Inspect all pipes, fittings and clamps; replace as needed.
- Clean the outside of the radiator and air conditioning condenser.
- 检查软管，如果有破裂的、膨胀的或变质的软管，就进行更换。
- 检查所有的管道、装置和夹子，如果需要就更换。
- 清洗散热器和空调冷凝器的外部。

To help ensure proper operation, a pressure test of the cooling system and pressure cap is recommended at least once a year.

为了保证工作正常，推荐至少一年一次，对冷却系统和压力阀进行压力检查。

5. Throttle System Inspection   节气门系统检查

Throttle system（includes accelerator and cruise control［巡航控制］）should operate freely without hesitation between full closed and wide open throttle.

节气门系统（包括加速器和巡航控制）应该在完全关闭和节气门全开之间无延迟地自由操控。

Inspect the following:

- Missing parts, such as retainers（固定器）or clips;
- Interference（干涉）of the linkage or the cable conduit（导管）to critical components such as fuel lines, brake lines, harness leads, etc.;
- Proximity of the cable to the exhaust system and other heat sources: check for melting and/or discoloration;
- Avoid sharp bends of cables;
- Clearance of the throttle system moving parts throughout their travel from other stationary components;
- Damage of the components due to cable kinking（扭结）, severe kinking, severe abrasion, misalignment, etc.

If any of the above conditions exists, notify your dealer（经销商）for a recommended rerouting, adjustment, or replacement.

检查如下问题：

- 缺失的零件，如固定器或夹子；
- 连接的干涉或到关键零件的线缆导管，如燃料管路、制动管路、电气配线导线，等等；
- 靠近通往排气系统和其他热源的线缆：检查是否有熔化和（或）变色；
- 避免线缆的锐弯；
- 对从固定部件开始的节气门系统运动零件的整个行程进行清洁；
- 由于线缆的扭结、严重的锐弯、严重的磨损、未对准等造成的损坏。

如果出现上面任何一种情况，通知经销商，寻求推荐的变更行程、调整或更换方法

6. Transfer Case and Front Axle（Four-Wheel Drive）Inspection
分动器和前轴（四轮驱动）检查

Every 12 months or at engine oil change intervals, check front axle and transfer case and add lubricant when necessary. A fluid loss could indicate a problem. Check and have it repaired, if needed. Check vent（出口）hose at transfer case for proper installation. More frequent lubrication may be required on off-road use.

每隔12个月或在发动机机油更换时，检查前轴和分动器，如果需要，添加润滑液。液体的损失可能代表着一个问题。如果需要，检查并修好它。检查分动器出口软管是否正确安装。如果用于越野，需要更频繁地润滑。

7. Brake System Inspection　制动系统检查

Inspect the complete system.

检查整个系统。

Inspect the brake lines and the hoses for the following：

- Proper hookup（连接）；
- Binding；
- Leaks；
- Cracks；
- Chafing（表面损伤）, etc.

检查制动管路和软管，看是否存在以下问题：

- 正确的连接；
- 粘结；
- 泄漏；
- 裂缝；
- 表面损伤，等等。

Inspect the disc brake pads for wear. Inspect the rotors for surface condition. Inspect other brake parts, including the calipers, the park brake, etc.

检查盘式制动器的制动块是否有磨损。检查制动盘的表面状况。检查其他制动器零件，包括制动钳、驻车制动装置，等等。

The brakes may need to be inspected more often if driving habits or conditions result in frequent braking.

如果驾驶习惯或条件导致频繁制动，就需要更经常地检查制动器。

20.8 Specifications of Tire Inflation Pressure 轮胎充气气压详述

When you inflate the tires to the recommended inflation pressures, the factory-installed wheels and tires are designed to handle loads to the tire's rated load capacity. Incorrect tire pressures, or under-inflated tires, can cause the following conditions:

- Vehicle handling problems;
- Poor fuel economy;
- Shortened tire life;
- Tire overloading.

当将轮胎充气到推荐的充气气压时，原厂的车轮和轮胎将能够承受轮胎额定负荷。不正确的轮胎胎压或充气不足的轮胎会造成下列问题：

- 汽车操控问题；
- 燃油经济性差；
- 轮胎寿命缩短；
- 轮胎过载。

Check the tire pressure when the following apply:

- The tires are cool;
- The vehicle has not been driven for more than 3 hours;
- The vehicle has been driven less than 1.6 km (1 mi).

在下列情况下检查轮胎胎压：

- 轮胎温度低；
- 汽车超过 3 个小时没有行驶；
- 汽车行驶里程小于 1.6 km (1 mi)。

Check the tires monthly or before any extended（长期的）trip. Adjust the tire pressure to the specifications on the tire placard. Install the valve caps or extensions on the valves. These keep out dust and water.

每月或者在长途旅行之前检查轮胎。使轮胎压力达到轮胎标识上的额定值。安装阀盖或者在气阀上加装延长物。这些装置可防止灰尘和水进入。

The kilopascal (kPa) is the metric term for tire inflation pressure. The tire pressure may be printed in both kilopascal (kPa) and psi. One psi equals 6.9 kPa.

千帕（kPa）是轮胎充气压力的公制单位。轮胎胎压可能用千帕（kPa）和磅/平方英尺表示。1磅/平方英尺等于6.9千帕。

Tires with a higher than recommended pressure can cause the following conditions：

- A hard ride；
- Tire bruising（擦伤）；
- Rapid **tread** wear at the center of the tire.

高于推荐压力的轮胎会导致以下问题：

- 不舒适的行驶；
- 轮胎擦伤；
- 在轮胎中间的胎面磨损。

Tires with a lower than recommended pressure can cause the following conditions：

- A tire squeal（尖叫）on turns；
- Hard steering；
- Rapid wear and uneven wear on the edge of the tread；
- Tire rim（边缘）bruises and tire rim rupture（破裂）；
- Tire **cord** breakage ；
- High tire temperatures；
- Reduced vehicle handling；
- High fuel consumption；
- Soft riding.

低于推荐压力的轮胎会导致以下问题：

- 转弯时轮胎发出尖叫声；
- 转向困难；
- 在轮胎面边缘的快速磨损和不均匀磨损；
- 轮胎边缘的擦伤和破裂；
- 帘线破损；
- 轮胎温度升高；
- 汽车操控性下降；
- 燃油消耗量升高；
- 柔性行驶。

Unequal pressure on the same axle can cause the following conditions：

- Uneven braking;
- Steering lead;
- Reduced vehicle handling.

同一根轴上压力不等会造成下列问题：

- 不均匀制动；
- 转向领先；
- 汽车操控性下降。

20.9 Explanation of Scheduled Services 定期保养的解释

1. Tire and Wheel Inspection and Rotation 轮胎和车轮的检查和旋转

Inspect the tires for **abnormal** wear or damage. Rotate the tires in order to equalize the wear and obtain maximum tire life.

检查轮胎，查找反常的磨损或损坏。旋转轮胎是为了均匀磨损，得到最大的轮胎寿命。

2. Accessory Drive Belt Inspection 附属驱动皮带检查

Inspect the accessory drive belts for the following conditions：

- Cracks;
- Fraying（磨损后的碎屑）;
- Wear;
- Proper tension.

检查附属驱动皮带，查找下列问题：

- 裂缝；
- 磨损后的碎屑；
- 磨损；
- 正确的张紧。

Replace the accessory drive belt as needed. Belts can have many small cracks in individual ribs（肋）without affecting the performance.

如果需要，就更换附属驱动皮带。皮带在个别的肋上可以有很多小裂缝，而不会影响性能。

3. Automatic Transmission Inspection 自动变速器检查

Change the fluid and the filter according to the maintenance schedule intervals.

根据保养计划的间隔时间更换变速器油和滤清器。

4. Spark Plug Wire Inspection 火花塞线路检查

Clean the spark plug wires. Inspect the spark plug wires for burns, cracks or other damage. Inspect the wire boot fit at the coils and at the spark plugs. Replace the wires as needed.

清洁火花塞线路。检查火花塞线路，查找烧蚀、裂缝或其他的损坏。检查火花塞和线圈处火花塞线路套管接合部位。如果需要，就更换线路。

5. Spark Plug Replacement 火花塞的更换

Replace the spark plugs according to the maintenance schedule intervals with the correct type. For information on the correct type of spark plug, refer to Maintenance Items.

根据维修计划的间隔时间用正确的型号更换火花塞。关于正确型号的火花塞的信息，可参见维修项目。

6. Fuel Filter Replacement 燃料滤清器的更换

Replace the fuel filter according to the maintenance schedule intervals with the correct type.

根据维修计划的间隔时间用正确的型号更换燃料滤清器。

7. Drive Axle Service 驱动轴的保养

Change the axle fluid according to the maintenance schedule intervals. Check the fluid level of the drive axle.

根据维修计划的间隔时间更换驱动轴的液体，并检查驱动轴的液面。

8. Cooling System Service 冷却系统的保养

Drain, flush and refill the cooling system with new coolant.

排空、冲洗冷却系统，然后用新的冷却剂装满冷却系统。

Key Words

off-road 越野的	tread 轮胎面
drain 排空	cord 帘线
wear 磨损	abnormal 反常的

Exercises

1. The services shown in this schedule up to 166, 000 km (100, 000 mi) should be performed after _____ at the same intervals.

2. It is important to perform these _____ checks at each fuel fill.

3. The brakes may need to be inspected _____ if driving habits or conditions result in frequent braking.

4. Oils of the proper quality for the vehicle can be _____ by looking for the STARBURST symbol.

5. Higher temperature weather conditions require _____ viscosity engine oils for satisfactory lubrication.

6. Rotate the tires in order to _____ the wear and obtain maximum tire life.

Unit 21
Effective Diagnosis & Troubleshooting
有效的诊断和修理故障

Key Terms

diagnostic tree
basic test equipment

The secret of effective diagnosis and troubleshooting（故障诊断维修）is to have a logical （合理的），well-ordered system. Following a logical step-by-step procedure will get you to the root cause of a problem quickly and efficiently. Repair manuals will have a diagnostic tree that goes in a logical progression. It will ask a question, usually yes or no, and depending on the answer will branch（分支）off in two or more directions. The last box in the tree will have the problem and how to correct it. A more complicated system will have branches going into specific tests and then have 2 or more branches from there depending on test results.

有效的诊断和修理故障的秘密就是拥有一个合理的、秩序井然的系统。遵循一个合理的按部就班的过程将会使你快速有效地找到问题发生的根本原因。维修手册上有一个过程合理的诊断树。它将会问一个问题，通常是或否，然后根据答案在两个或更多方向上分支。诊断树上最后的方框将会指出问题并给出修理的方法。一个更复杂的系统将会有进入特殊测试的分支，然后根据测试的结果产生两个或更多的分支。

You will need some basic test equipment to perform your diagnosis. A 12-volt（12 伏）test will tell you if a circuit has power or, when hooked up in reverse, will tell you if a ground circuit is good.

为了进行诊断，你需要一些基本的测试设备。一台 12 V 的测试仪将会告诉你电路中是否有电。反过来，在接线的时候，将会告诉你地线是否良好。

A good volt-ohm-meter（VOM）will be needed to perform specific voltage and resistance （电压和电阻）tests. You can get a good meter at any Radio Shack or Best Buy store. A digital meter is an excellent choice because they are easier to read than an analog（模拟式）meter. I have both digital and analog meters in my toolbox because sometimes an analog meter is best for a certain job. Most VOM's have an ammeter （电流表） that will test the alternator （交流发电机） output. Make sure the one you buy has it.

在进行特殊的电压和电阻检查时将会需要一块好的伏特欧姆表（VOM）。你可以在任何一家 RSH 无线电子或百思买商店得到一块好的测试表。一块数字表是一个好的选择，因为它们比模拟式仪表容易读数。在我的工具箱中，数字式和模拟式仪表都有，因为有时模拟式仪表对于某个工作来说是最恰当的。大多数 VOM 带有检测交流发电机输出的电流表。确定你买的那块表带有这个装置。

If you have an older car with a point equipped ignition system （分电器式点火系统）, you will need a dwell （触点闭合角） meter as well to measure and adjust the dwell angle of the points. As with any piece of equipment, read the instructions that come with your meter. It will tell you what the various functions are and how to connect the meter to the circuit for accurate test results. Most meters have a **fuse** in them to protect them from an incorrect connection. Make sure the one you buy has one and get a couple of spare fuses. You will, at some point, hook it up （连接） wrong and be very thankful you have the spares. I know I have.

如果你有一辆带有分电器式点火系统的比较旧的车，你就会需要一块触点闭合角测量表，来测量和调整触点闭合角。在使用任何设备时，要阅读随测量表提供的规程。它会告诉你各种功能是什么，为了得到准确的测量结果，如何把仪表连接到电路中。大多数仪表带有保险丝，以便在连接错误时保护它们。确保你买的表有保险丝，并准备两根备用。在某种情况下，你会连接错误，并庆幸你有备用保险丝。我知道我有备用保险丝。

Most of the troubleshooting on today's cars will be electrical in nature. A good wiring diagram （电路图） is essential to properly troubleshoot any electrical circuit. They usually come in two parts, a schematic （示意图） and the wiring diagram. The schematic shows the different components of a system and how they relate to each other. The wiring diagram shows the actual wire colors and connections.

当今汽车的大部分故障实际上是与电有关的。为了正确地进行电路故障的诊断维修，需要一个详细的电路图。它们一般由两个部分组成：示意图和电路图。示意图说明系统的不同部件和相互之间的连接关系。电路图说明实际线束的颜色和连接情况。

For testing the mechanical side of the engine, you will need some more specialized equipment. A vacuum gauge （真空表） with several adapters can be used to test manifold vacuum and test vacuum operated circuits. A vacuum pump is handy for testing vacuum operated components such as EGR valves and heating and air conditioning systems.

为了检修发动机的机械部分，你会需要一些更专业的设备。一块具有多个量程的真空表被用于测量进气歧管真空度和采用真空运行的管路。在测量采用真空运行的部件如废气再循环阀和加热与空调系统时需要真空泵。

I don't know how many people get burned looking for a complicated answer when it's a simple answer. If your house started leaning（倾斜）to the left, you wouldn't check the roof first. You would check the foundation（基础）. Same thing with a car, the foundation has to be sound before you look anywhere else.

当答案很简单时我不知道有多少人为了找到一个难解的答案而火冒三丈。如果你的房子开始向左倾斜，你不要先检查你的屋顶，而是应该检查地基。汽车也一样，在查看其他地方之前，你应该先检查一下基础。

With a drivability（驾驶）problem, the first thing you should check is the spark plugs. They will tell you a lot about the condition of the engine if you know how to read them. Check to make sure they are the correct plugs for that car. Don't automatically get the same ones that were in there. Check them. Maybe the guy who tuned it up（修理）before you put the wrong ones in. Use AC Delco plugs in GM（通用汽车）, Champion in Chrysler（克莱斯勒汽车）, Motorcraft in Fords and NGK's in Japanese cars.

出现驾驶问题时，你应该做的第一件事就是检查火花塞。如果你知道如何进行分析，火花塞会告诉你很多关于发动机的情况。检查并确认它们是该车上所应使用的那种火花塞。不要机械地使用与原来安装的火花塞相同的型号。检查它们，也许在你之前修理的那个人使用了错误的型号。在通用的汽车上使用 AC Delco 火花塞，在克莱斯勒汽车上使用 Champion 火花塞，在福田汽车上使用 Motorcraft 火花塞，在日本车上使用 NGK 火花塞。

After the spark plugs you need to check the ignition wires, **distributor cap** and rotor. Make sure the plug wires are tight on the plugs and there are no cracks or burns on them. A quick test is while the car is running, spray（喷射）water from a spray bottle on them. If the car starts to stumble（不稳定）or run rough, or you see sparks arcing（形成电弧）, you need new wires. Look inside the distributor cap for cracks and burns. If you see any, replace it. The same goes for the rotor. If the tip（末端）is burned out, replace it.

在火花塞之后你需要检查点火线、分电器盖和分火头。确保火花塞的导线紧紧地连接在火花塞上，并且导线上没有裂缝或烧坏点。进行一次快速的检查，在汽车运转的情况下，用喷壶把水喷在导线上。如果汽车运行开始变得不稳定或者运行粗暴，或者看到电火花形成电弧，你需要新的导线。在分电器盖内查找裂缝和烧坏点。如果你发现了，就进行更换。对分火头进行同样的检查。如果末端被烧断了，就更换它。

If in doubt（怀疑）, replace any of these parts. The cost is small and you will know that they are in good shape to continue troubleshooting. These are the most common causes of misfires（失火）and rough engine performance. The next thing to check is the vacuum lines. Make sure they are connected and in good shape. Trace（检查）the whole line for cracks, breaks and collapsed（失效的）areas.

如果怀疑，替换这些零件中的任何一个。这花费不多，并且你会知道它们完好无损，以便继续发现并修理故障。这些是使发动机性能粗暴和失火的最普通的原因。下一件事情是检查真空线路，确保它们彼此相连且完好无损。检查整条线路，查找裂缝、破裂和失效的区域。

Murphy's Law stipulates（规定）that a cracked or broken vacuum line will be in the most hidden place in the car. After that you need to check for loose electrical connections. Unplug the connectors and look at the terminals. Dirty, loose or corroded（被腐蚀的）connections will cause a world of strange symptoms（征兆）and intermittent（间歇性）problems.

墨菲法则指出一个有裂缝或破裂的真空管路会出现在汽车上最隐蔽的地方。然后，你应该检查松动的电气连接。拔下插头，检查终端。脏的、松动的、被腐蚀的线路将会造成各种奇怪的征兆和间歇性的问题。

Check the filters as well. A new air and fuel filter will solve quite a few drivability problems.

检查过滤器。一个新的空气和燃料滤清器会解决相当多的驾驶问题。

Do the same thing for electrical problems. Check the fuses and fusible links first. Check connections to see if they are clean and tight. Check light bulbs to see if they are just burnt out and the correct type. I had a customer bring a car in and said every time he stepped on the brake his **dash lights** came on. What he did was put the wrong type of bulb in his brake light and it would feed back into the dash. A dishonest mechanic（技工）would have had a field day with this one. He would replace the bulb and charge 5 hours labor locating and repairing a short.

发生电器故障时要进行相似的操作。首先检查保险丝和熔丝。检查线路，看看它们是否清洁牢固。检查照明灯泡，看看是否烧坏，型号是否正确。我有一个顾客，带来一辆车，他说每次他踩刹车时他的仪表板照明灯就会亮。他的问题是刹车灯使用了错误的型号，而这个问题反馈给了仪表板。一个不诚实的技工将会在这件事上花费一天时间，他会更换灯泡，并花 5 个小时定位和修理一个短路。

In short, check all the stupid things first. Don't take anything for granted（认为某事当然）. Car won't start. Check the gas gauge first. That one burned me a couple of times.

简单地说，首先检查所有愚蠢的事情。不要认为任何事情理所当然。汽车不能起动，首先要检查油箱。这个原因曾数次令我发火。

Look at it from all angles when you look for an electrical problem. Literally look at it forward and backwards. If you are tracing a wire, is the connector buried in the dash. Look at the wiring diagram and find another location to make the same test in a more accessible location. You'll get the same results in a much shorter time.

当你查找一个电器问题的时候，从各个角度观察它，前前后后地逐步观察它。如果你在追踪一条导线，连接器是否在仪表板的下面。察看电路图，找到另一个位置，从一个更容易接近的位置进行同样的检查。这样，你会在更短的时间内得到同样的结果。

Lastly check the computer for Diagnostic Trouble Codes（故障诊断码）. For this you will need a scanner（电控系统检测仪）or a service manual that explains how to pull the DTC's up manually. If you get a bad **injector** circuit code, don't assume it's a bad injector. That code is telling you it's in the injector circuit and that includes the wiring, injectors, dropping resistors (on older EFI cars) and computer. Any one of which will throw（产生）that code. Get your wiring diagram out and check the whole circuit.

最后查看（行车）电脑，查找故障诊断码。为此你需要一台电控系统检测仪或者一本维修手册，该手册说明如何手动导出故障诊断码。如果你得到了一个喷油器电路故障码，不要假定喷油器损坏。该故障码告诉你问题在喷油器电路中，包括导线、喷油器、滑动变阻器（在老式 EFI 汽车上）和行车电脑。它们中间任何一个都会产生故障码。拿出电路图，检查整个电路。

When you have found the problem and completed making the repair, check it again. Make sure it is fixed. Sometimes one fault will cause another one that you couldn't see at first. For example, there is a shorted wire between the injector and the computer. You fix the wire and take it for a ride and it still misses. Well you didn't see that the shorted wire burned out the injector. When you test the circuit again, you will see that the injector needs to be replaced also. Double-check your diagnosis; double-check your work and double-check the repair.

当你发现了问题，完成了修理，再次检查它，以确保它被修好了。有时一个问题会导致另一个问题，该问题你开始时无法发现。例如，在喷油器和行车电脑之间的导线存在短路。你修好了导线，然后开车，但问题依然存在。你没有发现短路的导线烧坏了喷油器。当你再次检查电路，你会发现喷油器也需要更换。复查你的诊断，复查你的工作，复查你的修理。

Troubleshooting a problem can be tough, even in the best of circumstances, but by following some simple rules, using the right test equipment properly and some common sense, you will locate and repair most problems with your vehicle yourself.

即使在最好的环境下发现并修理故障也可能是困难的。但是遵循一些简单的原则，使用正确的诊断设备和一些常识，你自己就能找到并修理你汽车上出现的大部分故障。

Key Words

fuse 保险丝	dash light 仪表板照明灯	distributor cap 分电器盖

Exercises

1. _____ will ask a question, usually yes or no, and depending on the answer will branch off in two or more directions.

2. After the spark plugs you need to check the ignition wires, _____ and rotor.

3. Why do you check it again when you have found the problem and completed making the repair?

Unit 22

OBD-Ⅱ 第二代车载诊断系统

Key Terms

OBD-Ⅱ
OBD-Ⅱ protocol
OBD-Ⅱ output

On-Board Diagnostic systems（车载诊断装置）are in most cars and light trucks on the road today. During the '70s and early '80s manufacturers started using electronic means to control engine functions and diagnose engine problems. This was primarily to meet EPA（美国环保署）emission standards. Through the years on-board diagnostic systems have become more sophisticated. OBD-Ⅱ, a new standard introduced in the mid-'90s, provides almost complete engine control and also monitors parts of the chassis, body and accessory devices, as well as the diagnostic control network of the car.

如今大部分轿车和轻型卡车装有车载诊断装置。在 20 世纪 70 年代和 80 年代早期汽车厂商开始使用电子方法控制发动机的功能和诊断发动机的故障。这主要是为了满足美国环保署的排放标准。车载诊断装置在这些年里变得更加复杂。OBD-Ⅱ，一个新的标准，在 90 年代中期出现，提供了几乎整个发动机的控制，也监控底盘的零件、车身和附属设备，还包括轿车的诊断控制网络。

22.1 Introduction 简介

22.1.1 Where Does OBD-Ⅱ Come From？ OBD-Ⅱ 从何而来？

To combat its smog（烟雾）problem in the LA basin, the State of California started requiring emission control systems on 1966 model cars. The federal government extended these controls nationwide in 1968.

为了解决 LA basin 地区的烟雾问题，加利福尼亚州开始对 1966 款轿车提出安装排放控制系统的要求。联邦政府在 1968 年把这些控制措施推广到全国。

Congress passed the Clean Air Act in 1970 and established the Environmental Protection Agency（EPA）. This started a series of graduated emission standards and requirements for maintenance of vehicles for extended periods of time. To meet these standards, manufacturers turned to electronically controlled **fuel feed** and ignition systems. Sensors measured engine performance and adjusted the systems to provide minimum pollution. These sensors were also accessed to provide early diagnostic assistance.

议会于 1970 年通过了净气法案，建立了环境保护署（EPA）。此事在很长时间内引发了一系列的循序渐进的针对汽车维修的排放标准和要求。为了满足这些标准，汽车厂商求助于电子控制燃料供给和点火系统。传感器测量发动机的性能并调整系统，以得到最小的污染。这些传感器也被用于早期的诊断。

At first there were few standards and each manufacturer had their own systems and signals. In 1988, the Society of Automotive Engineers（SAE，汽车工程协会）set a standard connector plug and set of diagnostic test signals. The EPA adapted most of their standards from the SAE on-board diagnostic programs and recommendations. OBD-Ⅱ is an expanded set of standards and practices developed by SAE and adopted by the EPA and CARB（California Air Resources Board）for implementation by January 1, 1996.

首先只有很少的标准，每个厂商有自己的系统和信号。在 1988 年，汽车工程协会（SAE）制定了一个标准的连接器插头和一系列诊断测试信号。EPA 大部分标准改编自 SAE 车载诊断程序和建议。OBD-Ⅱ 是由 SAE 开发的一组扩展的标准和惯例，被 EPA 和 CARB（加利福尼亚空气资源部）采用，于 1996 年 1 月 1 日实行。

22.1.2　Why Do We Need It?　我们为什么需要它?

The Environmental Protection Agency has been charged with（被授权）reducing "mobile emissions" from cars and trucks and given the power to require manufacturers to build cars which meet increasingly stiff emissions standards（日趋严格的排放标准）. The manufacturers must further maintain the emission standards of the cars for the useful life of the vehicle. OBD-Ⅱ provides a universal（全面）inspection and diagnosis method to be sure the car is performing to OEM standards. While there is argument as to the exact standards and methodology employed, the fact is there is a need to reduce vehicle emitted pollution levels in our cities, and we have to live with these requirements.

环境保护署被授权减少来自轿车和卡车的汽车排放，同时获得权利要求厂商制造满足日趋严格的排放标准的轿车。制造商必须在汽车使用期间继续满足排放标准。OBD-Ⅱ 提供了全面检查和诊断的方法，以保证轿车执行 OEM 标准。当存在关于精确的标准和使用方法的争论时，事实是在我们的城市里存在降低汽车排放污染水平的需要，而我们必须与这些要求共存。

22. 1. 3   Does My Car Have OBD-Ⅱ？   我的车上有 OBD-Ⅱ 吗?

All cars built since January 1, 1996 have OBD-Ⅱ systems. Manufacturers started incorporating（安装）OBD-Ⅱ in various models as early as 1994. Some early OBD-Ⅱ cars were not 100% compliant.

从 1996 年 1 月 1 日起制造的车辆装有 OBD-Ⅱ 系统。早在 1994 年制造商就开始在各种型号的车辆上安装 OBD-Ⅱ。一些早期的 OBD-Ⅱ 轿车不能 100% 适应。

There are three basic OBD-Ⅱ protocols（协议）in use, each with minor variations on the communication pattern between the on-board diagnostic computer and the scanner. While there have been some manufacturer changes between protocols in the past few years, as a rule of thumb, Chrysler products and all European and most Asian imports use ISO 9141 circuitry. GM cars and light trucks use SAE J1850 VPW（Variable Pulse Width Modulation）, and Fords use SAE J1850 PWM（Pulse Width Modulation, 脉冲宽度调制）communication patterns.

现在使用三种基本的 OBD-Ⅱ 协议，每一个协议在车载诊断电脑和电控系统检测仪的通信模式上都有少量改变。虽然有些制造商在过去几年间改变了 OBD-Ⅱ 采用的协议，一般来说，克莱斯勒的产品和所有欧洲和大部分亚洲进口车使用 ISO 9141 电路。通用汽车和轻型卡车使用 SAE J1850 VPW（可变脉宽调制），福特汽车使用 SAE J1850 PWM（脉冲宽度调制）通信模式。

You may also tell which protocol is used on a specific automobile by examining the connector socket（连接器插头）carefully. If the dash connector has a pin in the #7 position and no pin at #2 or #10, then the car has the ISO 9141 protocol. If no pin is present in the #7 position, the car uses an SAE protocol. If there are pins in positions #7 and #2 and/or #10, the car may use the ISO protocol.

你也可以通过仔细检查连接器插头说出一部特定的汽车使用的是何种协议。如果仪表板连接器在#7 位置有一根针，在#2 或#10 位置没有针，那么这辆轿车使用 ISO 9141 协议。如果#7 位置没有针存在，这辆轿车使用 SAE 协议。如果在#7 和#2 和（或）#10 位置有针，该轿车使用 ISO 协议。

While there are three OBD-Ⅱ electrical connection protocols, the command set（指令集）is fixed according to the SAE J1979 standard.

虽然有三种 OBD-Ⅱ 电子连接协议，但指令集根据 SAE J1979 标准确定。

22. 1. 4   How Do We Measure OBD-Ⅱ Output?
我们如何测量 OBD-Ⅱ 的输出?

Pre-OBD-Ⅱ cars had connectors in various positions under the **dashboard** and under the hood. All OBD-Ⅱ cars have a connector located in the passenger compartment（车厢）easily accessible from the driver's seat. Check under the dash or behind or near the ashtray（烟灰缸）. A cable is plugged into the OBD-Ⅱ J1962 connector and connected to AutoTap or another scan tool. AutoTap is available in PC/laptop（笔记本）or a Palm PDA versions. Other scan tools on the market range from simple hand-held meters that display trouble codes, up to a large console computer-based unit costing thousands of dollars.

OBD-Ⅱ 推出前的轿车带有位于仪表板下和发动机罩下多种位置的连接器。所有 OBD-Ⅱ 轿车的连接器位于车厢内, 所处位置易于从驾驶员坐椅处接近。检查仪表板下或者烟灰缸后面或附近。一根电缆被插到 OBD-Ⅱ J1962 连接器内并连接到 AutoTap 或者另一种检测工具。AutoTap 有台式机/笔记本或者 Palm PDA 样式。市场上其他检测工具既有简单的手持式测量仪表, 仅能显示故障码, 也有价值数千美元带有宽大控制台的计算机控制的检测工具。

22. 1. 5   What Good Does It Do to Measure OBD-Ⅱ Output?
测量 OBD-Ⅱ 的输出有什么好处?

OBD-Ⅱ signals are most often sought in response to a "Check Engine Light" appearing on the dashboard or drivability problems experienced with the vehicle. The data provided by OBD-Ⅱ can often pinpoint（查明）the specific component that has malfunctioned, saving substantial time and cost compared to guess-and-replace repairs. Scanning OBD-Ⅱ signals can also provide valuable information on the condition of a used car purchase（购买）.

对于 OBD-Ⅱ 信号最经常的需要是由于"检查发动机灯"在仪表板上亮起或者汽车出现了驾驶问题。由 OBD-Ⅱ 提供的数据经常能够查明出现故障的特定部件, 与猜测和更换修理方法相比较, 节约了时间和成本。检测 OBD-Ⅱ 信号也能提供与要购买的二手轿车有关的有价值的信息。

22. 1. 6   "Check Engine Light"   "检查发动机灯"

The service industry calls the Check Engine Light on your dash an "MIL" or Malfunction Indicator Light. It shows three different types of signals. Occasional（偶然的）flashes show momentary（瞬间的）malfunctions. It stays on if the problem is of a more serious nature, affecting the emissions output or safety of the vehicle. A constantly flashing MIL is a sign of a major problem which can cause serious damage if the engine is not stopped immediately. In all cases a "freeze frame" of all sensor readings at the time is recorded in the central computer of the vehicle.

汽车维修业把仪表板上的检查发动机灯叫做"MIL"或者故障指示灯。它显示三种不同的信号。偶然的闪烁表示瞬间的故障。如果故障更严重，影响到排放或汽车安全，它就会持续亮起。一个不断闪烁的 MIL 是一个主要故障的信号，如果不立刻关闭发动机就会造成严重损害。在任何故障情况下，一个故障发生时所有传感器读数的"冻结帧"被记录在汽车的中枢计算机内。

Hard failure signals caused by serious problems will cause the MIL to stay on any time the car is running until the problem is repaired and the MIL reset. Intermittent（间歇性的）failures cause the MIL to light momentarily and they often go out before the problem is located. The freeze frame of the car's condition captured in the computer at the time of the malfunction can be very valuable in diagnosing these intermittent problems. However, in some cases if the car completes three driving cycles（行驶循环）without a re-occurrence of the problem, the freeze frame will be erased.

由严重问题引起的硬件故障信号将使 MIL 在汽车运行的任何时候持续亮起，直到问题得到修理，并且 MIL 复位。间歇性的故障引起 MIL 暂时性亮起，而且经常在找到问题之前熄灭。在故障出现时在计算机内采集的汽车状况冻结帧对于诊断这些间歇性故障非常有价值。然而，在某些情况下如果汽车完成了三个行驶循环没有再次发生相同故障，该冻结帧将被删除。

22.2 OBD-Ⅱ Acronyms and Jargons   OBD-Ⅱ 的缩略语和术语

Like any government instigated project, OBD-Ⅱ quickly became a mouse's nest of acronyms（缩略语）, jargon（行话）, shorthand and code phrases that have meaning to the select few and sometimes seem to serve to keep the rest of us at bay（走投无路）.

与其他政府推动的项目相仿，OBD-Ⅱ 正在迅速变成一张由缩略语、术语、速记和编码的短语组成的网，这对于特定的少数人有意义，而在某个时候使其他人走投无路。

AFC — Air Flow Control   空气流量控制

ALDL — Assembly（装配）Line Diagnostic Link：former name for GM（only）Data Link Connector, the connector socket into which the scan tool plug is inserted；sometimes used to refer to any pre-OBD-Ⅱ computer signals   装配线诊断链接：通用汽车公司（专用）的名称为数据链接接口，用来插入诊断工具插头的接口插座；有时用于检测每一个前 OBD-Ⅱ 计算机信号

CAN — Controller Area Network   控制器局域网络

CARB — California Air Resources Board   加利福尼亚空气资源部

CFI — Central Fuel Injection（also Throttle Body Fuel Injection，TBI）中央燃料喷射（也叫做节气门体燃料喷射，TBI）

CFI — Continuous Fuel Injection   连续燃料喷射

CO — Carbon Monoxide   一氧化碳

DLC — Data Link Connector   数据链接接口

Driving Cycle — a specific sequence of start-up, warm-up and driving tasks that tests all OBD-Ⅱ functions   驾驶循环——一个特定次序的启动、暖机和驾驶作业，以检测所有的 OBD-Ⅱ 功能

DTC — Diagnostic Trouble Code   诊断故障码

ECM — Engine Control Module（模块）: usually the main in-car computer controlling emissions and engine operation   发动机控制模块：通常指汽车内控制排放和发动机运行的主要计算机

ECT — Engine Coolant Temperature   发动机冷却温度

EEC — Electronic Engine Control   电子发动机控制

EEPROM or E2PROM — Electrically Erasable Programmable Read Only Memory   电子可擦除可编程只读存储器

EFI — Electronic Fuel Injection   电控燃料喷射

EGR — Exhaust Gas Recirculation   废气再循环

EMR — Electronic Module Retard（延迟） 电子模块延迟

EPA — Environmental Protection Agency. Office of Mobile Sources is the branch concerned with auto emissions.   环境保护署。机动资源办公室是其处理汽车排放的分支机构。

ESC — Electronic Spark Control   电子点火控制

EST — Electronic Spark Timing   电子点火正时

DPFE — Differential（微分）Pressure Feedback EGR sensor（on Ford OBD-Ⅱ systems）微分式压力反馈 EGR 传感器（用于福特 OBD-Ⅱ 系统）

FLI — Fuel Level Indicator   燃料液面指示器

Fuel Trim — engine computer function that keeps the air/fuel mixture as close to the ideal 14.7:1 stoichiometric ratio（化学当量比）as possible   燃料修正——发动机计算机的功能，使空气/燃料混合物（的浓度）尽可能接近理想的 14.7:1 的化学当量比

HC — Hydrocarbons   碳氢化合物

HEI — High Energy Ignition   高能量点火

HO₂S — Heated Oxygen Sensor   带加热装置的氧传感器

IAT — Intake Air Temperature   进气空气温度

ISO 9141 — International Standards Organization OBD-Ⅱ communication mode, used by Chrysler and most foreign cars, and one of three hardware layers defined by OBD-Ⅱ　国际标准化组织 OBD-Ⅱ 通信模式，用于克莱斯勒汽车和大部分外国轿车，是由 OBD-Ⅱ 定义的三个硬件层之一

J1850 PWM —（Pulse Width Modulation）SAE-established OBD-Ⅱ communication standard used by Ford domestic cars and light trucks, and one of three hardware layers defined by OBD-Ⅱ　（脉宽调制）SAE 制定 OBD-Ⅱ 通信标准，用于福特汽车公司在本土销售的轿车和轻型卡车，是由 OBD-Ⅱ 定义的三个硬件层次之一

J1850 VPW —（Variable Pulse Width Modulation）SAE-established OBD-Ⅱ communication standard used by GM cars and light trucks, and one of three hardware layers defined by OBD-Ⅱ

（可变脉宽调制）SAE 制定的 OBD-Ⅱ 通信标准，用于通用汽车公司的轿车和轻型卡车，是由 OBD-Ⅱ 定义的三个硬件层次之一

J1962 — SAE-established standard for the connector plug layout used for all OBD-Ⅱ scan tools　SAE 制定的标准，用于所有 OBD-Ⅱ 解码工具的连接器插头设计

J1978 — SAE-established standard for OBD-Ⅱ scan tools　SAE 制定的标准，用于 OBD-Ⅱ 解码工具

J1979 — SAE-established standard for diagnostic test modes　SAE 制定的标准，用于诊断测试模式

J2012 — SAE-established standard accepted by EPA as the standard test report language for emission tests　SAE 制定的标准，被 EPA 接受，用于排放测试的标准测试报告语言

MAF — Mass Air Flow　质量空气流量

MAP — Manifold Absolute Pressure　进气歧管绝对压力

MAT — Manifold Air Temperature　进气歧管空气温度

MFG — Manufacturer　厂商

MIL — Malfunction Indicator Light, the "Check Engine Light" on your dash　故障指示灯，即汽车仪表板上的"检查发动机指示灯"

NOx — Oxides of Nitrogen　氮氧化物

O$_2$ — Oxygen　氧气

OBD — On-Board Diagnostics　车载诊断系统

OBD-Ⅱ — updated On-Board Diagnostic standard, effective in cars sold in the US after Jan. 1, 1996　最新的车载诊断标准，用于 1996 年 1 月 1 日后在美国销售的汽车

Parameters — Readings on scan tools representing functions measured by OBD-Ⅱ and proprietary readings　代表 OBD-Ⅱ 测量功能的解码工具读数和专有读数

PCM — Powertrain（动力传动系［包括发动机］）Control Module, the on-board computer that controls engine and drive train （传动系） 动力传动系控制模块，即控制发动机和传动系的车载计算机

PCV — Positive Crankcase Ventilation 曲轴箱强制通风

PID — Parameter ID 参数识别

Proprietary Readings — parameters shown by on-board computers which are not required by OBD-Ⅱ, but included by manufacturer to assist in trouble-shooting specific vehicles
专有读数——显示在车载计算机上的参数，OBD-Ⅱ 没有要求，但是被汽车厂商用来辅助诊断特定汽车的故障

PTC — Pending （未决的）Trouble Code 未决的故障码

RPM — Revolutions Per Minute 转/分

SAE — Society of Automotive Engineers, professional organization that set the standards that EPA adopted for OBD and OBD-Ⅱ 汽车工程学会，它制定了一系列标准的职业组织，EPA 在 OBD 和 OBD-Ⅱ 中采纳了这些标准

Scan Tool — computer-based read-out equipment to display OBD-Ⅱ parameters
汽车检测工具——基于计算机的读取设备，用来显示 OBD-Ⅱ 参数

SES — Service Engine Soon dash light, now referred to as MIL 尽快修理发动机仪表板灯，现在指故障指示灯

SFI — Sequential Fuel Injection 顺序燃料喷射

Stoichiometric Ratio — theoretical perfect combustion ratio of 1 part gas to 14. 7 parts air
化学当量比——理论上的完美的燃烧比例，即 1 单位汽油对 14.7 单位空气

TBI — Throttle Body Injection 节气门体喷射

TPI — Tuned Port Injection 调谐端口喷射

TPS — Throttle Position Sensor 节气门位置传感器

VAC — Vacuum 真空

VCM — Vehicle Control Module：the in-car computer that oversees （监视）engine management, transmission operation, anti-lock brakes, and other functions not directly related to emissions control 汽车控制模块：车内计算机，用来监视发动机管理、变速器操作、防抱死系统和其他不直接涉及排放的功能

VIN — Vehicle Identification Number 车辆识别码

VSS — Vehicle Speed Sensor 车速传感器

WOT — Wide Open Throttle 节气们全开

22.3 OBD-II Trouble Code   OBD-II 故障码

P0100	Mass or Volume Air Flow Circuit Malfunction 质量或容积空气流量线路故障
P0123	Throttle/Pedal Position Sensor/Switch A Circuit High Input 节气门/踏板位置传感器/开关 A 线路输出过高
P0147	O$_2$ Sensor Heater Circuit Malfunction（Bank 1，Sensor 3） 氧气传感器加热电路故障（气缸组 1，传感器 3）
P0206	Injector Circuit Malfunction — Cylinder 6 喷油器线路故障——气缸 6
P0231	Fuel Pump Secondary Circuit Low 燃油泵二级线路低
P0257	Injection Pump Fuel Metering Control "B" Range/Performance（Cam/Rotor/Injector） 喷油泵燃料测量控制"B"量程/性能问题
P0288	Cylinder 10 Injector Circuit Low 气缸 10 喷油器线路低
P0221	Throttle/Pedal Position Sensor/Switch B Circuit Range/Performance Problem 节气门/踏板位置传感器/开关 B 线路量程/性能问题
P0247	Turbocharger Wastegate（废气旁通阀）Solenoid B Malfunction 涡轮增压器废气旁通阀螺线管 B 故障
P0273	Cylinder 5 Injector Circuit Low 气缸 5 喷油器线路低

Key Words

fuel feed 燃料供给   dashboard 仪表板

Exercises

1. _____ provides almost complete engine control and also monitors parts of the chassis, body and accessory devices, as well as the diagnostic control network of the car.

2. There are three basic OBD-II protocols in use, each with minor variations on the communication pattern between the on-board diagnostic _____ and the scanner console or tool.

3. In all cases _____ of all sensor readings at the time is recorded in the central computer of the vehicle.

Appendix A

Terms 常用术语

English	Chinese
4-piston fixed caliper	四活塞固定式制动钳
accessories & electrical	附件与电气
adapter	转接器
adaptive damping system (ADS)	自适应阻尼系统
air bag restraint system	气囊约束系统
air conditioning & heat	空调与暖风
air conditioning (A/C)	空调
air suspension system	空气悬架系统
alternator & regulator	交流发电机与调节器
aluminum electrode wire	铝焊丝
anti-lock brake/TCS system	防抱死制动/TCS 系统
assembly	总成
automatic transmission	自动变速器
axle shaft	驱动轴
battery power connection	蓄电池电源接头
buzzer, relay & timer	蜂鸣器、继电器和定时器
canister purge (CANP)	碳罐净化
central locking (CL) & remote central locking (RCL) systems	中控锁与遥控中控锁系统
central multi-port fuel injection (CMFI)	中央多点燃油喷射
certified crash test	认证碰撞试验
circuit breaker	断路器
circuit protection device	电路保护装置
clearing code	清除故障码
composite unibody	组合式承载车身
constant volume sampling (CVS)	定容取样
control unit	控制单元
convertible top	折叠式车篷顶

continued

English	Chinese
corporate average fuel economy (CAFE)	社会平均燃油经济性
cowl	车颈板
cruise control system	巡航控制系统
crush zone	吸能区
curtain air bag	帘式气囊
data link connector	数据传送接头
daytime running light	白昼行驶灯
dealership body shop	经销商车身维修厂
diagnostic trouble code (DTC)	诊断故障码
digital volt-ohmmeter (DVOM)	数字电压电阻表
door trim panel	车门装饰板
door weatherstripping	车门密封条
draining & refilling	排空与再充注
drive cycle	行驶循环
electronic power steering	电子动力转向
electronic traction system (ETS) & electronic stability program (ESP) system	电子牵引控制系统与电子稳定性程序系统
engine mechanical	发动机机械
erasing diagnostic trouble code	清除诊断故障码
fixed caliper	固定式制动钳
floating caliper	浮式制动钳
freeze frame and snapshot	冻结帧和快照
front clip	前围
fuse details	保险丝详图
gear tooth contact patterns	轮齿接触面式样
general servicing	一般维护
headrest	头枕
heater system	暖风系统
hood hinge	发动机罩铰链
horn	喇叭
idle speed control (ISC)	怠速转速控制
ignition switch	点火开关
instrument panel	仪表板
interior trim	内饰
intermittent problem diagnosis	间歇故障诊断

continued

English	Chinese
longitudinal engine	纵置发动机
M-vacuum diagram	真空管路图
maintenance	维护保养
malfunction indicator lamp（MIL）	故障指示灯
manual A/C-heater systems	手动空调-暖风系统
manual trans service	手动变速器维修
manual transmission	手动变速器
metal conditioner	金属处理剂
misfire or rough operation	缺火或运转不稳
model designation	车型名称
multi-function unit system	多功能单元系统
multi-point fuel injection（MFI）	多点燃油喷射
navigation	导航
ohms（Ω）	欧姆
on-board diagnosis（OBD）	车载诊断
"P" series	"P"系列
park/neutral（P/N）	驻车/空挡
positive crankcase ventilation（PCV）	曲轴箱强制通风
power memory seat	电动记忆座椅
power top/sunroof	电动车顶/天窗
power windows	电动车窗
powertrain	动力传动系
powertrain control module（PCM）	动力传动系统控制模块
pulse width modulated（PWM）	脉冲宽度调制
quarter panel	后侧围板
radio & CD changer	收音机与CD换碟机
rear window & mirror defogger	后窗与后视镜除雾器
rear window defogger	后窗除雾器
retrieving diagnostic trouble codes（DTCs）	读取诊断故障码
scheduled service	定期保养
seat belt & supplemental restraint system（SRS）	座椅安全带与辅助约束系统
seat belt anchor	安全带固定器
sequential fuel injection（SFI）	顺序燃油喷射
shift interlock	换挡互锁
shift lock	换挡锁
shock tower/strut tower	减震器拱形座

continued

English	Chinese
single-point/multi-point fuel injection	单点/多点燃油喷射
starter	起动机
stoichiometric	理想空燃比
TBI	节气门体喷射
tech service bulletin	技术服务公报
torque specification	扭矩规范
transfer gearbox system	分动器变速系统
transmission	变速器
trigger	触发器
trouble shooting — basic procedure	故障诊断——基本程序
trunk, tailgate, fuel door	行李箱盖、尾门、加油口门
vacuum pump	真空泵
variable valve timing（VVT）	可变气门正时
vehicle control module	车辆控制模块
vehicle identification number（VIN）	车辆识别代码
warning system	报警系统
wide open throttle（WOT）	节气门全开

Appendix B
Glossary 词汇表

English	Chinese	Unit
3/2-way valve	3/2 换向阀	Unit 3
abnormal	反常的	Unit 20
accidentally	偶然地	Unit 9
air intake duct	进气道	Unit 2
alternately	交替的	Unit 9
ambient lighting	环境照明	Unit 9
anti-theft alarm system	防盗报警系统	Unit 9
backrest	靠背	Unit 9
block	卡住	Unit 9
body	车身	Unit 1
bolt	螺栓	Unit 2
boot lid	行李箱盖	Unit 10
brake caliper	制动钳	Unit 6
brake disc	制动盘	Unit 6
bumper	保险杠	Unit 9
cab	驾驶室	Unit 11
camshaft	凸轮轴	Unit 2
categorize	分类	Unit 1
center console	中央控制台	Unit 3
chassis	底盘	Unit 1
circuitry	电路	Unit 14
clearance light	示宽灯	Unit 9
clutch	离合器	Unit 3
compressor	压缩器	Unit 8
comprise	包含	Unit 9
condenser	冷凝器	Unit 2

continued

English	Chinese	Unit
connecting rod	连杆	Unit 2
cooling system	冷却系统	Unit 2
cord	帘线	Unit 20
courtesy light	前部区域照明灯	Unit 9
crankcase	曲轴箱	Unit 2
crankshaft	曲轴	Unit 2
crash	碰撞	Unit 10
current	电流	Unit 14
cylinder head	气缸盖	Unit 2
cylinder wall	气缸壁	Unit 2
dash light	仪表板照明灯	Unit 21
dashboard	仪表板	Unit 22
deactivate	使无效	Unit 9
denote	表示	Unit 9
diagnostic system	诊断系统	Unit 13
differential	差速器	Unit 4
distribute	分配	Unit 17
distributor cap	分电器盖	Unit 21
door handle	车门把手	Unit 9
downstream	下游的，后面的	Unit 2
drag lever	摇臂	Unit 2
drain	排空	Unit 20
DTC（Diagnostic Trouble Code）	故障诊断码	Unit 19
duty	负荷	Unit 18
duty factor	负载参数	Unit 9
EFI（Electronic Fuel Injection）	电子燃料喷射	Unit 13
electronic-hydraulic	电子液压的	Unit 3
emergency release	紧急解锁装置	Unit 6
engage	（齿轮）啮合	Unit 2
engine block	机体	Unit 2
ESA（Electronic Spark Advance）	电子点火正时	Unit 13
established current intensity	规定的电流强度	Unit 9
evaporator	蒸发器	Unit 8
exterior lighting	外部照明	Unit 9

continued

English	Chinese	Unit
flywheel	飞轮	Unit 2
fog lamp	雾灯	Unit 9
frame	车架	Unit 1
front axle	前轴	Unit 4
fuel feed	燃料供给	Unit 22
fuse	保险丝	Unit 21
gearshift	换挡杆	Unit 3
headlight	汽车大灯	Unit 9
higher-level	高级的	Unit 9
hold	保持	Unit 9
housing	外壳，壳体	Unit 6
immobilization	停车	Unit 9
incident lighting	透光照明	Unit 9
injection duration	喷油持续期	Unit 15
injector	喷油器	Unit 16
instrument lighting	仪表照明	Unit 9
intake pipe	进气管	Unit 2
intake port	进气口	Unit 16
interior lighting	车内照明	Unit 9
irrespective of	不考虑	Unit 9
ISC（Idle Speed Control）	怠速控制	Unit 13
knock sensor	爆震传感器	Unit 15
knurl	滚花轮	Unit 9
line	管路	Unit 9
luggage compartment	行李箱	Unit 6
magnesium alloy	镁合金	Unit 2
maintenance-free	免维护的	Unit 9
map	特性曲线	Unit 9
mechanism	机构	Unit 15
MIL（Malfunction Indicator Lamp）	故障指示灯	Unit 19
neutral position	空挡	Unit 3
off-road	越野的	Unit 20
oil cooler	机油冷却器	Unit 2

continued

English	Chinese	Unit
oil filter	机油滤清器	Unit 2
oil sump	油底壳	Unit 2
on the basis of	以……为基础	Unit 9
parallel to	平行于	Unit 9
parking brake	驻车制动器	Unit 6
parking lock	驻车锁止器	Unit 3
passenger compartment	乘员舱	Unit 8
perimeter-type frame	周边式车架	Unit 1
pillar	柱子	Unit 11
piston	活塞	Unit 2
piston ring	活塞环	Unit 2
primary current	初级电流	Unit 17
radiator	散热器	Unit 2
reactuate	再次开动	Unit 9
rear view mirror	后视镜	Unit 9
relevant	相关的	Unit 9
reservoir	储液器	Unit 8
residual heating area	余热区	Unit 9
restraint system	制动系统	Unit 12
restrictor	限流器	Unit 8
rigidity	刚度	Unit 10
rim	轮辋	Unit 4
seat heating	座椅加热	Unit 9
selector lever	选挡杆	Unit 3
sensitivity	灵敏度	Unit 9
shock absorber	减振器	Unit 7
signal	信号	Unit 15
spare wheel	备用车轮	Unit 4
spark plug	火花塞	Unit 2
spur gear	圆柱齿轮	Unit 6
stabilizer bar	稳定杆	Unit 4
steering	转向系	Unit 5
steering column	转向柱	Unit 5

continued

English	Chinese	Unit
steering gear	转向器	Unit 5
strength	强度	Unit 10
sun roof	天窗	Unit 8
swinging arm	摆臂	Unit 4
tailgate	后挡板	Unit 11
TDC (Top Dead Center)	上死点	Unit 15
terminal	终端	Unit 14
theoretical air-fuel ratio	理论空气－燃料比	Unit 15
thermostat	节温器	Unit 2
throttle	节气门	Unit 2
timer	延时电路	Unit 9
toothed chain	齿形带	Unit 2
track rod	转向横拉杆	Unit 4
trailer	拖车	Unit 12
transaxle	驱动桥	Unit 15
transmission	变速器	Unit 3
tread	轮胎面	Unit 20
TWC (Three-Way Catalytic Converter)	三元催化转化器	Unit 15
unibody	承载式车身	Unit 1
valve timing system	气门正时系统	Unit 2
VIN	车辆识别码	Unit 12
wear	磨损	Unit 20
wheel arch	轮罩	Unit 9
windshield	挡风玻璃	Unit 12
wiper	刮水器	Unit 9
worm	蜗杆	Unit 6

Appendix C

Makes and Models
汽车品牌与型号

Makes	Models
Acura（极品）	2.2CL, 2.5TL, 3.0CL, 3.2TL, 3.5RL, Integra, Legend, MDX, SLX, Vigor
Audi（奥迪）	100, 200, A4, A6, A8, Allroad, Cabriolet, S4, TT, V8 Quattro
BMW（宝马）	318i, 318i Convertible, 318is, 318ti, 320i, 323Ci, 323i, 323i Convertible, 323is, 325, 325 Series, 325Ci, 325e, 325i, 325i Convertible, 325iC, 325is, 325xi, 328Ci, 328i, 328i Convertible, 328is, 330Ci, 330i, 330xi, 525i, 525i Touring, 528i, 530i, 530i Touring, 535i, 540i, 635CSi, 735 Series, 735i, 735iL, 740i, 740iL, 750iL, 840Ci, 850 Series, 850Ci, L7, M Coupe, M Roadster, M3, M5, X5, Z3, Z3 M-Series, Z8
Buick（别克）	Century, LeSabre, Park Avenue, Regal, Rendezvous, Riviera, Roadmaster, Skylark
Cadillac（卡迪拉克）	Allante, Brougham, Catera, Concours, DeVille, DeVille Concours, Eldorado, Escalade, Escalade EXT, Fleetwood, Seville, Sixty Special
Chevrolet（雪弗兰）	Astro, Beretta, Blazer, Camaro, Caprice, Cavalier, Corsica, Corvette, Impala, Impala SS, Lumina, Lumina APV, Lumina Minivan, Malibu, Monte Carlo, Parcel, Pickup, Pickup C1500, Pickup C2500, Pickup C3500, Pickup K1500, Pickup K2500, Pickup K3500, Pickup Silverado 1500, Pickup Silverado 2500, S10, S10 Blazer, S10 Pickup, Sierra, Silverado 1500, Silverado 2500, Silverado 2500 HD, Silverado 3500, Suburban, Suburban C1500, Suburban C2500, Suburban K1500, Suburban K2500, Tahoe, Van G10, Van G20, Van G30, Venture
Chrysler（克莱斯勒）	300M, Cirrus, Concorde, Fifth Avenue, Imperial, Intrepid, Laser, LeBaron, LeBaron Convert/Coupe, LeBaron Sedan, LeBaron-Convertible, LHS, New Yorker, Sebring, Sebring Convertible, Sebring Coupe, Sebring Sedan, Town & Country, Voyager

continued

Makes	Models
Dodge（道奇）	Acclaim, Avenger, Caravan, Colt, Colt Vista, Dakota, Daytona, Durango, Dynasty, Grand Caravan, Intrepid, Monaco, Neon, Pickup, Pickup R1500, Pickup R2500, Pickup R3500, Ram Pickup, Ram Van, Ram Van B1500, Ram Van B2500, Ram Van B3500, Ram Van/Wagon, Ram Wagon B1500, Ram Wagon B2500, Ram Wagon B3500, Ram-50, Ramcharger, RWD Van, Shadow, Spirit, Stealth, Stratus, Stratus Coupe, Stratus Sedan
Eagle（鹰）	Premier, Summit, Summit Wagon, Talon, Vision
Ford（福特）	"E" Series, "F" Series, Aerostar, Aspire, Bronco, ChsCab, Contour, Crown Victoria, Econoline/Club Wagon, Escape, Escort, Escort ZX2, Explorer, Explorer Sport, Explorer Sport Trac, F Pickup, Festiva, Focus, Mustang, Pickup, Probe, Probe-2.0（M/T）, Ranger, Taurus, Tempo, Thunderbird, Windstar
Geo（吉优）	Prizm, Storm, Tracker
GMC（通用卡车）	Envoy, Envoy XL, Jimmy, Magnavan, Pickup, Pickup C1500, Pickup C2500, Pickup C3500, Pickup K1500, Pickup K2500, Pickup K3500, Pickup Sierra 1500, Pickup Sierra 2500, Rally, Safari, Sierra, Sierra 1500, Sierra 2500, Sierra 2500 HD, Sierra 3500, Sonoma, Suburban, Suburban C1500, Suburban C2500, Suburban K1500, Suburban K2500, Van G1500, Van G2500, Van G3500, Vandura, Yukon, Yukon XL
Honda（本田）	Accord, Civic, Civic del Sol, Civic/CRX, CR-V, Insight, Oasis, Odyssey, Passport, Prelude, S2000
Hyundai（现代）	Accent, Elantra, Excel, Precis, Santa Fe, Scoupe, Sonata, Tiburon, XG300
Infiniti（无限）	G20, I30, J30, Q45, QX4
Isuzu（五十铃）	Amigo, Hombre, Impulse, Oasis, Pickup, Rodeo, Rodeo Sport, Trooper, Vehi-CROSS
Jaguar（捷豹）	S-Type, XJ12, XJ6, XJ8, XJR, XJS, XK8, XKR
Jeep（吉普）	Cherokee, Comanche, Grand Cherokee, Grand Wagoneer, Wagoneer, Wrangler
Kia（起亚）	Optima, Rio, Sephia, Spectra, Sportage
Land Rover（陆虎）	Defender 90, Discovery, Range Rover
Lexus（雷克萨斯）	ES250, ES300, GS300, GS400, GS430, IS300, LS400, LS430, LX450, LX470, RX300, SC300, SC400
Lincoln（林肯）	Continental, LS, Mark VIII, Town Car

continued

Makes	Models
Mazda（马自达）	323, 626, 929, B2200, B2300, B2500, B2600, B2600i, B3000, B4000, Miata, Millenia, MPV, MX-3, MX-5 Miata, MX-6, Navajo, Pickup, Protégé, RX7, Tribute
Mercedes-Benz（奔驰）	190D, 190E, 260E, 300CE, 300D, 300E, 300SD, 300SE, 300SEL, 300SL, 300TE, 350SD, 350SDL, 380SE, 380SEC, 380SEL, 400E, 400SE, 400SEL, 420SEL, 500E, 500SEC, 500SEL, 500SL, 560SEC, 560SEL, C220, C230, C240, C280, C320, C36, CL500, CL600, CLK320, CLK430, E300, E320, E420, E430, E500, ML320, ML430, S320, S350, S420, S430, S500, S600, SL320, SL500, SL600, SLK230, SLK320
Mercury（水星）	Capri, Cougar, Grand Marquis, Mountaineer, Mystique, Sable, Topaz, Tracer, Villager
Mitsubishi（三菱）	3000GT, Diamante, Eclipse, Expo, Expo/Expo LRV, Galant, Mirage, Montero, Montero Sport, Pajero Sport, Pickup, Precis, Van/Wagon, Pickup
Nissan（日产）	200SX, 240SX, 300ZX, Altima, Frontier, Maxima, NX, Pathfinder, Pickup, Quest, Sentra, Sonata, Xterra, 风度 A32, 风度 A33, 公爵, 蓝鸟
Oldsmobile（奥兹莫比尔）	Achieva, Alero, Aurora, Bravada, Ciera, Custom Cruiser, Cutlass, Cutlass Calais, Cutlass Ciera, Cutlass Cruiser, Cutlass Supreme, Eighty Eight, Intrigue, LSS, Ninety Eight, Regency, Silhouette, Toronado, Touring Sedan, Trofeo
Plymouth（顺风）	Acclaim, Breeze, Colt, Colt Vista, Grand Voyager, Neon, Sundance, Voyager
Pontiac（庞帝克）	Aztek, Bonneville, Firebird, Grand Am, Grand Prix, LeMans, Montana, Safari, Sunbird, Sunfire, Trans Sport
Porsche（保时捷）	911, Acclaim, Boxster
Saab（绅宝）	900, 9000, 9-3, 9-5
Saturn（土星）	L100, L200, L300, LW200, LW300, SC, SC1, SC2, SL, SL1, SL2, SW1, SW2, Vue
Subaru（富士）	Forester, Impreza, Legacy, Outback, Outback Sport
Suzuki（铃木）	Esteem, Grand Vitara, Swift, Vitara, XL-7
Toyota（丰田）	4Runner, Avalon, Camry, Camry Solara, Celica, Corolla, Cressida, ECHO, Highlander, Land Cruiser, MR2, Paseo, Pickup, Previa, Prius, RAV4, Sequoia, Sienna, Supra, T100, T100 Pickup, Tacoma, Tercel, Tundra, 皇冠, 考斯特
Volkswagen（大众）	Cabrio, Cabriolet, Corrado, EuroVan, Fox, Golf, Golf III, GTI, Jetta, Jetta III, New Beetle, Passat, Vanagon
Volvo（富豪）	240, 850, 940, 960, C70, S40, S60, S70, S80, S90, V40, V70, V90

Appendix D

Index of Mitchell Repair Information
米切尔光盘数据库索引

Category and Section

Category		Section	
Accessories & Electrical	附件和电气	Electrical	电气系统
Accessories & Electrical	附件和电气	Accessories/Safety Equip	附件和安全装置
Air Conditioning & Heat	空调和暖风	Air Conditioning & Heat	空调和暖风
Automatic Transmission	自动变速器	Auto Trans Overhaul	自动变速器大修
Automatic Transmission	自动变速器	Automatic Trans Service	自动变速器维护
Automatic Transmission	自动变速器	Auto Trans Diagnosis	自动变速器诊断
Brakes	制动系统	Brakes	制动系统
Elec Component Location	电气元件位置	Elec Component Location	电气元件位置
Engine Mechanical	发动机机械	Engines	发动机维修
Engine Mechanical	发动机机械	Engine Cooling	发动机冷却系
Engine Performance	发动机性能	Fuel Systems	燃油系统
Engine Performance	发动机性能	Engine Performance Specs	发动机性能参数
Engine Performance	发动机性能	Engine Performance	发动机性能
Engine Performance	发动机性能	Emissions	排放系统
Engine Performance	发动机性能	Quick Spec	快速维修规范
Engine Performance	发动机性能	Tune-up	调修
Engine Performance	发动机性能	Prom Information	PROM 信息
Engine Performance	发动机性能	Computer Eng Control	发动机的电脑控制系统
General	通用信息	How To	指导与培训
General	通用信息	General Information	通用信息

continued

Category		Section	
General	通用信息	General Trouble Shooting	一般故障排除
General	通用信息	Tech-Cor Bulletins	Tech-Cor 技术公报
Maintenance	维护与保养	Maintenance	维护与保养
Manual Transmission	手动变速器	Manual Trans Diagnosis	手动变速器诊断
Manual Transmission	手动变速器	Manual Trans Overhaul	手动变速器大修
Manual Transmission	手动变速器	Manual Trans Service	手动变速器维护
Powertrain	动力传动系	Clutches	离合器
Powertrain	动力传动系	Transfer Cases	分动器
Powertrain	动力传动系	Drive Axles	驱动桥
Steering & Suspension	转向和悬架	Wheel Alignment	车轮定位
Steering & Suspension	转向和悬架	Suspension	悬架系统
Steering & Suspension	转向和悬架	Steering	转向系统
Wiring Diagrams	电路图		

Title

Title	
FRONT SUSPENSION RATTLE OR CLUNK：TENSION STRUT LOOSE	前悬架喀哒声或沉闷声：张紧杆松动
FRONT SUSPENSION RATTLES IN COLD TEMPERATURES	在低温时前悬架喀哒声
FRONT SUSPENSION SCRUNCH/POP NOISE（INSTALL WASHER）	前悬架嘎吱声/砰然声（安装垫圈）
FRONT SUSPENSION SEAT NOISE：NEW PLASTIC BUSHINGS	前悬架支座噪声：新的塑料轴套
FRONT SUSPENSION SHUDDER：HIGH RIDE HEIGHT ADJUSTMENT	前悬架抖动：高度调整
FRONT SUSPENSION SPACER REMOVAL DURING PDS	前悬架隔离器在提交用户前维护时拆除
FRONT SUSPENSION SQUEAK/CREAK — LOCATING PIN REMOVAL	前悬架尖叫/吱吱声——定位销拆卸
FRONT SUSPENSION UPPER ARM BUSHING NOISE	前悬架上臂套管噪声

continued

Title	
FRONT SUSPENSN SCRAPING	前悬架刮擦
FRONT SUSPERSION NOISE DIAGNOSIS	前悬架噪声诊断
FRONT TIRE WEAR	前轮胎磨损
FRONT TRUNK CARPET DAMAGE	前箱地毯损坏
FRONT TURN SIGNAL LAMP INSTALLATION PROCEDURE	前转向信号灯安装步骤
FRONT TURN SIGNAL LENS: WATER CONDENSATION REPAIR	前转向信号灯头：水冷凝修理
FRONT UPPER ARM BUSHING NOISE: NEW UPPER ARM	前上臂套管噪声：新的上臂
FRONT VALANCE PANEL MISSING OR LOOSE	前布饰板遗失或松动
FRONT WHEEL BEARING DUST CAPS — REPLACE	前车轮轴承防尘罩——更换
FRONT WHEEL BEARING HOUSING — OUTER CIRCLIP OMITTED	前车轮轴承座——遗漏的外弹簧圈
FRONT WHEEL BEARING HOUSING — CIRCLIP NO LONGER NEEDED	前车轮轴承座——不再需要弹簧圈
FRONT WHEEL BEARINGS — NOISY	前轮轴承——噪声
FRONT WHEEL CARRIER COVER/911 C2	前轮架盖/911 C2
FRONT WHEEL CLICKING NOISE	前轮滴答噪声
FRONT WHEEL HUBS REMOVAL/INSTALLATION PROCEDURE	前轮毂拆卸/安装步骤
FRONT WHEEL SUSPENSION TORQUE SPECIFICATION REVISION	前轮悬架力矩规范更正
FRONT WHEEL/STEERING WHEEL VIBRATION — PROCEDURE	前轮/转向轮振动——步骤
FRONT WHEELS ROAD NOISE: C-PILLAR FOAM SEALING	前轮路面噪声：C柱泡沫密封
SEALING	密封
FRONT WHISTLES/HOOD SEAL	前汽笛/发动机罩密封
FRONT WINDOW BIND REPAIR	前车窗镶边修理
FRONT WINDOW CLUNK	前车窗沉闷声
FRONT WINDOW IS INOPERATIVE/JUMPS DURING OPERATION	前车窗不能工作/操作时跳动

Appendix E

Keys to Exercises
课后练习答案

Unit 1

1. The body   2. the repair areas   3. unibody   4. transfer case

Unit 2

1. the throttle section   2. spur gears   3. 3,500 rpm

4. The manifold   5. the resonator type   6. an exhaust flap

7. The camshaft   8. repairs   9. balancing weights

10. the drag lever   11. a worm gear   12. On no account

13. a toothed chain   14. the water pump   15. The map-controlled thermostat

16. the low-temperature coolant radiator circuit   17. the last cooling level

18. "open deck"   19. hollowed   20. three

21. oil jets   22. the oil pump   23. The oil check valve

24. unscrewed   25. the oil thermostat

Unit 3

1. a torque converter   2. a so-called mechatronics module   3. the commands

4. the torque converter   5. the hydraulic shift unit

6. a single carrier planetary gear train   7. The parking lock

8. The central gateway module   9. The warm-up program

10. the gearbox   11. the hydraulic valves   12. The electronic pressure control valves

Unit 4

1. That nearly all the axle components are made of aluminium

2. A reinforcement plate

3. the tension strut   4. The stabilizer bar

5. That the rear axle differential is mounted with two mount points at the front and only one at the rear

6. the swinging arm   7. stabilizer links   8. forged wheel   9. balancing

Unit 5

1. total steering wheel revolutions   2. dynamic drive   3. compressed

Unit 6

1. hydraulic dual-circuit   2. inner-vented   3. the brake caliper
4. rolling away   5. (1) Locking (brake applied); (2) Dynamic braking
6. the balance arm   7. direct intervention   8. the DSC control unit

Unit 7

1. the shock absorbers   2. low pressure dampers

Unit 8

1. lower   2. refrigerant   3. failure
4. Climate control   5. the refrigerant circulation   6. The restrictor
7. an overload safety   8. expansion valves   9. reservoir
10. the narrow point, the narrow point

Unit 9

1. semiconductor components   2. a duty factor of 50:50   3. hazard-warning flashing
4. The door warning light   5. The term "ambient lighting" 6. the K-CAN system
7. the anti-theft alarm system   8. the left rear wheel arch   9. an alarm telegram
10. the hazard-warning lights   11. The lock cylinder in the tailgate
12. disengaged   13. unlocked   14. unlocked
15. the switch block   16. Emergency closing   17. trapping
18. open the window   19. the driver's switch block   20. the rapid heating
21. Stage 3 (maximum temperature) 22. a balance controller   23. the control buttons
24. a slide switch   25. outside temperature   26. The wiper module
27. EEPROM   28. reversing of the wiper motor 29. its functional content
30. touched once   31. stopped   32. the angle of rotation sensor
33. stopped   34. the distances   35. the time span
36. certainty   37. The instrument cluster   38. parallel to

Unit 10

1. additional safety   2. the bumper cross-member

3. manufacturing both the front side panels and all the individual parts of the bonnet from aluminum

4. replace the shackle hinge   5. the sides

Unit 11

1. car size   2. more rear

Unit 12

1. how and when   2. 25 km/h   3. look up and convert

Unit 13

1. During warm-up, acceleration, deceleration or high-load driving conditions

2. knocking   3. stable   4. advanced and complex

Unit 14

1. actuators   2. engine ECU   3. sensor ground terminals

Unit 15

1. the basic injection duration   2. manifold pressure   3. throttle position

4. G signal plate   5. engine speed   6. thermistors

7. the theoretical air-fuel ratio   8. the oxygen concentration   9. transaxle

10. ignition timing   11. ignition timing control

Unit 16

1. regulated   2. the valve   3. the plunger stroke does not change

Unit 17

1. the ignition timing   2. the ignition signal (IGT)   3. the ignition coil   4. False

Unit 18

1. (1) B   (2) D   (3) A   2. A. True   B. False   C. False   3. B

Unit 19

1. A. True   B. True   C. True   2. the MIL (Malfunction Indicator Lamp)
3. 5   4. cut off   5. back-up mode

Unit 20

1. 166,000 km (100,000 mi)   2. underhood   3. more often
4. identified   5. higher   6. equalize

Unit 21

1. A diagnostic tree   2. distributor cap
3. Sometimes one fault will cause another one that you couldn't see at first.

Unit 22

1. OBD-II   2. computer   3. a "freeze frame"